Isadora Tattlin was born and raised in California. She is married to a European executive and lives wherever his job takes them and their two young children.

Havana

Cuba Diaries

by Isadora Tattlin

BANTAM BOOKS

LONDON • NEW YORK • TORONTO • SYDNEY • AUCKLAND

For 'Thea' and 'Jimmie'
our good-natured fellow travelers

Contents

GULF OF
MEXICO

Minas de
Matahambre

Havana

Matanzas

Varadero

Dimas

Viñales

Santa Clara

Mantua

★ Pinar del Río

Cienfuegos

Re

Trinidad

CARIBBEAN SEA

Cuba

ATLANTIC OCEAN

edios

Morón

★ Camaguey

Holguín ★

● Bayamo

★ Guantánamo

Baracoa

★ Siboney

Santiago de Cuba

Principal Characters

The Tattlin Family
    Isadora, the narrator
    Nick, her husband
    Thea, their daughter
    Jimmie, their son
    Sam, Isadora's brother

The Help
    Concha, the downstairs maid
    Danila, the upstairs maid
    Estrella, the laundress
    José, the driver
    Lorena, the cook
    Manuel, the butler
    Miguel, the gardener
    Roberto, the driver for guests and errand boy

The Nannies
    Juana, the Cuban nanny, who joined the family later and left
        with them
    Muna, the Bangladeshi nanny, who came with the family but
        left for home early

Instructors
    Carlita, the swimming instructor
    Gonzalo, who replaced Carlita as the swimming instructor
    Lety, the gymnastics instructor
    Mrs. Fleites, a teacher at the children's school
    Olga, the Spanish instructor

Doctors
  Millares Cao, the specialist in skin diseases
  Maria del Carmen, the psychologist
  Yamila Lawton, the allergist
  Silvia, the pediatrician

Cuban Officials (some no longer in office at the time of this
writing)
  Fidel Castro, president
  Raúl Castro, his brother, vice president, and head of the
    armed forces
  Alfredo Guevara (no relation to Che), head of the Instituto
    Cubano del Arte y de la Industria Cinematográfica
    (ICAIC), or Cuban Film Institute
  Eusebio Leal, historian of the city of Havana and founder
    and president of Habaguanex, a corporation dedicated to
    the restoration of Old Havana
  Maida, a Bienes Culturales employee
  Nestor, a Customs agent
  Orestes, a plainclothesman in Havana
  Piñeiro, aka Barbaroja (Redbeard), former head of Cuban
    intelligence
  Rigoberto, head of the Consejo Popular in Pinar del Río

Cuban Artists, Writers, Musicians, and Intelligentsia (see also
Survivors)
  Natalia Bolivar Arostegui, a former teenage revolutionary,
    now an anthropologist, writer, and expert on Santeria
  Saidel Brito, an artist
  Alexis Esquivel, an artist
  Reynaldo González, a writer and director of Cineteca, or the
    Cuban Film Archives
  Kcho, an artist
  Dulce María Loynaz, Cuba's greatest living lyric poet
  Meira, Ángel Toirac's wife, a writer and poetess
  Antonio Nuñez, an artist
  Oliva, an artist in Pinar del Río
  YeYe Perez, a professional blackface actor
  Zenaida Castro Romeu, the conductor of Camerata Romeu
  Lázaro Saavedra, an artist

Esterio Segura, an artist
Ángel Toirac, an artist

Other Cuban Friends and Acquaintances (see also *Survivors*)
Alfonse, aka El Ingles
Aurora, a book dealer
Báez, an official Cuban journalist
Barbara, aka our Elegguá, an unofficial guide who also works
    at Nick's firm
Lilian and Saida Carrera, two very old sisters living in the
    Vedado area
Eddie, Reynaldo Gonzalez's boyfriend
El Viejo Loco, an antique dealer
Nelson Figueroa, an architect living in Baracoa
Flora, Ladisel's wife
Gloria, an artisan living in Baracoa
Ivan, an employee at Nick's firm
Jaime, a gay friend
Ladisel, a tour guide in Cienfuegos and Varadero
Lola, an enterprising, voluble friend
Reny, a cultural liaison
Davide, an architect, uncle of Carlita
Naty Revuelta, Fidel's ex-lover and the mother of his only
    daughter, Alina
Bibi Sebaya, an original resident of the Country Club area
Sergio, an Argentinean tour guide in Pinar del Río
Tomás, a lawyer living in Baracoa
Usnavy, a friend of Aurora's
Arquitecto Vasquez, an architect who runs a gallery-cum-
    paladar

Foreign Friends and Acquaintances
Alex, a diplomat
Bernard, Nick's second assistant
Carey, the Italian ambassador's American wife
Fritz, Nick's first assistant
Ana María Guevara, Che's stepmother
Mike Kozak, principal officer of the U.S. Special Interests
    Section, the de facto U.S. ambassador; Sullivan was his
    predecessor

Lorna, an American, the ex-wife of Piñeiro (see *Cuban Officials*)

Marianne, a Canadian friend

Mark, an American anchorman who comes to Cuba on two occasions, the second time to cover the pope's visit

Nicoletta, half-X——ian, half-Cuban, sent to Cuba by a Swedish firm

Querido Vecino!, the Tattlins' neighbor

Rolf, Danish cultural attaché

Vivarelli, an Italian film director and the only foreign member of the Cuban Communist Party

Survivors (see also *Cuban Artists, Writers, and Intelligentsia and Other Cuban Friends and Acquaintances*)

Natalia Bolivar Arostegui

Lilian and Saida Carrera

Dulce María Loynaz

Naty Revuelta

Bibi Sebaya

Introduction

IN THE EARLY AND MID-1990S, Cuba suffered several major setbacks. The first, in 1990, was the abrupt withdrawal of economic subsidies by the Soviet Union following the fall of the Berlin Wall. Cuba, which was being subsidized by the Soviet Union at the rate of $3 million a day (it is estimated), entered economic free fall. The value of the peso dropped from 1 peso to the dollar to 140 pesos to the dollar. Gasoline, transport, food, and material goods were in dramatically short supply, and Cuba entered what was defined by Fidel Castro as its *periodo especial en tiempo de paz*, or 'special period in time of peace,' a time in which the Cuban people were asked to endure shortages for the sake of the survival of the socialist revolution while their government adjusted to new realities.

In 1993, in an attempt to stem the economic free fall and to put more hard currency in circulation, the possession of dollars by average Cuban individuals, which until then had been illegal, was decriminalized. Dollar stores containing goods that before then had been available only to foreigners were opened to Cubans as well. Foreign investment of up to 49 percent in manufacturing, agriculture, and the tourist industry was encouraged and facilitated.

Legalization of the dollar and foreign investment, however, were not timely enough to prevent the *balsero* crisis of 1994, in which tens of thousands of Cubans took to the Straits of Florida in anything that floated and were not impeded by Cuban authorities. This led to a change in the U.S.-Cuba emigration accords. Cubans leaving Cuba for the United States were no longer welcomed as political refugees but classified as economic migrants and required to undergo the same screenings as economic migrants from other countries.

Further liberalizations of the economy included the opening, in 1994, of *agropecuarios*, or fruit, vegetable, lamb, and pork markets, in which farmers, who had been obliged to produce only for government entities, could now sell on the open market a portion beyond what they produced for the government. Cuban shoppers no longer had to rely solely on undersupplied bodegas, or neighborhood food stores, where Cubans shopped for subsidized basics with ration books. *Agropecuarios* brought variety to Cubans' diets and helped to alleviate malnutrition, which was beginning to take hold in the provinces. Self-employed workers, or *cuentapropistas*, such as manicurists, shoe repairmen, seamstresses, tire repairmen, piñata makers, or rent-a-clowns for children's parties, were allowed to operate. *Paladares*, or private restaurants in peoples' houses, were legalized.

The downside to legalization of the dollar and liberalization of the economy was (and continues to be) the rise of inequality between Cubans with access to dollars and Cubans possessing only pesos. The relationship between salaries became skewed. People in less-skilled jobs but in daily contact with foreigners, such as domestic servants for foreign families, hotel workers, and taxi drivers, made salaries up to twenty times greater than the pesos-only salaries of doctors and engineers.

The early and mid-1990s saw social liberalizations as well. Gays no longer faced active discrimination. In 1992, the Cuban National Assembly changed the definition of Cuba from an atheist state to a lay state. Those who openly professed religious affiliations no longer faced professional or political ostracism, and a surge in church attendance occurred. Artists, musicians, playwrights, and writers were allowed to travel more freely. More and more tourists visited Cuba, which put more and more Cubans in contact with foreigners. In 1998, the pope visited Cuba.

My family and I arrived in Cuba at this time of liberalization and of opening. It lasted until the Miami-based Hermanos al Rescate airplanes were shot down by the Cuban Air Force for an alleged incursion into Cuban airspace. The result was a tightening of the U.S. embargo by way of the Helms-Burton Bill, signed into law in 1996. Subsequent developments (with the exception of the visit of the pope) witnessed, for the most part, stepped-up repression on the part of the Cuban government and a contraction on the part of Cuban society.

It is still difficult to gauge, at the vantage point of a few years, how intentional or foreseeable the results of the Cuban government's liberalizations in the early and mid-1990s were. Foreign investment was encouraged, dollars were legalized, some categories of *cuentapropistas* were permitted or tolerated, and *agropecuarios* were opened as direct decisions of the government. Further developments, however, in which it appeared that average Cubans seemed to be taking the reins of society in their own hands, seem not to have been intended, and seem to have been the result of the government's inability, for a brief but raucous lag time, to integrate the myriad ripple effects of its liberalizations with the goals of socialism.

It is this rowdy, ambiguous, ironic, and sometimes even exhilarating time that, the longer we lived there, the more I felt the compulsion to document. It was a time that seemed to be defining itself as a *time*, unique in itself, which would not and could not last, but which called out to be preserved, in memory and on paper. Every day was extraordinary.

Our identities and the identities of most Cubans and others have been disguised for protection. Criticism of the government or of its leadership is punishable by imprisonment of up to thirty years. The Cuban government remains the principal employer of the population. Activities that are perfectly legal in most countries, such as the buying and selling of goods and services from and by individuals, were and are in some instances permitted by the government; in other instances not permitted but tolerated (with the limits of toleration constantly shifting); but in most instances neither permitted nor tolerated – neither permitted nor tolerated at the time of our living there, and neither permitted nor tolerated now – and can lead to loss of employment, fines, and imprisonment.

My husband's generous salary, a small legacy from my own family, and the low cost of goods and services in Cuba allowed us to live in a style far more grandiose than the style to which we are accustomed. Because of the low cost of living, nondiplomatic foreigners in Cuba with even modest incomes can afford to rent spacious houses (either discreetly, from private sources, or less discreetly, from the government) and have one or two domestic servants. Nondiplomatic foreigners are generally the employees of foreign companies; some foreigners, however, do manage to maintain houses in Cuba as vacation homes. The low cost of living is one reason foreigners have servants; the other reason is that the spacious houses foreigners rent, though start-of-the-art in the 1950s, are no longer chock-full of smoothly running labor-saving devices nor served by an efficient infrastructure. One or two servants, at least, were necessary during the time we lived there if a resident foreigner wanted to do something more with his day than coax more life out of a forty-five-year-old Kenmore refrigerator or spend half a day on the telephone trying to get a tanker truck to come to fill his cistern, the aqueduct leading to the cistern having not been patched since 1957.

I am a U.S. citizen, born and raised in the United States. I hold a U.S. passport, but I also hold an 'X—ian' passport, acquired after my marriage to my husband, to facilitate my moving around the globe with him. Our children hold both U.S. and X—ian passports. Though the United States maintains a forty-year-old embargo against Cuba, which bars most U.S. citizens from traveling in Cuba, Cuba maintains normal diplomatic relations with most other Western countries. My children and I used our 'X—ian' passports for entering and leaving Cuba. We presented U.S. passports to U.S. immigration officials when entering the United States. This was perfectly legal for us, as X—ians and Americans, to do. Though I at times, especially in the beginning, played down my *norteamericana* identity and played up my X—ian identity, thinking that Cubans would feel less inhibited in expressing themselves about the United States if I did that, I never did attempt to hide the fact that I was *norteamericana* and soon discovered that the fact of my being *norteamericana*, far from being inhibiting, was, more often than not, a source of curiosity and at times even delight.

My editor has asked me to write a word about religion. It would take another book – and there are in fact many books – to describe the vast range of religious expression in Cuba. In spite of Cuba's having defined itself until 1992 as an atheist state, Cuba is a deeply religious country. This is the product not only of its traditions, but also, I believe, of its astounding physical beauty, which compels you to marvel at the virtuosity of the

Creator at every turn of a country road or every glimpse of a ceiba tree.

Catholicism and Santeria are the predominant religions of Cuba. Santeria is the blending of Catholicism with the polytheistic beliefs of West Africa, brought to Cuba by West African slaves.

In the attempt to make Cuba's slaves Catholic, the worship of West African gods, or *orishas*, was forbidden by early Spanish colonists. The resourceful slaves continued to worship their *orishas*, however, while appearing to be Catholics by masking their *orishas* as Catholic saints. Female saints often became stand-ins for male *orishas*, and male saints often became stand-ins for female *orishas*, in order to mask them more thoroughly. Hence Santa Barbara, who in Catholicism is the protectress of powder magazines, stands for Changó, the *orisha* of thunder and war.

In Santeria, the message of Jesus is amplified by the inexorable forces of nature (as represented by the *orishas*) and of fate. Each Santeria devotee has his or her chosen *orisha*, to whom he or she makes offerings and obeyances. *Babalaos*, or Santeria priests, are consulted regularly for guidance and knowledge of the future. The predictions of a council of *babalaos*, made on the first day of every year and circulated on photocopied sheets throughout Cuba, are read with intense interest by practically all Cubans.

Santeria is not solely the religion of Afro-Cubans. A growing number of Cubans of European descent not only listen to the New Year's predictions of *babalaos* but follow Santeria with varying degrees of adherence. Cubans of all shades can be seen wearing beads in the colors of their *orishas*.

In addition to conducting religious services, the Catholic Church is active as a source of medicines and as a caregiver, especially of the elderly, in Catholic homes run by nuns and priests. Though Catholic schools are not allowed, the Catholic Church is increasingly active in after-school programs and in adult classes in a variety of subjects. People in all sectors of society pay attention to Catholic publications and the sermons of outspoken priests, as they are among the few (though limited) alternatives to government messages.

All faiths in Cuba respect the mysticism and power of La Virgen de la Caridad del Cobre (The Virgin of the Charity of

Cobre). *Cobre* means copper, and it is also the name of a town where a shrine to her was built, in the middle of a copper-mining region. According to popular legend, three fishermen were caught in a dangerous storm in a small boat in Nipe Bay in the year 1628. In some versions of the story, the three men in the boat were a Native American, a Spaniard, and an African slave, representing the three races of Cuba. Just as they began to believe they were doomed, a small statue of a *mulata* Madonna came floating to them across the water on some wooden planks. Though there was a storm, the statue of the Madonna and the dress clothing her were dry. In her left arm she held the infant Jesus, and in her right arm, a cross. On the wooden planks on which she was floating were written the words, 'I am the Virgin of Charity.'

At the entrance to the church in Cobre is a vast display of ex-votos, medals, photos, offerings, and other testimonials from those who have been helped or healed by their faith in the power of La Caridad. The Nobel Prize of Ernest Hemingway, which Hemingway left as an offering to La Caridad, is also there (but kept locked, at the time of this writing, in a closet for safe-keeping, after the brief theft of it several years ago).

La Caridad's Santeria counterpart is Ochún, the *orisha* of femininity and of rivers. According to *The Orishas of Cuba*, by Natalia Bolivar Arostegui, a Cuban anthropologist and expert on Santeria, Ochún 'is the symbol of flirtation, grace and feminine sexuality.' In Cuba, 'she is represented as a beautiful *mulata* who is kind, a good dancer, likes parties and is always happy.'

Ochún 'can also *resolver* anything.'

I will not translate for you at this point the meaning of the word *resolver*. Though you can guess its superficial meaning, the full, Cuban meaning (amplified by vicissitudes, just as La Caridad herself is amplified by Ochún) is for you to discover in the following diary.

The First
School Year

I. 1

Call me Isadora.

Nick says, 'What about Cuba?'

'What do you mean, 'What about Cuba?''

'What about being there for a few years? L. proposed it.'

L. is Nick's boss. 'Are you kidding me?'

'What do you think?'

I cannot speak. I am thinking about how I have said to Nick sometimes that it would be nice to be a little closer to the United States on Nick's next assignment. It was as if some overly zealous fairy godmother had heard me. Either that, or I had not specified enough when I made my wish. You have to be careful with those wishes, for they can come true.

'*Cuba?*'

'How about it?'

'I . . . I just don't know. When do we have to get back to them?'

'This afternoon.'

One hour later, I'm in the station wagon, going to pick my six-year-old up from school, and suddenly I'm not there anymore but under my desk during bomb drill, staring at the red rubber soles of Jonathan Muller's Buster Browns. It's California, 1962. Something about the Cubans, the Russians, and nuclear missiles pointed directly at Saint Stephen's School. People with beards are very dangerous. Also, panic buying in the supermarket. Cans of chicken noodle soup smashed, lying on the floor. Soon after that, it is determined that the fifth grade should stop learning French and start learning Spanish. A big Cuban boy appears at school. Carlos. But he is the nice kind, we

23

are told, not the mean kind, who want to bomb us. He does not know any English but quickly learns to say, 'Shadap.' His mother comes, too, to teach us Spanish. She has long black leg hairs smushed under her stockings and a mole hidden in the fold of her double chin, which pops out when she looks up at the clock, so that we can hardly get past the '*Yo soy, tu eres,*' so much are we waiting for that mole. The other teachers cannot speak about her among themselves without making violiny sounds with their voices. She had to hide her wedding ring in her shoe to get out of Cuba. I picture people leaving Cuba with little circles printed on the soles of their feet, tiny holes gouged by diamonds.

Cuba. Now I find myself breathing fast, and I have a racing feeling up and down my arms, which is what happens whenever I have to move or do anything new. I don't *like* doing new things. I don't like traveling and living in weird places. I would have been happy to sit in my loft in New York City for the next hundred years, except that there were no men in New York who were not married or gay. I had to go to another city to find Nick, and then he had to be a foreigner, and not a foreigner from a standard country, like France, but one from a weird little country, X—, and not even a foreigner who stayed in one place, but an energy consultant for a multinational corporation, Energy Consulting International (gas, electric, geothermal, hydro, solar, wind: everything but nuclear he'll tell you how to produce in the most efficient way), who stays a few years in one country, then moves to another. So I keep on having to do new things and keep on traveling and living in weird places, being married to Nick. He makes me do it, only this time, it's *more* new somehow, more racing-feeling-up-my-arms making. Cuba really *is* scary: it's not just me.

I see the bright blue South China Sea coming up ahead of the station wagon and realize how clean past the six-year-old's school I've gone.

I. 2

A friend of ours who lived in Cuba tells me on the phone that I really won't have to spend my time in Cuba hunting for this item and that item because if it's not in the Diplomercado, they just don't have it, and that's that. The Diplomercado, our friend explains, or 'Diplomarket,' is a supermarket in Havana, more plentifully stocked than other markets, and with higher-quality goods, where, until the legalization of the dollar in 1993, only diplomats or other foreigners (who were the only people with access to dollars) could shop. It is now open to anyone with dollars. If you really get desperate for something, and it's not in the Diplomercado, our friend explains, you have to go find it in another country. One time, he says, he flew to Mexico to buy a toilet seat. He has heard, though, that the material situation is changing, and that there are more stores opening and you can find more stuff around.

I read that in the city of Trinidad, a perfectly preserved Spanish colonial town that has been declared a world monument by UNESCO, housewives stand in doorways asking for soap from passing tourists in the gathering dusk.

I have three months to get our supplies in before we pack and leave.

I. 3

Our shopping list for Cuba, to be packed in the container with our clothes and furniture and sent to Cuba for free by Nick's company:

18 gallons Clorox
3 dozen boxes gallon-size
    Ziploc freezer bags
3 dozen boxes quart-size
    Ziploc freezer bags
64 gallons fabric softener
120 rolls paper towels
216 bars bath soap
4 cartons Scotch-Brite
    sponges
24 rolls wax paper
60 cakes hand soap
1 carton insecticidal spray
25 cans insecticidal powder
6,000 paper napkins

2,000 plastic glasses
3,600 feet plastic wrap
1,000 garbage bags
120 liters pine disinfectant
20 liters oven cleaner
120 liters all-purpose cleaner
36 liters toilet cleaner
6 liters toilet rust remover
12 liters ceramic cleanser
120 scouring pads
36 liters glass cleaner
4 gallons grease cutter
672 rolls of toilet paper
384 Kleenex boxes
6 liters Woolite

360 clothespins

3 dozen boxes sandwich bags

2,400 feet aluminum foil

120 kilos Tide powder detergent

6 gallons shampoo

4 gallons cream rinse

48 boxes Tampax

24 boxes panty liners

24 kilos rice

12 kilos lentils

24 500-gram boxes (each) of spaghetti, linguine, penne, farfalle, and rigatoni

1,200 bottles wine

3 cases each of gin, whiskey, vodka, and vermouth

48 liters olive oil

8 kilos tea

8 kilos canned tuna

12 kilos Kalamata olives

3 kilos capers

2 kilos anchovies

12 dozen boxes assorted cookies

24 liters silver polish

20 liters brass polish

600 meters roast-tying string

1 kilo oregano

½ kilo each of thyme, basil, rosemary, marjoram, all-spice, cinnamon, and cloves

6 cans baking powder

6 cans baking soda

240 packets dry yeast

360 candles

60 bobeches (glass collars to catch candle drips)

6 bottles Tylenol

12 tubes toothpaste

12 boxes Alka-Seltzer

6 boxes hemorrhoidal suppositories

2 gallons Mylanta

½ kilo athlete's foot powder

2 liters calamine lotion

4 bottles Visine

12 boxes Band-Aids

6 dozen Gillette Trac II razor blades

6 bottles children's chewable vitamins

4 bottles amoxicillin

4 bottles antihistamine

2 tubes Genticol (for yellow eye)

4 bottles children's Tempra

5 bottles Dimetapp

12 bottles sunblock (SPF 20)

24 cans insect repellent

120 packets water disinfectant

And I am sure I have forgotten many things.

Our forty-foot container is packed by a team of six Indians. The toilet paper is the last to go. The packages are light and flexible and can be packed in anywhere. Four Indians stand and watch as two carry the clear plastic packages out on their backs. The look on their faces is of embarrassment, astonishment, and glee. 'Cuba' is the only word I can catch. All six start to laugh, pushing one mover, who, laughing, pushes them back. I look at the leader of their group. 'He India vote Communist,' the leader says, putting his arm around the one who was pushed. We all laugh.

I. 4

We stop in Madrid on our way to Cuba to visit a friend of Nick's who lived in Cuba for four years.

'But what is the basic problem?' we ask Nick's friend.

'Fidel is an old man who can't admit that he made a mistake.'

'But surely it can't be as simple as that.'

'Oh yes it can.'

I. 5

The captain announces that we will soon be beginning our descent. The Spanish executives in the first-class cabin stand, lean, anything to be better able to look out the windows. There is an audible sigh.

Christopher Columbus, on first seeing Cuba, wrote, 'Never have human eyes beheld anything so beautiful.'

I have never been to Florida or the Caribbean: I never felt the need to go, but no one ever told me that the sea was *violet*. Violet, then a greenish violet band, then turquoise, then aquamarine, then clear, utterly clear, to rocks and white sand, then green, green grass dotted with silvery white palm trees, then jungle-covered bluffs and ravines with rivers shining through.

Can this be real? Am I looking at what I am looking at? I have seen photos of the Caribbean in magazines but always thought the colors were enhanced. I feel aesthetic floors, ceilings, and walls being snatched off me like dry mats, leaving me in a giddy new space.

How can anyone have a problem, living here?

Closer, we see houses and roads. We search for cars. There are none; then, closer, we see one, moving patiently. Closer, we see Olympic-sized swimming pools with (now it begins) no water in them, with high platforms for diving boards but no diving boards, just bent, rusted metal supports. We see rusted metal supports for billboards, the billboards having fallen off long ago. Closer still, the real funk begins. Now here we go: rust, lack of paint, mildew, stucco falling off, grass and trees growing out of roof drains, large rusted tanks and rusted, twisted metal structures – supports for more billboards, which have fallen off, too. Closer still, banana trees, papaya trees, mango trees, orange trees, plants with red plumes, orange flowers, yellow hanging bells, purple sprays. Climbing plants that look very much like the plants you see in dentists' offices, only twenty times as big, climbing up palm trees, dentists' office plants gone wild, a green blur past the plane now. An Aeroflot fuselage and a basic little airport.

A 1956 two-tone Chevrolet, a hospital-green brush-painted mid-1940s Oldsmobile, a canary yellow 1957 Ford, the year of the first tail fins, and a Studebaker, a Studebaker, with its bullet nose, moving majestically. Nick and I contemplate it as if it were a Titian. And we've only been on the road for three minutes. And there's a gas crisis.

It's Moscow, but instead of grim-looking white people walking down the road, you have happier-looking white and black and brown people walking down the road, waiting for buses in groups in front of giant slogans painted on walls or plastered on billboards. HASTA LA VICTORIA SIEMPRE (Always toward victory) one slogan reads, and another, VIVA FIDEL Y LA REVOLUCIÓN SOCIALISTA (Long live Fidel and the socialist revolution).

You think, for the first two seconds that you see the slogans, that the people who made the slogans, the people who put the slogans up, and the people standing in front of the slogans are somehow *kidding,* but then you realize, just as quickly, that they are not kidding.

There are advertising billboards, too, on trusses that are still intact, for Habana Club rum, Pepsodent, and Cubatur, a travel agency. Some thoughts about Pepsodent's being an American brand, and about there being a U.S. embargo against Cuba, rise desultorily in our conversation, but we are too jet-lagged to speculate seriously.

Seeing advertising billboards among the slogans brings on another private wave of thinking-they-must-be-kidding, but again, the thinking-they-must-be-kidding vanishes in one second more.

It's China, too, with the bicycles, whole families packed on some. No one is fat, and you are sure of it because they don't have a lot on in the way of clothes. Shorts, halter tops, tank tops, sneakers – Cuban national dress.

IT'S ENORMOUS, OUR HOUSE. Six help lined up just inside the front door as we arrive: a butler, a gardener, a cook, a downstairs maid, an upstairs maid, and a laundress. That's not including the chauffeur, who is bringing the bags up behind us, and Muna, our baby-sitter from Bangladesh, who to our intense relief has agreed to come with us. She will be lonely here, we know, and we have told her that, but she loves Thea, who is six, and Jimmie, who is four, and we have thought that it would be better for the children if she came along. We have told her that if she can't stand it, she can leave, and we'll understand.

I asked Nick several weeks ago if six in help wasn't a little too much. We weren't diplomats, and in the last country, we had only three, including Muna, but Nick said his predecessor had six, it was mean to let anybody go, the house was huge, the kitchen was medieval, and we could afford to live a little because the help cost so little, only $150 per month per person. Of the $150 per month per person, $85 would go directly to the employee, and $65 would go to Cubalse, the state-run conglomerate in charge of almost all construction in the country and almost all services, which provides domestic and other help to foreigners and watches over the help it provides. Eighty-five dollars a month was a *fortune*, Nick explained to me several weeks ago as we were packing, because in Cuba, the average salary was $10 per month.

'*Watches over them?*'

'Watches over them to make sure they watch over us.'

Muna is paid much more because she travels with us, goes to the States and Europe with us, and her salary is a compromise between what she would make in Europe and what she would make in the States. I have told her that the best thing to do when the other people in the house ask her how much money she is making is to lie and say $300.

We look through the house. The children career, yelling, through the echoing halls, searching for their rooms.

The help come at us, as we are touring, keys in hand. Five years of Spanish in school, but I cannot understand a single

29

word. They open closets, safes, close them, put keys in our hands. They seem to want to get the keys out of their own hands as fast as possible. There is a lot of ceremony around a walk-in air-conditioned closet off the kitchen. It is called the *despensa* and it is closed with a key, too.

We walk onto the veranda. Dwarf palms rustle like sheets in the evening breeze. We sit down in metal rocking chairs. The butler, tray in hand, asks us what we would like to drink. We ask for the most Cuban drink. It is a *mojito*, made of dark rum, light rum, lime juice, sugar, and crushed mint.

It was very hot when we arrived, but now it is cooler and a soft breeze hits us, though the words *soft breeze* flop dully as soon as I think them, just as before, on the plane, the word *violet* didn't come anywhere near describing a whole new sensual experience. A pleasant panic as I rummage, jet-lagged, for what it's like: it's like getting hit by a well-powdered marshmallow.

'I think we're going to like it here,' one of us – I don't know which one of us – says.

WE HAVE TWO BATHROOMS off our bedroom. The bathroom we determine will be Nick's, the His-looking bathroom, is green, purple, and pink. The gardener takes the lid off the toilet and shows us the date, 1928, and the words SANDUSKY, OHIO, stamped on the lid's underside. 'Sandusky, yeah!' I say in English. The gardener smiles. The bathroom we determine will be my bathroom, the Hers-looking bathroom, is pink and green with a pink sunken tub underneath a frosted arched window, against which you can see the shadows of palm trees waving.

The she of the Hers-looking bathroom, who lived here (we have been told) until 1958, was short, we realize, and the he of the His-looking bathroom loved her very much and liked to lie in bed and watch her in the tub, her hair pinned up, high-heeled satin slippers ready at the side. He was an adviser to Batista. 'Mr. Castro's going to kill me,' he is reported to have said. Which is what happened. She went to Miami and died there in 1981. They live in our house now, as ghosts.

The showerhead in his bathroom is a Speakman, crusted with mineral deposits, so that it can't be adjusted beyond a fat spray. Only boiling-hot water comes out of it – there is no cold – so we shift to her bathroom. A modern European 'telephone'-type showerhead has been attached to the pitted art deco faucet, which emits only a very weak spray. Still, it is a bearable temperature, and I hold it for Nick, who then holds it for me, training it on key parts.

I. 6

The Diplomercado is not far from us, in an area of inexplicably empty volcanic plains on the edge of the sea, with only the occasional tourist hotel. I have to go immediately, for there is nothing to eat in the house, absolutely nothing. Our shipment is still two months away. José, the driver, says that he will go with me. He says it will be a little crowded because it is Saturday morning.

There is a wedge of about three hundred people in front of a single swinging glass door. A guard is letting them in one by one. 'Follow me,' says José. I get in immediately behind José, and we move, remarkably quickly, along one side of the wedge. '*Permiso, permiso*,' José says. People move out of our way.

I am embarrassed. I have heard that foreigners are served first, allowed to go places Cubans cannot go. I am wondering if I look so different: I am wearing a T-shirt with sweat patches under the arms and a pair of shorts. I have dark hair. It is José, I guess, who is making me seem foreign, but on the faces I see, there is no annoyance, though I think I hear a sigh or two. José nods to the guard, and in we go.

Once inside, people start running. José makes three quick leaps to the shopping carts, pulls one, and we make for the meats. People are standing four thick at the meat bins, scooping plastic-wrapped packages of frozen and semifrozen chicken and meat out of them – thin blood dripping from the packages – almost as fast as the clerks are throwing the packages in, then inching their way out of line, middle-aged white and brown women, mostly, their faces flushed. There is a little jostling, but there is no pushing or shouting. 'Excuse me,' I hear, 'please.' It is polite semipanic.

'What do you want?' José asks.

'Ground beef,' I say, 'chicken . . .'

José feints, ducks, dodges, passing frozen chickens and packs of ground beef back to me in the one space I have found for the cart as I try not to think of freezer burn.

It is the only place to buy beef in a city of two million people. The cook has made a list: flour, milk, cream, baking powder, salt, sugar, onions, carrots, potatoes, pasta, rice, beans, vegetable oil, and canned tomatoes, in addition to the meat. It's a two-person operation, I realize. I stay with the cart while José moves around, gathering the items and returning to the cart.

Squid in ink, I see. Octopus, too. And a twenty-foot section of white asparagus in cans. Rows upon rows of cardoons in glass jars from Italy. Pigs' feet floating in brine in glass jars with Russian writing on them. Something labeled 'Luncheon Meat.' Purple hot dogs from Romania, standing on end in a kind of cookie tin, and layers of pale yellow peas and greenish carrots in gallon jars with no labels whatsoever. There's a smell of sweat and mold and pickle juice, and the terrazzo floor looks like it hasn't been mopped in thirty-five years.

There are American products, too, and some of them look the worse for wear – cans of Planters corn chips with the paper coming off the canisters and brown around the edges – but some of them look brand-new. Pepsi. Heinz ketchup. Del Monte canned fruit.

When it comes to what you really need, there's vegetable oil, I see, but only a single row of bottles on the edge of the shelf, with no other bottles behind them. From a distance and if you squint, it looks like profusion.

José returns. He speaks slowly so that I can understand. There is no flour, he says, no sugar, and no salt. He tells me to leave the cart and follow him. José leads me to a swinging door at the back of the Diplo. He knocks, and a man in a green smock looks out cautiously. José mumbles something to him. The man shakes my hand. Just then, a cart loaded with packs of sugar is being wheeled out. José takes two off the top. The man in the smock disappears into the back of the shop and emerges with five packs of flour. José says maybe he can buy some salt from a friend. There's no baking powder at all.

A shopping list in Cuba, I realize, is just a wish list. It has little to do with what might actually be there. There is toilet paper, though, lots of it, and I start to feel as if I have gone a little overboard with what I put in the container.

We pass the produce section on the way out. Four tomatoes

wrapped in plastic on a Styrofoam tray for $5.00, three apples for $4.50. I tell José I can understand it, about the apples, but $5.00 for four tomatoes, which surely must grow here? José tells me to buy just enough fruits and vegetables to last for the next day or two, until I can get to the *agro*.

Creemos en Fidel y en la revolución (We believe in Fidel and in the revolution) reads a slogan Nick and I see during a walk we take in the evening.

I. 7

I am beginning to get the names straight after three days. José, about thirty-eight, is medium height, wears too-tight *guayaberas* (traditional Cuban shirts buttoned down the front, with pockets), and has some hairs growing out of the top of his nose, which he tries to keep after. Manuel is the butler, and though he shares the title of *custodio* with the gardener, Miguel, Manuel is, by way of age (he's fifty-five) and experience, the head guy and is perfect for the role. He looks like an Asian version of Robert Mitchum and Cubans call him Chino (Chinese), but he tells me that he has no Chinese blood and his ancestors were all from the Canary Islands. He is quiet, digni-fied, knows when to advise on the way things are usually done and when not to. He comes every day at four o'clock, as the others are leaving, serves dinner, and sleeps in one of the three maids' rooms (the other two are used now for storage).

I ask Muna to find out if Manuel has a wife. Muna seems to be getting along with everyone and brings me back small bits of information.

Miguel, the gardener, about thirty-five, is small and slim with a razor-thin face and looks just like his mother, Estrella, the laundress, who has a razor-thin face as well, and bright blue eyes. A telephone and computer technician from Nick's firm comes to do some work at the house and has a razor-thin face as well. *This must be some kind of Cuban face*, I think, *some Galician or Canary Islands or Asturian face*, until they tell me the electrician, Ysidro, is Miguel's brother, Estrella's other son. 'I like their faces,' Nick says. 'So extreme.'

Concha, the downstairs maid, in her mid-fifties, is tense, with eyebrows that have been plucked, then painted back on. She has one son in Tampa and a daughter in Venezuela. She has some pretensions to propriety (an urban background, some education, unlike Estrella and Danila, the upstairs maid, who are both country girls), which can be an asset when you're having to deal with downstairs (taking phone messages, serving meals) but can lead to lording it over the others.

Danila, the upstairs maid, in her mid-thirties, is the simplest of the lot. She seems scared and doesn't speak much above a mumble – scared, maybe, that she will lose her job to Muna, but we would never do that. Danila doesn't have much to do, though, and she knows it. Muna won't have much to do, either, during the day, when the children are in school. We have told Muna that her job in Cuba will be more mental than physical. It is her judgment we will be paying for, her consistency with the children. Danila is *leche con un poquito de café* (milk with a little bit of coffee) – a little bit black, with green eyes and a shapely figure.

Lorena, the cook, is jet-black, with a lively personality.

I don't know much yet about the black/white thing in this country. So far it doesn't seem to *be* a thing: you see black people and white people and brown people hanging out together in much more fluid ways than in the States – playing dominoes at card tables on the sidewalk, waiting at bus stops, holding hands, riding four on a motorcycle, each one of the four a different shade. There is no black neighborhood, no white neighborhood, and I find myself with a new feeling: it is the feeling of being relaxed.

TE SERÉ SIEMPRE FI$^D_\wedge$EL (I will always be faithful to you). *Fiel* means faithful, but they have inserted a *d*.

I.8

'We don't have to wear uniforms?' Thea asks as I lay a T-shirt, shorts, and sandals out for her on the first day at the International School of Havana. Thea and Jimmie wore gray uniforms at the British-run school that they were in last.

'No.' I have somehow forgotten to tell her and Jimmie this.

34

'*Wow!*' Thea runs into Jimmie's room. '*No uniforms! No uniforms! No uniforms!*'

'IT WAS LIKE BEING at a party, but with new kids!' Thea says, jumping into the car after her first day at the International School of Havana.

'Yeah!' Jimmie says.

Thea's second-grade teacher and Jimmie's kindergarten teacher wave at me from behind the chain-link gate. 'It went very well!' they call to me in English.

'Did you put something in their juice?' I ask the teachers.

They laugh. 'They are happy children!'

I drive home with Thea and Jimmie, bouncing on the back-seat.

'So how did it go?'

'We sang, Mommy! We danced! I am going to be in a play!' Thea says.

'I made puzzles with my teacher!' Jimmie says. 'And there was a *big pig* in one puzzle! Ha! Ha! Ha!'

Nick and I have heard about how hard it is on the children, changing schools and friends.

We are home. Thea and Jimmie leap from the car. They dump their lunch boxes on the hall bench, take off their shirts, and run upstairs with their shirts streaming behind them like flags. 'We're in *Kew-baaaaaaaa*, we're in *Kew-baaaaaaaaaa* and we don't have to wear any *uni-for-or-or-orms!!!!!!!!!!!!!!!!!!!!*'

I. 9

Miguel takes me to an *agropecuario*, or fruit, vegetable, lamb, and pork market. The pesos-only *agropecuario* is a middle way between the entirely state-run dollars-only Diplomercado, with its five-dollar-a-pound tomatoes, and the state-run pesos-only bodegas, where only Cubans can go, with ration books, to buy staples (when available) at subsidized prices. Less and less, though, is available in the bodegas, so Cubans are obliged to shop at *agros* and at the Diplo (if they have dollars) more and more.

Agropecuarios, where farmers are allowed to sell on the open market a percentage of what they produce, have been operating

– this time around – only about a year. *Agros* were first opened in the eighties and were very successful, but they were shut down after only a few months. Then, when the *periodo especial* began, and people, especially children, started showing signs of vitamin deficiencies, Raúl Castro declared that people's not having enough to eat was a matter of national security, and the *agros* were allowed to open again.

A farmer can raise pigs and lambs and sell their meat at the *agro*, but only the state can sell beef. Who can sell chickens seems to be undefined. Miguel says they are seen at the *agro* once every few months. Watermelons I see, and garlic and squash. Onions, limes, and white, red, and black beans. A pyramid of cabbages. Yuccas, malangas, and sweet potatoes. Cucumbers, and tomatoes at ten pesos (twenty-fifty cents) a pound instead of five dollars. Ten pesos is 5 to 10 percent of a Cuban's monthly salary, but still, I feel relieved. Parsley, spinach, and leeks. Pork, lamb, and sausages in one section. People yelling, 'Buy my stuff! It's the best!' just like in any market in the world.

Miguel says it's a good time of year now for fruits and vegetables.

'But who would ever buy fruits and vegetables at the Diplomercado?' I ask Miguel.

'*Turistas*,' he says, who don't know any better, businessmen . . .

'They have to really, *really* not know any better . . .'

Miguel says it's amazing how many visitors or recent arrivals in Cuba really, really do not know any better. 'They get off the plane and . . .' Miguel makes like a blind man, groping for his way.

I. 10

'Why are there always so many women standing by the side of the road, Mommy?' Thea and Jimmie ask me on the way home from school.

We see them on Quinta Avenida, which is the main artery of Miramar, a former upper-class neighborhood, and on the Malecón, which is a boulevard running along the sea, flanked by wide sidewalks and, on one side, a low seawall. We see them lingering on the curbs in latex spandex hot pants, halter tops, bike shorts, tube dresses, and sometimes décolleté, full-length evening dresses, the *jineteras. Jinete* means 'jockey' in Spanish. *Jinetera* is a word invented in Cuba to mean 'female jockey' because she rides the tourists.

It is said that they are not out-and-out prostitutes because they do not talk about price right away and say no if they do not like the man's face; if police stop, they tell them they are hitchhiking, for Cuban women tend to dress revealingly anyway and hitchhiking has become a common means of transportation since the beginning of the *periodo especial*, when bus service was drastically curtailed.

A *jinetera* will start out as a date, for the most part, going to a bar, to a nightclub, or to a *paladar* with the sexual tourist who has picked her up. Usually she will stay with the same sexual tourist for the entire length of his stay. She will take the sexual tourist home to meet her family. The sexual tourist will give the family presents.

'They are hitchhiking,' I tell the children.

THE BODY OF A DEAD dog has been lying fifteen feet from the entrance to our house for two days. Its body is swollen now and stiff. I keep thinking it is going to be picked up any minute. The guard, who has a walkie-talkie, paces by it. I distract the children when we drive past it on our way to and from school, singing, telling them to count the number of white cars on the other side of the street.

I ask Manuel if there isn't some kind of service in Havana to call to pick it up. I say I can't believe that the bodies of dead animals would be left to rot by the side of a major street . . .

Manuel laughs politely and says that he will put gasoline on it and burn it.

I. 11

It's early Beverly Hills, our house: that's it. The body of the dead dog kept me for a while from seeing it as I walked around the garden, looking up at the house, trying to remember where I had seen its style before. The Beverly Hills of Gloria Swanson, Theda Bara, Mary Pickford, and Harold Lloyd. It is the period and style, too, of the house my parents lived in before they were divorced, which my father continued to live in after the divorce, in lonely splendor; it was demolished after his death to make room for luxury tract houses. Spanish style, it was called, which I always assumed was a made-up California thing. I've never seen any houses in Spain that looked like it, but here they are in Cuba, built by practically Spanish people.

I go through the house now with the rush of recognition and a racing feeling not just up my arms but all over. I am home. Home with the cascading bougainvillea, thick walls, terra-cotta tile roofs, cooing of mourning doves, and *tsk, tsk* of sprinklers in the morning. Home with the hugely comfortable closets, mirror-lined dressing rooms, and Spanish-speaking help. Home with the hospital-green aerodynamic pantry with the matching Waring blender. Home with the roaring laundry room, the close-smelling back stairs, the attic I so much wanted to *be* an attic, with baby buggies and dress molds in it, which was instead just a ventilation space I couldn't stand up in. (Those real attics, I surmised, the ones in book illustrations, were East Coast attics.) Home with the abandoned staff rooms and bathrooms with emerald green water in their toilets, unflushed for years, and the utility room in the garage with its petrified rags and machine parts stamped ELMIRA, N.Y., OR ST. LOUIS, MO., 1937. Home with the brick-solid door handles and hinges, the surprised-eyed firm-gripping electrical outlets, the light switches composed of two bobbing Bakelite buttons, the beaten-iron ceiling lamps and sconces of a Hispanicized Arts and Crafts movement. Home with the '57, '58, and '59 Fords, Lincolns, Cadillacs, and Buicks passing majestically on the street outside.

I had gotten used to the idea that I couldn't go home again. Now I know that what the overly zealous fairy godmother (for lack of knowing what else to call her) really meant was that I couldn't go home again *in California*.

SEÑORES IMPERIALISTAS, reads a billboard facing the U.S. Interests Section, showing a muscle-bound, lantern-jawed Cuban soldier facing a cowering Uncle Sam, NO LES TENEMOS ABSOLUTAMENTE NINGUN MIEDO! (Mr. Imperialists: we are absolutely unafraid of you!).

I. 12

I have one set of keys to the *despensa*; the other set is held by Miguel, the gardener, during the day, and Manuel, the butler, from 4 P.M. on. I never remember to bring the chain of keys I have with me down the mile-long winding staircase, so that every time I want to check the food supply during the day, I have to ask Concha, the downstairs maid, who goes to look for Miguel in the garden. Sometimes the process takes more than ten minutes, but it is too hot to climb the stairs, and I can't send someone to go look for the keys where I have hidden them, because they are supposed to be in a secret place. It's a pain to all of us, embarrassing to me and (I think) insulting to the help, but here people take a lot. Lorena, the cook, doesn't even have a key, and I would like to give her one, but I don't dare, fearing it would upset some delicate chain of command that has been handed down from generation to generation. I try not to think of the advice from the wife of Nick's predecessor: 'Lorena's the head spy, and everyone else in the house is afraid of her. She lies and she steals, too, as blacks always do.'

People from X— (a monocultural, xenophobic little country, where women in loden coats visibly shiver when they see an African) make those kinds of take-your-breath-away remarks all the time.

Lorena keeps a small supply of oil, rice, pasta, potatoes, herbs, and spices in a smaller unlocked closet for immediate access. It's some Latin American thing, I think hopefully, this keeping the *despensa* locked. Something about my aunt, who lived for many years in Honduras, is rumbling around in my mind and then surfaces: my aunt had a *despensa* that she wanted to keep unlocked. Twenty-four cooks she fired (she said) until she found one who could manage not to steal from it, and that cook she had for twelve years.

Our closet of cleaning supplies is locked with a key, too.

I. 13

No toilet paper in the Diplomercado. There is therefore no Kleenex, no paper napkins, no paper towels, and the stand selling the Cuban newspapers *Granma* and *Juventud Rebelde* is doing a brisk business. There are also no telephone directories and haven't been any for years.

I feel vindicated.

I. 14

All this trying to get settled has meant that we haven't gotten out to see anything except the Diplomercado, the *agropecuario*, the school, Nick's office, and the neighborhood around our house.

Tonight, though, we go with a documentary filmmaker to see a play put on in a metalworker's factory. We drive on unlit roads for nearly an hour, looking for the place, diving into potholes and swerving around bicyclists and crowds waiting silently at what used to be bus stops for passing farm or construction vehicles – requisitioned for the transport of people – to pack them in. Heads turn in unison to watch the Toyota Land Cruiser pass.

Nick and I think it's going to be something experimental, a performance staged *in* the factory, like a show that was done years ago in the rail yards outside Paris, but instead we are led into a small auditorium within the factory complex. Then I remember: this is the workers' paradise, factories are *supposed* to take care of workers' cultural needs, and instead of chic or hip-looking Cubans drawn to an alternative experience, the audience is made up of factory workers, short, white mostly, Spanish-looking, as if out of some Spanish travel brochure, as if they could be on some cute street, the men in berets, but they are wearing clothes that don't fit – *really* don't fit – and they are sweating a lot, as if they still aren't used to the humidity, even after two or more generations.

The documentary filmmaker explains that the show is a revival of a kind of entertainment that developed in Cuban music halls in the last century and lasted until *el triunfo de la revolución* (the triumph of the revolution). Originally, only men were allowed to attend music halls, because the shows in them were considered too obscene for women. The shows always involved three characters, El Gallego (the Galician, or Spaniard – all Spaniards are called *gallegos* because so many did come from Galicia), El Negro, and La Mulata (the Mulatta). The shows were closed following *el triunfo de la revolución* because they were considered racist. They are now again being permitted to be performed (but in out-of-the-way places) because there's a current argument circulating that it's racist *not* to show historical or popular racism, that representing historical or popular racism in art is criticism of it: there's that argument, and there's also the government's penchant for picking some cultural area in which it can safely show how liberal it's being, and at the moment, it's this cultural area.

It seems that Cubans – it doesn't matter who they are – never say the word *revolución* without putting the words *el triunfo de la* before it, and hearing nonofficial or unorthodox Cubans say it is like the way it was for us seeing the first slogan on our way from the airport: we think, for a second, that they are kidding, but it's always only for a second.

We know they aren't kidding, but whenever Nick or I hear *el triunfo de la* or see a slogan, something still catches in our chests, and there's a glow, like a flash from a cherry bomb, which is just as quickly over. It's getting to be less, though, the catch and flash, all the time.

The show is called *El Encuentro de Dos Mundos* (The Meeting of Two Worlds) and it's about Columbus's discovery of America, though the Indians this time are contemporary Cubans (represented by La Mulata), and Columbus (El Gallego) is a European sexual tourist, who lures La Mulata with bullion and jewels, causing her to forsake her family and her ideals. We can't understand all the words, but La Mulata wears a grass skirt and a bone in her hair and jumps up, spread-eagled, on El Gallego's crotch repeatedly. The audience doubles over, screaming with laughter. El Negro is a white man in blackface who plays various roles, one of them that of a priest, who at one point shifts from a Catholic blessing to the trance dancing of a *babalao* (a Santeria priest, Santeria being a blending of West African religions, imported to Cuba by slaves, and Catholicism) whirling, muttering, and shaking. Once again the crowd goes wild.

Afterward, we meet the star and author of the show, YeYe Perez. He hands us his card. 'YeYe Perez, El Negro Vernáculo,' it reads. He is a professional blackface actor, and he is trying to revive this music-hall tradition, he explains.

CUBA IS DEFINITELY DIFFERENT racial territory from the United States. There is racism, but it is less institutionalized, more in-your-face. A white or a black man will call a black man standing nearby 'a cute little nigger,' and the black man won't seem offended, and then the white or the black will put his arm around the black man he has just called *negrito* and they will both beam at me, as close and seemingly well adjusted as two peas in a pod. Black men and white men sigh, '*Ay, mi negra . .*' when a good-looking black woman or *mulata* passes them on the street. A white or a black will try to get the attention of an unfamiliar black person across the street by shouting, '*Oye, negrito!*' and the black won't seem to mind. Unknown Asians are called *chino* or *chinito* by blacks, whites, and other Asians. Blacks call, '*Oye, blanco,*' to unknown whites, but they do not say '*blanco*' or '*blanquito*' as often as blacks or whites say '*negro*' or '*negrito.*' When someone is really blond, he or she will be called *negrito* or *negrita*, as a sign of affection, just as when a woman is beautiful she is called *fea* (ugly). Reference to skin color is made by touching two fingers to the forearm. 'She's a nice girl,' a white person will say, and the other white person will reply, '*pero . . .*' ('but . . .') and touch his forearm. White people and black people both touch two fingers to the forearm as a way of referring to skin color, but only whites will follow it with a '*pero . . .*' There are no exclusively black or exclusively white neighborhoods, though when it comes to Miramar, Siboney, or Cubanacán, the formerly upper-class and upper-middle-class neighborhoods, there are mostly whites living in them, and when it comes to Old Havana, there are mostly blacks or *mulatos* living there, but whites live there, too. There are no waves of black crime, no black anger, no white vigilantism, no hate crimes. Still, when a crime is committed, the policeman, *no matter what color he is*, will say, '*Fue un negro, no?*' ('It was a black, wasn't it?').

I. 15

We finally get a chance to walk around Habana Vieja. We have been through it a couple of times in the car, but this time we are able to get out and walk, and not just in the Cathedral Square.

'Pretty run down,' 'It's in bad shape:' You hear that a lot, but no one prepares you for Berlin, 1945. Berlin, 1945, but routine, with tourists walking through it, taking photographs of the baroque and neoclassical and art nouveau and art deco remains, and people trying to sell you cigars, and kids and mothers and grandmothers living in the ruins, acting like it's a perfectly normal day, descending the stairs with water buckets to fill from tank trucks in the street because while there may be bathrooms in their apartments, there's no running water, and there hasn't been any for years. Sometimes a street is blocked off because a building has collapsed, its insides reduced to rubble by a fire brigade and shoveled into a big mound on the street to await pickup, which often, because of gas shortages, does not come for several days. The rubble heap attracts other garbage: corncobs, carrot tops, blood-soaked rags, uncrumpling issues of *Granma* that have been used as toilet paper.

Putti, caryatids, Corinthian columns, sphinxes, fasciae, garlands, meanders, centurions, blare past elegance. Sidewalk mosaics announce the stores that were: JOYERÍA (Jewelry Store), PELETERÍA (Shoe Store), WESTINGHOUSE Y HOTPOINT. Wooden braces hold some facades in place. *Yagruma* trees grow out of second-story balconies – not out of pots, but *out of the balconies themselves* – their roots finding enough nutrients in the interstices between blocks to grow several stories, sometimes higher than the roofs.

It is hard to believe that thirty-odd years of mere neglect could destroy so much. It looks more like an assault or, if not an assault, as if someone really hated the place, hated it in spite of its beauty, or because of it, as if being beautiful were a taunt. Touring Habana Vieja is like stepping into a feud you don't know all the details of and being stunned at the strength of the hatred, at the force of the negative energy, and at the monu-mentality of the ego, or egos, behind the feud.

We walk under a series of porticoes. More mosaics set into terrazzo pavement: PIELES (Furs – we suppose for Cuban ladies who traveled to New York or Europe), AGENCIA DE VIAJES (Travel Agency), HERMANOS — sastres (— Brothers Tailors; the name is blotted out by a blob of cement). People have set up card tables and stools along the street side of the porticoes. Women sit behind some, doing manicures. One man repairs eyeglasses, others refill Bic lighters from spray cans of insecti-cide. Another man restitches tennis shoes. Another with tarot cards, incense, and Santeria images speaks earnestly to a client.

One of the few active establishments along the store side of the portico is in a niche between two empty stores. People line up at the niche for tiny vanilla ice cream cones, one small scoop of vanilla per cone. Each customer walks away with two cones. Nick finds out that the ice cream vendor is a state establishment and that only one size ice cream cone can be offered. It costs one peso (five cents). The ice cream seller is not allowed to sell two scoops on a cone. Each customer is, however, allowed to buy two ice cream cones. Each customer walks away licking one cone, then the other, in rapid succession, before they melt in the heat.

We enter a department store called Fin de Siglo (End of the Century). At first we're not sure it's open because it is so dark inside and the display windows have nothing in them but dust, curled poster board, and sun-bleached crepe paper flowers. But we see people coming and going through smudged swinging glass doors, so we go in, too.

Eyes adjusting to the dim light, I feel the fifties washing over me again. I'm with my mother this time. She has on a crisp white hat about half as big as a regular hat, curved to her head like a piece of seashell and held in place by two tortoiseshell combs. I am holding her hand, and we are cruising through aisles lined with polished wood biomorphic-form display counters.

Fluorescent lights flicker on the first floor, salesgirls are there, a wooden escalator is running to the second floor, but only a quarter of the counters have anything in them. The counters that have anything in them contain only items that can be produced in Cuba: aluminum kitchen utensils, papier-mâché puppets, baby shoes, sport shirts, buttons laid out individually like jewels. There is a lot of space around each button, and I find myself, as I look at the buttons and at the space around each one of them, thinking about how my mother is dead and I am not going to see her anymore: my mother died in the middle of our packing for Cuba, and I have been so busy until this moment that I have not thought about how I am really and truly not going to see her anymore.

Raised, carpeted platforms with plaster neoclassical columns and mannequin body parts on them. Some wide, absolutely empty spaces. A store directory announces the departments: children's clothes, home furnishings, men's shoes. Scratchy salsa from a cassette player. Salesgirls sit, legs wide apart, on sagging vinyl armchairs in what was once the shoe trying-on area. No one is shopping: the people going in and out of the store, we realize, are just using it as a way to cut a corner and stay for a moment in the shade, for the store has another entrance on a cross street.

I get a Nick-and-I-are-in-a-film feeling – a surrealistic French or Spanish film or an Eastern European film from the seventies – and we talk in low voices about how we can't understand why filmmakers are not using this place right now to make all kinds of films, and when Cuban officials refuse to let them because they would be showing an unflattering side of Cuba, why those same filmmakers are not shooting from their pockets, from holes in their lapels, any way they can.

Nick and I are in one of the weirdest places on earth, weird not so much because it is stuck in the fifties and is empty, but because it is *open*, *staffed*, and *routine*. It is one of the weirdest places on earth, but it is at the same time familiar, as if a nuclear missile really *did* hit Saint Stephen's School and forty-year-olds now climb out from under their desks, blinking at what's left. It will become routine, too, I know, in time, not having a mother.

A sign at the bottom of the escalator reads MORE UPSTAIRS.

I. 16

The International School of Havana, which serves the English-speaking foreign community, is an adequate school academically, and Thea and Jimmie definitely enjoy it, but Nick and I start to look around for other activities for the children to do after school. The Community Center of Siboney offers dance classes to children in the afternoons, Nick discovers. Thea will be able to keep up the ballet she started in the previous country and meet Cuban children at the same time. We can't have the children living in Cuba and never spending time with Cuban children.

There is only one Cuban child in the school, Yolanda. Cuban children are not normally allowed. Yolanda is there because her father, a Cuban actor working in Mexico, is a *gusañero*, a new category of expatriate Cuban, the term being a combination of *gusano* (worm, a term for all Cubans who have left Cuba) and *compañero* (comrade), meaning a Cuban who makes foreign currency and returns a portion of it to the Cuban government in exchange for being able to keep his Cuban citizenship and travel freely to and from Cuba. Yolanda is in the school because her father can pay for it and because the Cuban government either hasn't yet developed a policy about children with a *gusañero* parent or simply hasn't noticed Yolanda is there.

José drives down a pitted driveway and around a circle and stops in front of a midsize mansion, its garden a jungle with rusting appliance and machine parts poking through the foliage. As usual, we're not sure we're at the right place. Few buildings in Havana are used for what they were originally intended, and even fewer have signs in front of them. José goes in ahead of us and comes out with his thumb up.

An upright Remington typewriter and a battered, unplugged mimeograph machine sit on a desk behind a particleboard partition in the marble-floored foyer. The *directora*, a cheerful *mulata*, kisses both of us and Thea on both cheeks. We thank the *directora* for making it possible for Thea to take classes. She says it's odd, but few foreign families have ever expressed an interest in their children's taking dance classes at the *centro*.

We are shown into the dressing room. Thea has asked Nick and me to stay with her the whole time. We are led through a pantry to what must have been a state-of-the-art kitchen in 1959. There is space in the French provincial wooden cabinets for a wall oven, another space for a stove top once set into a yellow Formica countertop now gouged with cigarette burns, the remains of a garbage-disposal unit, and a space for a built-in refrigerator. Vents near the ceiling show that there must have been central air-conditioning. A coffin-style freezer remains, its lid ripped off, brownish liquid at the bottom. Only a few linoleum tiles are still in place, so the floor is for the most part crumbling cement. The *directora* tells us to leave Thea's clothes heaped on a counter. We do not have to worry about the clothes, for she . . . she points at her eye. '*Entienden?*' ('Do you understand?').

'I feel weird,' Thea says to us.

Other girls arrive soon, lithe-limbed, giggling, with tulle bows in their hair. They change out of their clothes and into leotards, helped by earnest mothers, most of them a good fifteen years younger than I am. Most of the leotards have been mended more than once, the straps taken up or extended, and the legs rehemmed.

We move into the dance studio, in what must have been the library. Scalloped borders of oak paneling outline alcoves where the bookshelves must have been. A cast-iron chandelier, festooned with cobwebs, is the room's remaining ornament.

'It's like a witch's house, Mommy.'

What parquet is left has buckled, but most of it has been removed and replaced with shellacked plywood. It is April, eighty-five degrees, and humid.

The teacher, an El Greco–faced blond, kisses us on both cheeks. One window is open; the other window is shut. 'I try never to use the word *heat*,' she murmurs to us in French. She climbs onto a chair and opens the other window. 'There!' she says, smiling, to her students as she steps off the chair. It does not cool off at all.

Nick and I sit in the garden at the back of the house, dangling our feet in an empty swimming pool, getting up every five minutes to stand on a tree stump and look in through a window at Thea. Parents are not allowed to stay in the room, but we have assured Thea that we will look in on her every ten minutes. 'Every five minutes,' Thea said.

'How much longer?' Thea mouths to us through a forest of lithe, nut-brown, arching limbs every time we look in on her.

AFTER WE GET HOME, Muna motions to me to follow her into an empty hallway. She tells me Manuel was in jail for nine years. A political prisoner. He keeps his conviction in the *despensa*.

'In the *despensa*?'

'He says it's safe there.'

I. 17

Nick and I go downtown every chance we can get, to complete our tour. We go to a *cuentapropista* (people allowed to do business for themselves) complex in a large store on Avenida Galliano. People rent counters in the store and sell either what they have made or what they are allowed to sell. Aisles of glassed-in counters hold handmade party decorations, aluminum utensils, used record albums, bottles and packages of mysterious liquids and dried leaves, some bicycle parts, used baby clothes, plaster Santeria images, rolled beeswax candles, hair ornaments, goldfish swimming in little glass bowls.

A lunch counter with built-in stools wraps around three sides of the store. Some of the stool seats are missing; only the bases are left. A repeating frieze of menu runs along the top of all three sides of the food area: PERROS CALIENTES (hot dogs), 5 centavos, PANATELA DE BOSTON CREMA (Boston cream pie), 20 ¢, ENSALADA DE ESPAN (spam salad), 15 ¢, PANQUÉ, 5 ¢ CADA UNO (pancakes, 5 centavos each), HAMBURGUESA (hamburger) 20 ¢. It is the menu and the prices of 1961.

Only one side of the lunch counters is occupied. The other two sides are empty and dark. Stool seats have been taken from the empty sides to keep the stools along the lighted counter intact.

The waitresses do not take orders, nor do customers give them. One waitress stands at blackened pots on an unplugged griddle filling plates with rice, beans, squash, and pinkish meat and handing them to another waitress, who hands them silently to customers. During lulls, the second waitress pours tiny glasses of Tropicola. Dirty plates are removed, and more blackened pots are brought through a swinging door as the pots on the unplugged griddle empty.

In the pavement at each of the store's two entrances, mosaic in flowing script spells out WOOLWORTH.

I. 18
Word has gotten out that a couple of people in the government think that Nick is a good guy, and word has gotten to Nick that he should invite them for dinner.

We have to serve twice as much food when Cubans come over, Lorena says, because they eat a lot.

'Yes?'

'Oh yes. *No tienen control*' ('They have no control').

Thin, pale white men in 65 percent polyester *guayaberas*, Chinese nylon socks with lines of arrows or Ping-Pong paddles running up the ankles, and gunmetal, powder blue, or pale yellow basket-weave loafers. Placid, heavy first wives, for the most part, with feet stuffed into pointed patent leather shoes with poofs of flesh out the top. There are, however, some younger trophy wives as well. I didn't think there would *be* trophy wives in Cuba. One sports a décolletage held up by Chanel-bag–like chains suspended from a band around the throat. This looks somehow more socialist. I don't know why.

Concha shows the seating plan at the entrance to the dining room. The first woman into the dining room, wife of the guest of honor, tries to take the seating plan from her, thinking it's some kind of party favor, but Concha holds on. 'Oh,' the woman says. Concha smiles slightly, arching one eyebrow.

The first course is served, and each person served digs right in without waiting for anyone else. I don't know whether to hold my ground or not, but eventually I do, waiting for Nick. Some don't put their napkins in their laps. One stands up and reaches across the table to grab the salt. Others spear the pâté on their plates with knives and carry it directly to their mouths. Still others wave their knives around as they talk. One woman, clacking loudly, with her face very near her plate, sucks pâté from her side teeth, clearing the rest with the nail of her pinky.

'*Qué rico!*' ('How rich!' i.e., sumptuous) several of them say, complimenting me on the food.

'*Sí, sí, muy sabroso*' ('Yes, yes, very delicious'), one of the men who has just been waving his knife around says to me, in a honeyed basso profondo. '*Señora, felicidades . . .*' ('Congratulations . . .'). He makes a flourish with his knifeless hand, as though he were doffing a hat.

'You're from the United States?' the high official to my right says. He is very thin, with bad posture and a few strands of hair combed over his baldness. His voice is thin, too, plaintive.

'Have you ever been there?'

'Never,' he says. 'They won't *let me . . .*'

'Maybe you will get there some day . . .'

'But the United States, it has this policy, this embargo, it won't *let* Communist ministers like me in. Only to the UN . . .'

'That's really too bad,' I say, 'because Cuba is a beautiful country, and the United States is a beautiful country, and I think they would enjoy each other so much.'

He sighs. 'I just don't know why they don't *like us* . . .'

'The United States is a very large country, a very vast and complicated country, and there are some people in the United States who are for the embargo, but there are also a lot of people who are against the embargo . . .'

The man to my left is saying something across the table about North Americans.

'The *señora* is North American!' the man to my right, leaning forward, calls to the man to my left.

'The *señora* is North American!' the man to my left repeats. He looks at me. 'You can help us! You know Sullivan's wife – you can talk to her!'

Sullivan is the chief officer of the U.S. Interests Section of the Swiss Embassy, the de facto U.S. ambassador.

'But Sullivan doesn't *have* a wife. He is divorced . . .'

'He has a wife! You should talk to her!'

MIGUEL APPROACHES ME in the garden after breakfast. '*Mira, señora* . . .' I follow him to where the hose we use for watering the lawn and vegetable garden is lying on the ground. He picks up the end of the hose. It is completely bare. 'One of the chauffeurs last night, they stole the attachment for connecting the hose to the sprinkler. It will take much more time to water the garden now.'

'One of the chauffeurs from last night? One of the chauffeurs *of the officials?*'

'*Señora*, when Cubans come, you have to hide things.'

'But people *from the government?*'

Miguel looks at the ground, shaking his head.

'Can you find attachments in Cuba?'

'No.'

'That's why they stole it, then.'

Miguel considers this. He sticks out his lower lip, nodding. 'That's why, of course . . .'

I. 19

Lorena's son is in prison. He was sentenced to ten years in prison when he was eighteen years old. He has already been in prison for three years. Muna hasn't found out yet what he is in for. Lorena goes once a month to visit him.

After Lorena has gone home for the evening, we ask Manuel what Lorena's son did. Manuel shrugs, saying he thought it was just an ordinary crime.

After a minute or two, Manuel returns. He clears his throat. We know what's coming. Manuel has the habit of shuffling his feet and moving one hand, then the other, beyond his ample paunch as he talks, in a kind of sedate cross-country skiing action. 'With your permission, there is something I have been meaning to talk to you about . . .'

'Yes, Manuel?'

'I don't want you to think I've been trying to hide anything from you. I, too, have been in prison. For political crimes. After *el triunfo de la revolución*, I didn't agree with the way things were going. I aided some counterrevolutionaries and I was put in jail for nine years. My conviction is here if you would like to read it . . .'

Manuel returns with his conviction on a silver tray.

Manuel, too, says *el triunfo de la revolución.*

SOCIALISMO O MUERTE (Socialism or death), reads the sign in six-foot-high letters supported by scaffolding over the entrance to a tunnel under the Almendares River.

You see it, you see it, you see it as you drive toward the tunnel, and then you have darkness, as if you have picked death.

I. 20

We visit a complex of stores for tourists in a newly restored *palacio* just off the Malecón. Tourist buses are parked outside it. We have heard the best store for Che T-shirts is here. Some friends want them.

There are Che T-shirts, there are Camilo Cienfuegos T-shirts, there are Tropicola T-shirts, there are fringed T-shirts with sleepy-eyed, unrecognizable cartoon characters on them, saying things that you don't understand if they are written in Spanish or that don't make any sense if they are written in English. There are T-shirts with naked women on them, or parts of naked women, saying, '*Yo* ♥ *Cuba.*'

There is a store selling tapes and CDs; there is a store selling beer, rum, soft drinks, film, and suntan lotion. There is a store selling jewelry, and a store selling leather items. There is a store selling refrigerator magnets of the cathedral and the Hotel Nacional, highly lacquered wooden key holders, rum pourers, cigar holders, and even ashtrays with images of Che and the words HASTA LA VICTORIA SIEMPRE burned into them with soldering irons. An image of Che's face is in the bottom of each ashtray, so that cigarettes will be stubbed out on his face. There are papier-mâché images of fish, clowns, butterflies, and alligators and of black *rumberas* in long, flouncy dresses with head kerchiefs, with huge behinds and huge lips, smoking cigars. There are African-style masks and statues, macramé bracelets, a $120 Black & Decker sandwich maker, an $85 blender, a $75 crushed-ice maker, a $40 toilet paper holder, playing cards, beaded necklaces . . .

Nick and I stop at the last few items on display. The pink plastic toilet paper holder is out of its box, with the mounting screws taped onto the back of it with yellowed Scotch tape. The Black & Decker sandwich-maker box is crushed and worn on the edges but looks unused.

We are the only people in the store. Nick says, '*Buenos días,*' to the saleswoman behind the counter.

'*Buenos días,*' she says.

'This is a very nice store.'

'Thank you.'

'There are nice things in the store.'

'Yes, there are very nice things in this store.'

There is silence. We've got time on our hands, so Nick says after a while, 'This is a store for tourists, isn't it?'

'Yes, for tourists.'

'We're intrigued by the sandwich maker.'

'Intrigued?'

'Is it for tourists?'

'*Sí, claro.*'

'It's for tourists to buy for themselves?'

'Certainly.'

'A tourist comes in here and says to himself, 'I'm just going to pick up a little one-hundred-twenty-dollar, one-hundred-ten-volt sandwich maker to take back to Düsseldorf to remember Cuba by'?'

She laughs. 'Why not? It's something original, isn't it?'

I. 21

Our container has arrived after two months, and our three days of unpacking are attended by an expert from Bienes Culturales and a veterinarian. We serve them coffee, lunch, more coffee, and Tropicola as they wander for eight hours a day among boxes and growing mountains of Bubble Wrap and newspaper.

The expert from Bienes Culturales is looking for Cuban national treasures.

'Cuban national treasures *coming back* to Cuba *from Southeast Asia?*'

'*Eso es.*' Cuban national treasures, the expert tells me conspiratorially, have been known to come back to Cuba *from all over the world.*

The veterinarian is on the lookout for canned meat.

I tell the veterinarian the family doesn't *like* canned meat. Canned meat has preservatives – carcinogens – in it.

The veterinarian tells me she just has to make sure there isn't any in our shipment.

The Bienes Culturales expert, Betina, hands me her card and, winking, tells me to be sure to ask for her when we move out.

TWO MEN FROM THE central bank come to make a note of all the jewelry and silver we are bringing into the country. We spread it out on the dining table, silver on one end and jewelry on the other. The list of silver and jewelry we have brought in will be checked, before we leave in a few years' time, against a list of the silver and jewelry we will be taking out of the country.

One man is in his sixties, and the other man is in his thirties. We offer them coffee and Coca-Cola. The older man describes the pieces and measures them while the younger man writes.

'How do you like it here in Cuba?' the older man asks me.

'It is a beautiful country.'

'Are you from X—— as well?'

'No, I am from the United States.'

'The United States?'

'Yes.'

'Hm . . .' He turns over a silver dish. 'Does Cuba remind you of the United States? The look of it, I mean. This is what some North Americans tell me . . .'

'Nature is different, and I have only seen Havana, but I am struck by similarities in the urban landscape every day. The design of so many of the houses, the way the streets are laid out, the stores. Americans will be fascinated by this place when they finally do come here. It will remind people my age of the way streets and stores looked in their childhoods. It reminds me of my childhood. The Woolworth's. The coffee shops. I even saw a piece of a Montgomery Ward sign the other day.'

'*El sea me encantó . . .*'

'Sorry?' I don't know what *el sea* is, but he liked it, or literally was enchanted by it.

'*El . . . ¿como se dice in inglés? El* Sea-errs *me encantó, con su catálogo.*'

'Oh, Sears Roebuck.'

'*Eso es.*' He turns to the young man. 'If they didn't have it in the store, you could order it from the catalog and it would get here in a few days. I'm telling you, it was like that.' He turns to me: '*Y me encantaron las revistas,* getting them from the United States. *El* National Geographic. *Qué revista tan interesante, tan hermosa*' ('And I loved the magazines . . . What an interesting and beautiful magazine').

I wait for him to say something else. His eyes mist.

'The *National Geographic* is still there, and it is exactly the same,' I say heartily. 'The format hasn't changed. Water?'

'*Sí, por favor.*' He picks up another piece of silver, stares at it. He slaps the young man's arm, clearing his throat. '*Vamos. A la pincha, chico*' ('Let's get back to work, kid').

I. 22

We finally start Spanish lessons. The director of our children's school has found someone for us, Olga. Olga wears a peasant blouse and a dirndl skirt. She will teach the children first, then Muna, then Nick and me, one hour for each group, two days a week. We tell her the children take Spanish in school, but we want them to have extra Spanish, at home. We say that it should be playful, to hold their interest.

We assess, together with her, what we need to work on. She nods, taking notes.

'But no ideology,' Nick says.

'Of course not,' Olga says, flushing.

'It was the blouse,' Nick says to me later.

I. 23

It is late April but not terribly hot today. We put the children's bicycles, which arrived in the container, in the back of the Land Cruiser and take them to one of the large, shady squares we have driven by in Miramar. There are busts of Cuban poets in the square. It is shaded with giant ficus trees, and there is a small bandstand in the middle of it.

Thea and Jimmie get on their bikes and start riding enthusiastically. Nick and I walk in the shade of the ficus trees. The cement paths are pulverized in many places, and there are small trash heaps, some of which are smoldering, but they are far enough off the paths. Thea rides ahead of Jimmie until we cannot see her anymore. We climb steps to the bandstand. We see Thea at one side of the square. She has stopped her bike and is waiting for Jimmie. We also see a group of boys, about eight of them, between the ages of ten and fourteen, moving toward Thea and her bike, stopping behind bushes on the way, and looking at Jimmie's bike at the same time.

'*Hijos de puta!*' ('Sons of a whore!') Nick yells in the loudest voice possible. The boys scatter. Thea and Jimmie, their mouths agape, watch the boys scattering. Then, in a loud but casual voice, Nick calls to Thea and Jimmie, 'Hey kids, ride back to us. Let's see how fast you can do it, come on . . .'

I. 24

When Nick comes home for lunch, and then later, at dinner, after the children are in bed, we search each other's eyes, looking for scraps of information – rumors, secrets, speculations, anecdotes – to use as indicators of how much longer things will go on this way, to give some significance to our being here, to make us feel that we are in an unfolding drama instead of a dull slog.

'Muhammad Ali will be coming here . . .'

'Fidel kept his hand behind his back during the meeting. There's a rumor that he has Parkinson's . . .'

'Elizardo Sánchez' – a Cuban dissident – 'was arrested, and while he was being taken away, a group of people outside his house sang the Cuban national anthem . . .'

'There were only half as many vendors in the *agro* today . . .'

'M. says Raúl Castro is called La China because he is supposed to be gay and his real father was the family's Chinese cook. He *does* look entirely different from Fidel and Ramón . . .'

'There was white spittle in the corners of Fidel's mouth when he spoke. R. says a doctor told her Parkinson's medication can cause that . . .'

'A group of Republican senators' aides will be visiting . . .'

'Cooking oil will no longer be subsidized . . .'

'A Spanish priest was expelled . . .'

'A vice president was caught with ten thousand dollars cash in his home . . .'

MIGUEL ASKS US IF he can take tomorrow off. His wife has to have an operation, to remove a benign cyst on her femur. She has asthma, and so it has been hard to find the right moment for the operation, but she hasn't had any asthma attacks lately, so the doctor wants to operate on her tomorrow.

I. 25

We spend the first night of our first overnight trip outside of Havana since arriving five months ago at Hotel Rancho Faro Luna, which is just outside of Cienfuegos. The trip is a combination of business and pleasure. Hotel Rancho Faro Luna is modest, but clean and recently renovated. We take a swim in the sea with a teenage girl who is a relative of the hotel's director. I have the sensation of being stung in the water, but Nick says he doesn't feel anything. The girl pulls her hand out of the water. She has raised welts like mosquito bites on her forearm. 'Microorganisms,' she says, 'they come in the spring.' I have itching, raised welts on my skin, too. She tells us it's called *agua mala* (bad water).

We leave the children with Muna, who will take them to

have dinner in the dining room of Hotel Rancho Faro Luna.

We have been invited to dinner by a member of the local *nomenklatura* (a Soviet word meaning 'Communist leadership'). His house is modest, but very clean. Our host, a short, stout, clean-cut man, yells heartily to us in Spanish. I do not understand most of it. We are served snapper, shrimp, and lobster, grilled, fried, in *enchilado* sauce (a moderately spicy tomato sauce), and flambéed. The lights are dimmed when the flambéed shrimp comes out, glowing with a blue flame. We have two *mojitos* each and move on to beer. Our host wants to give us each another *mojito*, but we say we'd better not. He keeps yelling. Nick eggs him on. They are all laughing, so I start laughing, too. '*Qué simpático es este señor*,' our host says, about Nick. Ladisel, our guide on the trip, and Flora, his wife, smile timidly. We are also served yucca con mojo (a root vegetable similar to a potato, with a garlic sauce), a salad of avocado, cucumber, and tomato, and a dessert of *cáscara de toronja* (pressed grapefruit rind in syrup) with cream cheese, followed by coffee and *ron añejo* (rum aged over seven years). The rum is like hot silk. Nick is offered Cohibas, which are the finest Cuban cigars and sell for four hundred dollars a box.

We roll back to the Hotel Rancho Faro Luna, feeling like we need wheelbarrows under our stomachs. Nick puts a hand on the small of my back to push me up the stairs.

We stand on the balcony of our hotel room. A nearly full moon is rising out of the sea. First it is orange, and then it becomes white. It shines on the sea and on our very full stomachs, which protrude over the aluminum railing and over the sea below like the prows of pirate ships. The children snore in the next room. We burp. We have done nothing we approve of, but still, we are happy.

I. 26

Standing inside the unfinished nuclear reactor outside of Cienfuegos (which has sat three-quarters complete since the Russians pulled out) is like standing inside a dark, nearly dried-out navel orange, cracked open.

The reactor is explained very rapidly to Nick in Spanish. We walk on catwalks over rods that stick up, and I remember what I can of Chernobyl and make a note to ask Nick later: were those *the* rods? Water drips and I make a note: was that *the* water? *Flojos* (literally, 'loose guys' – thin guys with bad posture who pretend to work but just lounge around) hover in the shadows. Everything is covered with grease to keep it from rusting, but it's still like a dried-out navel orange.

Nick's firm has told him not to *touch* the nuclear issue, but we have to be polite.

'It will make a wonderful discotheque,' Nick says to Ladisel, Flora, and the head of the suspended works. 'Put a Plexiglas floor over this whole level.' Nick indicates the level we are standing on. 'Light the rods up from below.'

Ladisel, Flora, and the head of the suspended works laugh uneasily.

I. 27

Driving from Cienfuegos to Varadero (this is our reward for having visited the reactor) on the second leg of our trip, we pass through a citrus-growing region. It is neither cold nor hot, and the smell of the orange blossoms blows in through the open windows of the van. The children put their noses at the edge of the window and start breathing and breathing with little moans of delight, like they do when they eat guava ice cream. Jimmie says, 'There's perfume all around, Mommy,' and I feel like swooning and jumping out of my skin, all at once; it's the same pleasantly panicky feeling I get sometimes at dusk on our back patio.

Flora is telling me that the hardest thing to find right now is clothes.

Flora and I have gotten to the point of talking about how things are – materially – for her family. It takes longer, usually, to get to this point with a Cuban official, or a Cuban official's wife, but we've had nearly two solid days together. Some will never say that they lack for anything, or if you mention material hardship, they will launch right into education and health care, as if no other country in the world offered free education and health care.

'Food, we have,' Flora says.'It's a bit boring because it's always the same thing – rice, beans, rice, beans, sometimes chicken or meat – but there are practically no clothes or shoes.'

Flora is wearing a shirtwaist of flowered cloth. It looks brand-new.

'That's a nice dress.'

'This cloth was given to me by a friend who traveled to Spain. It's the only way.'

We drive over a rise, and a thick black plume of smoke appears. It is an affront in the middle of the orange groves. The smoke is not behaving in the same way as other paleo-industrial smoke we have seen in Cuba, though. It is intermittent but regular, and it is coming toward us. I am trying to think of what it could be or where I have seen smoke like it before, when suddenly, a huge black . . . thing appears in an alley between the orange trees. I feel my hand go up to my throat and my mouth drop open. 'Look!' we yell to the children.

It's got a bulbous burner, a gaping funnel, a cowcatcher, a big number on the side, arms pushing the wheels round and round, and an engineer hanging out the side, and it's pulling ten railroad cars on a track I haven't noticed before. It's huge, it's magnificent, and it's every cowboy movie I've ever seen and every American history book, and it's in front of us in the bright light of the middle of the day, in the middle of an orange grove in Cuba, just as casual as you please.

'Does it burn wood? Does it burn wood?' we ask Ladisel. We are practically bouncing up and down on our seats.

'Wood. And also sugarcane fibers.'

'Fantastic!' Nick says.

Ladisel smiles.

The engine is gliding majestically in front of us now, metal screeching against metal, an operatic aria out of the Industrial Revolution, and I want to remember everything about it, forever. It is matte black, there is not a spot of rust on it, the number 1 is painted on the side of the engine with nineteenth-century flourishes, and the smoke and soot (of the kind Grandma used to make, with cinders in it) is blowing back on the soot black railroad cars.

There's paleoindustry, and then there's paleoindustry.

'It's like something out of a museum!' I yell over the noise.

Ladisel's smile turns sheepish and he gets the beat-up, hollow-chested, chain-smoking look that some Cuban officials have. 'It's just for freight, you know,' he says. 'Passenger trains are more modern.'

'My wife's never seen one,' Nick says, 'but in X— we had them up until a few years ago. I used to ride them when I was a little boy.'

'But it's beautiful,' I say quickly, 'and it's exciting for us to see it.'

I want to look and look – there is never enough time – but the steam engine is curving away from us now. It is at the angle trains are always at when Indians or robbers jump onto them in movies.

'You realize what you have, don't you?' Nick asks Ladisel.

Ladisel looks at us looking at him. He nods uncertainly.

'You musn't throw it away. Even after things change.'

Ladisel still looks beat-up.

'In the United States, an engine like that would be very valuable.'

Ladisel sits a little straighter on the seat.

THEA AND JIMMIE RETURN breathlessly to us in the downstairs hall of the government-protocol house we have been given in Varadero, complete with cook and maid, for the remainder of the weekend, informing us that there are no toilet seats on any of the toilets, just like I had said there wouldn't be!

Ladisel and Flora mercifully do not speak any English, nor do the cook or maid, who are standing by.

'*Disculpe*' ('Excuse me'). I take Thea and Jimmie by the wrists and lead them to the far end of the hall.

'They're so *cold* . . . ,' Thea says, meaning the rims of the bowls.

I tell Thea and Jimmie that they will have to stand over them every time, then, like they do over public toilets.

'You mean I am going to have to stand the *whole weekend?*' Thea persists.

'Thea . . .'

Lunch, we are told, is ready for us on the table.

Ladisel and Flora reveal during lunch that this is the first time they have been in Varadero since their honeymoon, and their children are now twelve and fourteen. Ladisel says he has been to the Soviet Union, though.

I ask Ladisel what Cubans thought of the Soviet Union when they got there. Did they really like it? I say that I went there in the time of Ronald Reagan, and that before I got there, I heard what Reagan said about the Soviet Union, and since my politics are left of center, I thought, of course, that what he said was an exaggeration . . . but then when I got there and I saw how it was, I thought, *Dios mío* . . . (*My God* . . .).

He says most Cubans thought, *Dios mío*, about it, too.

Thea and Jimmie go into the garden of the guest house after lunch and pick large, flexible, waxy leaves, which they drape over the rims of the toilet bowls in every bathroom. 'There!' they say.

'*Genial*' ('Very smart'), Ladisel and Flora, who have been pulled by Thea and Jimmie to inspect the toilets, say.

Nick steers Jimmie and Thea into their room. He shuts the door. Nick gets down at eye level with them and tells them that if they are ever in a Cuban's house again – and this, too, is a Cuban's house – and they see that something is broken or that something is missing, they are not supposed to complain about it or even mention it, that it is not nice to point out to people what they are lacking.

'But *Mommy* talked about it . . .'

'Mommy talked about it among *us*, but Mommy shouldn't have talked about it at all. Mommy was a little bit naughty, but more than being naughty, she was tiresome, which is kind of like being naughty.'

'It's true, I was tiresome,' I say.

DRIVING HOME PAST the U.S. Interests Section, we see the SEÑORES IMPERIALISTAS sign has been taken down.

'They've taken it down!' I exclaim.

Ladisel and Flora smile uncertainly.

I. 28

There is no flour in the Diplo, no sugar, and no salt.

Lowering her voice and looking around, Lorena says she is sure she can *conseguir* some flour for us.

Resolver (to resolve) and *conseguir* (to get, obtain, attain, find) are two of the most frequently used verbs in Cuba and are used more often than the word *comprar* (to buy), for more often than not, it is not mere buying that you have to do in order to acquire material things.

A REPAIRMAN WHO VISITS the house regularly, lowering his voice, says his brother-in-law's uncle's second wife's present husband can get us three-hundred-dollar boxes of cigars for twenty dollars.

THE SEÑORES IMPERIALISTAS SIGN has been put back, freshly painted and with its trusses reinforced.

The flour arrives, Lorena dragging a big sack in through the door.

Manuel tells me later in another room, also in a lowered voice, that I shouldn't buy flour from the *calle* (street). They cut it with poor-quality flour and chemicals and it can be bad.

I. 29

Even though Nick said 'no ideology,' Olga, the Spanish teacher, still sometimes tries to fit it in, in little phrases we have to practice, and we encourage her with our repartee.

Us: 'In the United States, there are more goods.'

Olga: 'In Cuba, there is more equality among people.'

Us: 'But some are more equal than others.'

Olga looks around. 'I just read *Animal Farm*,' Olga whispers in English. 'Oh, how perfect it is for the present situation . . .'

Olga was a committed party member at one time, she tells us. She worked as a translator for the Venceremos Brigades of American college students when they came to cut cane in the seventies.

'They're all stockbrokers now. Or real estate agents,' we say.

Olga purses her lips. 'I don't want to hear about it,' she says tiredly in English. She looks around, then continues in a lowered voice, still in English: 'I have been outside the socialist world only once in my life. For one day in Saint John, New Brunswick. I was on a boat that had gone to pick up Venceremos people, just on the other side of the U.S. border. Only one day, can you believe it?'

'How was it with the Venceremos people?'

'I never heard that ugly word – I can't say it in English, it is so ugly – so much in my whole life . . .'

'What word?'

'I can't say it . . .'

'Oh yes you can.'

'Oh, you know, that Anglo-Saxon word . . .' She takes a deep breath, looks around.

'What word?'

'*Fuck*,' she whispers in the quietest voice possible.

I. 30

We have a swimming teacher for the children, Carlita. Carlita is a teacher at the Escuela de Natación Marcelo Salado on Primera Avenida. The Escuela de Natación is a boarding school. Promising swimmers are sent to the school from all over Cuba from the age of eleven. They have regular classes, but they also swim at least three hours a day.

Carlita tells me the children won't be able to use the dressing room at the *escuela*, but she will be able to teach them there. She says it's also better if José lets us off *not directly in front of* the school, but a block or two to one side or the other of the school, and for us not to talk too much in the lobby. It was better, in fact, for us not to talk in the lobby at all.

'Are foreigners not allowed to take lessons?'

'This has not yet really been decided.'

Carlita is waiting for us in the lobby. She ushers us quickly through a side door to an Olympic-sized outdoor pool. The water of the pool is cloudy and greenish.

'Is the water clean?' I whisper to Carlita in Spanish, stopping a few feet back from the pool.

'Oh yes, clean,' Carlita says. 'The school lacks chemicals right now to keep the water *transparente*, but it is clean.'

In all lanes but one, the students of the Escuela de Natación are ripping back and forth faster than I have ever seen human beings, let alone not fully grown ones, move in water. At the shallow end of the free lane, there is a gaggle of mothers and small children. We join them. I take off the children's clothes. They have swimsuits on underneath.

'Can I talk now?' I whisper to Carlita.

'Now it's OK. They don't care out here.'

TU EJEMPLO VIVE, TUS IDEAS PERDURAN SIEMPRE (Your example lives on, your ideas are everlasting), reads a billboard with an image of Che on it.

I. 31

Nick doesn't attend our Spanish lesson today.

'I am not a Cuban American, and I never had anything to do with Cuba until I got here, but I will be so happy one day when it all opens up, I think I will cry,' I find myself saying to Olga, my voice breaking slightly.

'But I don't think it will be as simple as that . . .' Olga's eyes fill with tears. 'My brother is in Miami. He left a year ago and I don't know when I will see him again . . .' She reaches into her handbag for a handkerchief. 'Sorry.'

I pat Olga's hand.

I. 32

Berti, the wife of the man who used to have Nick's job, is back for a visit. She misses Cuba, she says. She says I will miss Cuba, too, when I go.

Berti goes to the Diplo, buys some steaks to give as presents, and takes me to meet her Cuban friends. One is Lola, whom we visit in her new house, which she has *permutaed* with her old house. 'If she were in Miami, she would be a millionaire,' Berti whispers to me, ringing the doorbell.

In Cuba you can't buy or sell property, but you can *permutar* (exchange) it. You can exchange up (to a bigger, better house or apartment) or down (to a smaller, crummier house or apartment). If you exchange up, you give money, goods, or services to the person who is exchanging down to your crummier house or apartment to make up the difference (without telling anyone, of course).

Berti walks into Lola's house, taking everything in. 'But this is a *palace!*' she says. Lola beams. It *is* the nicest house I've seen a Cuban living in: spotless terrazzo floors stretching to a patio overlooking a stand of royal palms, not a bit of grime anywhere, a terrazzo staircase with a molded-aluminum balustrade, polished glass louvers allowing breezes from every direction, a kitchen with a vast counter, a full stove with every burner working.

Lola has giant breasts, a compact figure, smooth, hairless olive skin, and hair dyed a solid reddish brown. She moves slowly, duck-footedly, through the house, showing us its various features, paunch and breasts thrust before her like a trophy, and I am reminded of how the Arabs were in Spain for almost a thousand years. Lola walks as if she were in Moroccan slippers, kicking a caftan out of the way. I am reminded, too, of how 20 percent of Spanish words are Arabic, and of how nearly all words in Spanish relating to home comforts – the words for *rug* and *cushion*, for example – are of Arabic origin. I find myself thinking affectionately of an Arab friend, Iman, and her three refrigerators – one for drinks, one for meat and vegetables, and one for leftovers – their shelves with plastic doilies on them, lace borders gracing the edges. I have the feeling that Lola is basically an Arab woman, one who truly reigns at home, who raises housekeeping to an art form and cooking to the sublime and finds the power of the position she has attained in late middle age (her husband and children being utterly dependent on her, for where else would they find such a spotless home and such good food?) far more fulfilling than the willowy charms of youth.

Lola serves us coffee, then leads us into a bedroom. Berti has been trying to explain to me what Lola does, but between the X— ian and the Spanish, I haven't really made out what it is. Lola pulls gym bags out of a closet and sets them near the bed. She opens them, and a powerful smell of cedar and mildew fills the bedroom. She puts her hands in the gym bags and starts pulling cloth out of them, white cloth mostly, but tea-colored, too, and also pastel and black. We are soon able to make out embroidered sheets, pillowcases, tablecloths, napkins, hand towels, infants' baptismal clothes, layettes, booties, coasters, place mats, runners, lace shawls, mantillas, antimacassars, bloomers, slips, and other oddly shaped bits of linen and lace, their purposes known only to the Creole chatelaine of the 1890s.

Lola holds one item up, then another, for the light to shine through. '*Look* at the work,' Berti marvels, caressing them. They are antique, Spanish, and elegant, and they speak of a time light-years away yet lingering still in people's closets, of nuns, plantations, slaves, high ceilings, endless corridors, giant families, and babies like precious icons, wrapped and rewrapped fourteen times a day by untiring *niñeras* (baby-sitters).

Some of the linens are more than 150 years old, Lola says. The people who are selling them are trying to raise money to go to Miami.

I. 33

We are on our way to the city of Trinidad on our first unescorted trip outside Havana, just Nick, me, the children, and Muna. It is dark. There is something in the road. It is orange and moving. There are many orange pieces, moving slowly on an orange road. Some pieces swivel in the beam of our headlights as we approach, while a current of other orange pieces streams through the mass slightly faster, away from us, pushing still other pieces out of the way. Nick stops, leaving the headlights on. We get out.

They are orange crabs and they are on the road ahead of us as far as the eye can see. Orange crabs moving over orange crab bodies already flattened on the road by earlier cars. The living crab bodies are the size of Little Leaguers' baseball mitts. They are moving from one side of the road, where the sea is, to the other side, where there is sandy soil and bushes and trees. They move with their claws raised, as if they are the victims of a holdup, their eyes on stalks, swiveling. We wonder, for a split second, if they can attack, but they scuttle from us as we approach, and we quickly realize that we can herd them. 'Gee-ha,' I say, waving my arms, pushing a stream of them ahead of me. 'Gee-ha!' the children say tentatively, waving their arms and stepping gingerly on pulverized crab, steering their personal herds. The crabs move ahead of us, but just as soon as we herd some off the road, others move onto the road to take their place. It is some timeless mating or egg-laying ritual, crabs attracted by the heat of the asphalt, and judging from the number of crabs stretching into the darkness on either side of the road, the thick orange carpet of pulverized crab, and the vast scuttling noise, which nearly drowns out our own voices, it doesn't seem to be something that has just begun or is going to be finished soon.

We get in the car. Crush, crunch, we hear under the tires. We do not speak. *Yes, life is sacred, but sometimes* . . . I rehearse saying to the children, but they are too tired to grill me.

We get to Trinidad and stop several times to ask for directions to the Hotel Ancón. Each time we are directed farther away from town. Finally there are no more buildings, and we find ourselves driving on a completely empty, dark road. No one in the tourist office explained to us that the Ancón is so far out of town. We continue to ask lone bicyclists and horsemen if we are truly on the right road, until in the end we have gone fifteen kilometers.

We arrive at a monstrous building. 'There must be some mistake . . .' Nick and I start to say simultaneously, but flickering panels atop the structure spell out AN ÓN.

The style is part European auto grill on pylons with a cavernous breezeway underneath, part to-be-renovated airport in Uzbekistan, with the smell of a rest stop on the New Jersey Turnpike. Images of armless and legless men, women, and children on fluorescent panels announce an array of services in grim internationalese. A surly desk clerk completes our welcome. In our minuscule room and in the minuscule room of Muna and the children, a sticky, cigarette-burned TV table blocks the way to the door that leads to the balcony overlooking the sea. The bathroom door cannot be opened all the way, either, because it bumps into the bed.

We realize how much we have been shielded so far. Our thoughts turn to the tourist office and the thousands of tourists who have already been sent by it to the Ancón. We should not be surprised, though: we visited the Soviet Union. Still, it's impressive that such ugliness – harrowing ugliness in the building design and miserable ugliness in the rooms – has been achieved next to what is supposed to be one of the loveliest towns on earth. It's impressive, too, that wave after wave of tourists do not come out of the Ancón talking about its ugliness, writing about its ugliness, becoming Anita Hills in their exposure of its ugliness: it's almost as if there were a conspiracy or as if the Ancón were some kind of afterlife and the tourists who came here before us were dead souls.

* * *

THE COLUMNS DELINEATING the central square in Trinidad are
topped by baroque ceramic jars. The treelessness of the square
brings to mind early photos of urban American areas just com-
pleted, as well as the spareness of Spanish, Greek, and Italian
squares.

We visit the cathedral, where a mass is being held. The congregation is singing hymns accompanied by maracas, guitars,
and drums. The people sway back and forth to *son*, salsa, and
mambo rhythms. We listen, enraptured. It is light, joyful, and a
ton more fun than other masses I have attended. The bishop
delivers a sermon. We can hardly understand a word, but the
packed congregation becomes very silent and listens with an air
of intense concentration. We wonder how alternative the
message is, but we cannot tell. We intended just to visit but end
up staying for the whole mass, then get in line to shake the
bishop's hand on the way out. The children are getting squirmy.
Nick says he wants to speak to the bishop. I see a horse-drawn
carriage waiting outside and tell Nick I will take Muna and the
children for a carriage ride, then we'll meet him in half an hour
in front of the cathedral.

We pass one splendid block after another, peeking through
doorways to tiled courtyards lush with bougainvillea and
through the grillwork of floor-to-ceiling windows to high-
ceilinged rooms with painted wainscoting. The wainscoting is
either delicate Pompeian, with vines and spare classical motifs,
or meaty baroque, with formal topiary gardens glimpsed
through trompe l'oeil balustrades.

A group of women and children are standing in the square
when we return. Their eyes are fixed on us. It is noon and very
hot, and there is no one in the middle of the shadeless square
but them. They put their hands on the sides of the carriage.
'Soap, soap,' they plead. I open my mouth, but only a strangled
'No' comes out. We get out of the carriage and push through
them. More of them come out from the shadows at the sides of
the square. 'Soap, soap.' They are almost moaning it. They put
their hands on us.

Muna and I grab the children and run to a half-open door in
which a priest stands, motioning to us. He opens the door wide,
and in we shoot, the women and children at our heels. He

pushes the women and children back and closes the door in their faces. Nick is behind him, looking worried.

'When your husband told us you had gone off in the carriage,' the priest says, 'I knew this would happen to you on the way back. I was watching you.'

'What should I have done?'

'You can't do anything,' the priest says.

'And do they really think tourists carry bars of soap around in their handbags?'

'This is the question all tourists ask me. They believe tourists have everything.'

By the time we are outside again with Nick, the group of women and children has disappeared. We walk in the shade close to the buildings, looking for a place to have lunch. We finally see a sign for a restaurant and enter a spacious colonial house, with two shaded courtyards, frescoed wainscots, table-cloths, flowers. There is, however, no one in the restaurant, and as we sit down, we see that the flowers are dusty plastic and the tablecloths look as if they haven't been changed for many weeks.

'What do you have for lunch?'

'Chicken, rice, and squash.'

We have eaten chicken, rice, and squash for three days. On the way here, from the Ancón, we passed through lush scenery and saw pigs, sheep, goats, and cows. 'Do you have anything besides chicken?'

'We have ham.'

'Is it fresh ham?'

'Yes.'

We sit at our table, thinking about how wonderful it will be to have fresh ham. Fifteen minutes pass. The children go for a walk with Muna. Twenty minutes pass. We play five games of hangman. It is too hot to try to find someplace else. Maybe the word we should have used was not the Spanish word for 'fresh,' for ham is never fresh, but the word for 'local,' made from local pigs in the local method, the whole haunch of the pig hung up to cure, in some local protected-by-UNESCO larder. Spain is Ham City, but now that we think about it, we haven't seen a proper ham since we've come to Cuba. Forty-five minutes. The children have dusted all the plastic flowers on all the tables with their napkins.

There is an outdoor oven in the courtyard, with steaming kettles on top of it. Cubans line up in front of it with plates. They are dished up rice, squash, and meat.

'What about us?' we ask the waitress.

'That's for the workers,' she explains.

After fifty-five minutes, we see a can of ham from Denmark going by our table.

'Is that the ham?' we ask.

'Yes.'

'You said it was fresh ham.'

'It's ham fresh out of the can.'

We are too hungry to try to look for another place.

After ten more minutes, the ham finally arrives at our table, with rice on the side.

'Mine has circles on it,' Thea says.

We look. Her slice has rings from the top of the can. I touch the ham. It is cold. The rice is cold, too. We turn our slices over. Someone else must have rings from the bottom of the can. 'I win,' Nick says.

We don't ask for any dessert. The bill comes. It is fifty dollars.

EASTER SUNDAY THE NEXT DAY. We visit the cathedral again. It is crowded to overflowing. There is more percussion in the music this time, and people are swaying more emphatically. Yesterday was a day of mourning, after all. Once again, people crane forward to catch every word of the bishop's sermon.

We tour the Sierra del Escambray in the afternoon and return in time for an early dinner. I am now reading the guide *Lonely Planet Cuba*, which we have brought to Cuba with us but never read, thinking it was of little use, since it was published before the beginning of the *periodo especial*. It 'recommends' a place to eat, or at least says it's not disgusting.

When we get to the restaurant, it is closed. A lone young man on the street explains to us that it closes every night at 6 P.M.

'How can they close a restaurant at 6 P.M.?'

'It's for the busloads of tourists. They always go back to their hotels before nightfall. If you like, I know a place where you can eat very well.'

'You mean a *paladar*?'

'Yes.'

'Let's go,' I say to Nick.

'I don't know . . .' Nick says, but I am already following the young man. It feels OK to follow him; I don't know why. It feels OK to follow him even down the dark side street we have turned onto.

'We're going who knows where, with children . . .' Nick mumbles.

'Trust me.'

We knock at an unmarked door. A friendly-looking older man opens it. The young man speaks rapidly to him. He opens the door wider, to allow us in. We stand in an airy, high-ceilinged room that looks onto a courtyard.

He has pork, he says to us, and he has fish.

'Is the fish fresh?' we ask.

'Very fresh,' he says. '*Mira.*' He calls to someone in a room behind him to bring the fish to us. A young woman brings out a large red snapper. Nick inspects its clear eye and red gills.

We order fish, rice, beans, salad. He says it will take about half an hour to prepare. We can sit in his living room, he says, and watch some television while we wait.

We sit in commodious armchairs, watching television and drinking cold Cristal beers. Muna and the children drink Tropicolas. A little girl is asleep on the floor in front of us, her cheek on the art nouveau tiles. It is the coolest place to be. Men, women, and children cross the room back and forth in front of us, stepping gingerly over the little girl and calling cheery greetings to us as they pass. Some of the women even stop to kiss us on both cheeks, stroke the childrens' chins, and say '*Qué lindos*' about them. The little girl is finally picked up and moved to a sofa. Our guide sits with us in another armchair, drinking the Cristal we have offered him. He is studying English. Our host comes in and chats with us. He was an engineer, but he is doing this now to make ends meet.

We are relaxed for the first time since we have been in Trinidad.

The meal is ready in half an hour. We sit down at the family dining table. We offer dinner to our guide, but he declines the invitation. He says he will come back after our meal to show us back to our car.

It is one of the best meals we've had in Cuba outside of our own home.

The engineer sits at our table and explains. Before, private restaurants were entirely forbidden. People were arrested for running them. Since the legalization of the dollar, *paladares* are not exactly encouraged, because they compete with the tourist hotels, but they are not forbidden, either. The engineer raises a hand and tilts it one way, then the other. It's a gray area, he says, like a lot of things in Cuba at the moment. Better to be discreet, though.

The engineer presents us with a bill at the end of the meal. It is twenty dollars.

We thank the engineer and his family profusely as we leave. The engineer writes his name, address, and telephone number on a piece of paper. He asks us to please recommend his *paladar* to our friends.

The young man who led us to the *paladar* returns after our meal to lead us to our car. Nick gives him a five-dollar tip.

We drive to the Ancón aglow, feeling, like the children in *The Lion, the Witch and the Wardrobe,* as if we have gone through a door that is sometimes there and sometimes not there, into a whole new place.

NICK HAS AN APPOINTMENT in Cienfuegos on the way home. I tell Nick not to worry: Muna and the children and I will wander around and look for a place to have lunch.

Muna and the children and I end up on a kind of pedestrian mall. Many shops are closed and empty, or only a quarter full. The street and the shop windows are very dirty. We pass a bar with chairs on the sidewalk. The children are thirsty. We walk into the bar. People are sitting on stools all along the bar. A huge, horizontal Kenmore refrigerator, circa 1953, takes up most of the wall behind the bartender.

'What do you have to drink?' I ask.

'We have nothing to drink,' the bartender says.

I wonder if they are denying us because of the apartheid system under which Cubans are served in one place and foreigners in another, and they don't know how else to tell us, but then I look at the people sitting all along the bar and realize they are sitting with nothing in front of them. It is true: they are drinking nothing.

'We will be getting something to drink in a few minutes. It hasn't been delivered yet.'

Muna and the children and I continue our walk. 'I'm thirsty, Mommy,' the children say. I am beginning to get nervous. There is not a store, either, serving bottled water or any kind of drink. It is very hot. How do people stay on their feet with nothing to eat or drink?

We return to the bar and sit at one of the outdoor tables. There is nothing to drink, but it is shady at least. I leave Muna and the children and cruise the stores. I find some earrings and rings made out of cow horn. The earrings have been in the display case so long they have mold growing on them, which is an attractive burnished green. I will tell the friend I give the earrings to that she has the option of leaving the mold on or washing it off. I return to Muna and the children. There are some Germans at the next table. I assume drinks will never arrive, but to our surprise, four drinks that look like Coca-Cola appear in paper cups. We take sips. Whatever it is, it is disgustingly sweet, sweeter even than Tropicola. Even the children find it too sweet. The Germans have also been served. They make terrible faces as they taste the drinks, then put the cups back down without drinking any more. We all get up at the same time, leaving the full cups, with money beside them. The girl who is serving us acts surprised.

We meet Nick and start to look for a restaurant or a loitering young man to lead us to a *paladar*. It is one o'clock. The restaurants written about in *Lonely Planet Cuba* are all closed. No young men approach us. We find only one restaurant open. We go in. All the tables are full. We ask the waiter how long it will take before we are served. Half an hour, he says. We ask if there is anywhere we can wait. He leads us to an adjoining bar, which is dark and filthy. Earsplitting music is blaring from a radio. We back out of the bar, back into the restaurant. One man gets up from a table, his napkin tucked into his pants.

'Do you speak English?' he says.

'Yes,' we say.

'Just wait, you will be served.'

'But it is so unpleasant here. We will go.'

'Where are you from?' he says, slightly offended.

'X—. Where are you from?'

'Russia. This is the special period, you know . . .' he says, following us as we walk out the door.

We try the waterfront, near the tourist hotels. There is bound to be something there. One restaurant, Covadonga, made famous because Fidel ate shrimp there on his march to Havana, a jewel of Santa Monica–type 1950s restaurant architecture, has a door open. A man stands behind a dilapidated bar.

'Do you have any food?' I ask. The man looks at me as if it's the oddest question he's ever heard. He mumbles something about a building a few doors away.

'I'm hungry, Mommy. Hungry and thirsty,' the children are saying.

It is two-thirty. I approach the building a few doors away. There is no sign on the building, but I see tourists lining up outside it. We go in. There is a kind of buffet being served. Cold spaghetti and some meat beside it in a sauce. We line up behind the tourists. There is one plate left by the time we get to the buffet. 'More plates should be coming in a few minutes,' a waitress says without conviction. We take the one remaining plate and load it with enough cold spaghetti and meat in sauce for the two children. There is no table to sit at, so we sit on a low wall on the porch outside. There are no knives or forks to be found, so we tell the children to eat the spaghetti and meat with their hands.

'I want to be in Miami,' Thea says.

JUST AS NICK, MUNA, and I resign ourselves to driving back hungry to Havana, we pass, in a little village a few kilometers outside of Cienfuegos, a woman selling *yucas rellenas* (stuffed yuccas) for a few pesos from a cart at the side of the road. They are not bad at all. They are, in fact, delicious. There are more carts after her, selling *yucas rellenas, empanaditas* (meat- or cheese-filled turnovers), *pasteles de coco* (coconut pastries), fruit juice, and coffee.

It's an elusive door you have to find, to access motivated Cubans, edible food, and charm. Or maybe it's a squeeze through a crack, or a leap of faith, or a stroke of blind luck. It varies, at any rate, the access code, from town to town and from hour to hour.

We have made progress, but it is beautiful, our house, when we get back to it – our house with its polished, echoing halls, its ironed sheets, its Posturepedic mattresses, its showers with now-robust pressure, its air-conditioned bedrooms, satellite TV, and larder full of food, painstakingly accumulated. It was big before, our house, pleasant, but now it really is *beautiful*.

The children are so happy to be home that they play nicely together for two whole hours.

I. 34

I am not the only American here who is not Robert Vesco, or a fugitive Black Panther, or a plane hijacker, or a Weatherman who held up a Brink's truck, or an American working at the Interests Section or the spouse of one. There is a Patsy, an American woman who is married to a Canadian who works for Labatt's beer. There is Carey, the American wife of the Italian ambassador. We are the three Americans who are here because of what our spouses do, and have two passports to smooth our passages.

Then there are other Americans, whose various situations I do not know all the details of. If they are over sixty, their weird-nesses are easier to figure out. There is Lionel, the left-wing journalist who has been here since the revolution. He is married to Mrs. Hunter, who is Canadian and runs the International School, and though he says, mistily, 'There was so much fervor then . . . ,' maybe he is here now because of his wife's job. There's Lorna of Connecticut, the ex-wife of Piñeiro, the former head of intelligence during the revolution and for most of the years thereafter. Some say Piñeiro was responsible for the deaths of hundreds of people, some say thousands. Lorna has straight white-blond hair cut in a timeless bob, teaches dance at the International School, and trains a small dance troupe out of her house. Lorna is constantly on the look-out for oatmeal to make oatmeal cookies for her dance troupe, and travels often to Connecticut. She lives for dance, she says. There's Mrs. Retamar, whose mother was American, who is married to the head of the Casa de las Americas. Listening to Mrs. Retamar and her husband speak English is like listening to Victor Posner, the utterly un-foreign-accented Soviet journalist, when he used to be on TV: even though you knew it took all kinds, you still somehow couldn't believe that being an apologist for totalitarianism could go with knowing all those *synonyms*.

Among the younger ones, whose circumstances are somehow harder to define, there's an affable lady from New Jersey (I don't yet know her name) who is the wife of Miguel Alfonso, an irascible Cuban bureaucrat with a slim gray ponytail who specializes in virulent anti-U.S. cocktail party remarks. They travel to the United States every summer for vacation on the Jersey Shore. There's a U.S.-born woman with a New York accent whom I met at a cocktail party, who works at Cuba's main bioengineering lab. When I asked her if Cuba was taking any steps to provide more soap for its people, she replied exasperatedly, 'The lack of soap in Cuba is because of the U.S. embargo!' There's a teacher at the school, Mrs. Fleites, who looks like Bette Midler and talks like her. Mrs. Fleites told me her parents left Cuba for Brooklyn because of Batista and came back because of Fidel; then she added brightly, 'It seemed like a good idea at the time!'

There are others, too, whom you don't notice at first, who dress and act like Cubans. 'Son of a bitch!' one mumbles beside me as he stubs his toe on a piece of raised pavement on the Malecón. '*Ooon leebrrrro day zana-orrriaaas*' ('A pound of carrots'), another one says at the *agro*, holding out a tattered plastic bag.

I. 35

Nick and I know a little more now about Santeria, and we have learned that it is an Elegguá that we need (literally, an 'opener of roads' – one who makes the way for you).

We have an Elegguá at Nick's firm in the form of Barbara – a Mexican of X——ian origin. Barbara is tall and fragile, with an essential understanding of both Cuba and the world outside. It is impossible, we have come to feel, for non-Cubans to have the road opened in the right way if they have an Elegguá who knows nothing of life outside Cuba. Well-meaning Cuban Cubans have directed us to exhibitions of cornball landscapes, fake African sculpture, socialist psychedelic realism (happy workers, José Martí, and Che in psychedelic colors: their version of the sixties, but still going strong), and artists' studios with old guys in them in (I swear) berets, their thumbs through palettes.

We follow Barbara through the rubble of the Plaza Vieja to the Centro del Desarrollo de Artes Visuales (Center for the Development of the Visual Arts). We climb stairs inside a naive neoclassical frescoed stairwell to the second floor. Like many *palacios* in Habana Vieja, the building housing the *centro* is an irresistible blend of noble and rustic: naive neoclassical painted wood ceilings, frescoed wainscoting, stained glass fanlights, thick white walls, and worn, undulating brick floors.

Something different is going on at the *centro*. Just a couple of polyester *guayaberas*, the rest unindoctrinated-looking young people in natural-fiber clothes, and on the walls, good art. It is an annual show of young artists.

Everyone is talking about Kcho, a twenty-two-year-old artist who has just won the year's UNESCO prize. The artist is not present, but on one wall is the work that won the prize. It is a crown of thorns in the form of a *balsero*'s raft, or inner tube, complete with the carved wood handles *balseros* use to hang on to in case of rough seas. It is elegant and tragic, delicate and monumental, Cuban and universal. We and everyone else in the gallery are stunned by the fact that Kcho is only twenty-two.

We visit a gallery of works for sale on the ground floor. The works for sale are interesting as well, especially some painted bas-relief plaster panels, with the sheen and somber tone of religious works. One shows the Virgen de la Caridad del Cobre, who usually holds the Christ child, holding an alligator (a symbol of Cuba, whose outline on a map resembles the outline of an alligator) instead, floating above three cannons instead of above the usual three men in a boat. One shows the Virgen del Cobre being offered a red baby in exchange for a white one. Another shows a bearded man in a classic Cuban Army uniform, with a rifle on his back, feeding sugarcane into an ox-driven mill, the kind of sugar mill used two hundred years ago. The mood is gentle, resigned. The artist, Esterio Segura, is there by chance. The gallery manager introduces us to him as he is wheeling his bicycle out of the courtyard. He is a combination of white, black, and Chinese, with high cheekbones, a birth-mark near one eye like a permanent tear, a long, sparse, mustache and goatee like a Buddhist sage, and a relaxed Afro swelling upward from behind a tortoiseshell headband.

I. 37

It is May, ninety degrees, and humid. Sweat pouring into the girls' eyes is hampering the girls' performance, the teacher explains, and the dance studio is too crowded now that more girls have signed up for lessons. The lessons will be on the back patio from now until the fall. Girls should no longer wear ballet shoes because the cement floor of the patio is so rough it will tear them up. The girls should wear sneakers. They will not do floor exercises again until they move back into the dance studio in the fall.

The Cuban mothers and children absorb this information without comment.

'You've got to be kidding,' Thea says in English.

The children look at her. 'Are you from Japan?' one of the children asks Thea.

The class moves onto the back patio and begins its exercises. Thea does them jerkily, rolling her eyes. I frown at her and she adjusts her expression.

I. 38

Since the big cocktail party the firm recommends we have every year is going to be in one month, Manuel says that it's a good idea to start *resolviendo* and *consiguiendo* now.

Para resolver y/o conseguir: 500 drinking glasses, paper napkins, ice, limes, mint (for *mojitos*), ice containers, rum (4 cases dark and 4 light), 8 cases beer, 12 cases Tropicola, 4 cases scotch, 4 cases vodka, 6 cases champagne, 1 pig, 2 *jamon bikis* (a salami-shaped ham made of different parts of the pig pressed together), 10 pounds white cheese, 40 liters canned tomatoes, 5 pounds grated coconut, 10 dozen eggs, 50 kilos flour, 50 kilos sugar, 20 kilos malangas, 20 kilos potatoes, 20 kilos green bananas, 8 waiters.

The list is broken down into manageable units, with the *resolviendo* and/or *consiguiendo* of each item assigned to the employee most able to do it, to the firm, or to me. Alcohol and mixers are to be ordered through the firm. Readily available fruits and vegetables will be bought at the *agro*. The *jamon biki* is to be *conseguido*ed through a friend of Miguel's. Flour and sugar *resuelto*ed by Lorena. Potatoes are to be *conseguido*ed by

Manuel. Ice, ice containers, and mint will be *resuelto*ed at the last minute, but the pig remains up in the air.

I tell Manuel that I would like to find some other way to get enough flour and sugar, and others have whispered to me that they would be able to *resolver* flour and sugar, but so far Lorena has been the only one who has been able to successfully *resolver* these two items.

'I'VE GOT A NICE PIG,' the plumber who is Miguel's friend says, lying under the sink with a wrench in his hand.

Miguel is nearby, nodding. 'It's true,' he says. 'He has a very nice pig, large, good for the party.'

We arrange to buy the pig for three hundred dollars, which I gather is one dollar a pound. The plumber will kill it, scald it (which, I learn, is what you have to do to get the bristles off), and bring it to the house with the head and feet removed on a day when the children are in school.

SACKS OF FLOUR AND of sugar are dragged in through the door by Lorena, who is whispering, eyes opened wide and the whites of her eyes showing all the way around her pupils.

CONCHA APPROACHES ME while I am having lunch. 'I have a good boy who can help for the party.'

'Good.' I have asked the help to find extra waiters, people they know, for the party.

'He knows how to serve. He has a white shirt . . .'

'Fine.'

'Do you mind if he's black?'

'What?' I say, thinking that it's just my Spanish, but Concha touches two fingers to her forearm.

'*Negro. El es Negro. Le da fastidio?*'

I give a slight jerk. She *is* asking me if it bothers me that he is black.

'Black, white, yellow, green, it doesn't matter to me.'

'Sorry to ask you, *señora*, but some ladies, they *do* mind.'

THE PIG ARRIVES AND is laid out on the table on the veranda in back of the kitchen, where the help usually eat lunch, two legs of the table on the slightly raised cement floor of the veranda, two legs on the grass, so that the blood drains off into a basin Manuel has placed in the grass at the lower end. I walk back and forth in front of the door leading to the veranda, half watching, half not wanting to watch, as Manuel, wearing an old *guayabera* and wielding a large knife, skins the pig, then cuts the fat off. He cuts the fat into large cubes, which are rendered into *chicharrones*, or cracklings, by Lorena and put into tubs of lard in the *despensa*, like goose livers in France. The legs are cut off, wrapped, and put in the freezer, then the rest of the meat is cut up into pieces of three to four kilos each, wrapped, and put in the freezer.

I am – *afraid*, I guess, is the word – to ask whether the three hundred dollars includes the head and feet of the pig or not. I have not *seen* the head, but there is a mysterious black plastic bag on the kitchen floor. I don't want them to know that I didn't know, when I paid the plumber, if I was paying for the head and feet or not. I did ask the plumber to cut the head and feet off before the pig came to the house, but I didn't tell him to *keep* them. I don't want the help to know that I didn't know exactly what I was paying for. I think the plumber did say something to me about head and feet and price, but I don't want him or the help to know how little in control I am.

I am also afraid to find out (if the head *is* around), what it is they *do* with the head. I'm sure they do something with it: Cuba is a do-something-with pigs'-heads type of place.

I. 39

Nick and I go with our Elegguá to the opening of a group show in the gallery-cum-*paladar* of Arquitecto Vasquez.

Once again, people in natural-fiber clothes, and on the wall, a picture of a bearded centaur (his face is covered, but you can see pieces of beard protruding), his body pierced by arrows decorated with the flags of former Communist countries. A cherub seated on the centaur's back holds the cloth covering the centaur's face, but you cannot tell whether the cherub is holding the cloth in order to keep it in place or to remove it. El Caballo (the Horse) is one of the many names for Fidel because in the numerology of the Cuban lottery, the number one is represented by a horse. Another picture shows Lenin in a coffin floating above a contemplative Karl Marx, over whose shoulder the face of Groucho Marx mugs.

Castro is never named in Cuba; he is referred to as Él (Him), El Señor (the Mister, the Sir, or probably more accurately, the Lord), El Caballo (the Horse), or El Niño (the Child), or one simply makes a silent hand gesture down from the chin to indicate a beard. Among the art we have seen so far, we have never seen a painting depicting Him openly, and we have been wondering if it is even allowed to paint direct images of Him. We have asked our Elegguá and others if it is allowed, but no one has been able to tell us so far. At Galería Vasquez, though, there is also a painting depicting Him openly: it is a close-up of Him, presumably in some European museum, contemplating a painting of the head of a woman in Renaissance dress. The painting is in black, white, and gray. It is a copy of an actual well-known news photograph of him, Arquitecto Vasquez tells us. Arquitecto Vasquez tells us that the artist, Toirac, has painted an entire series of paintings of Fidel, copied from well-known photographs of Him.

We ask Arquitecto Vasquez if he thinks it might be possible for us to visit Toirac in his studio. Arquitecto Vasquez gives us the telephone number of Toirac's neighbor's mother. Not everyone in Havana has a phone, and this is the easiest way to get him a message.

ÁNGEL TOIRAC AND HIS WIFE, Meira, live in a fifth-floor walk-up in Old Havana.

Ángel has large features, and his abundant, curly black hair is, like Esterio Segura's, held back by a lady's tortoiseshell headband. Meira, who is a poet, has creamy skin and a very wholesome air about her.

Ángel's latest series of paintings is called *Tiempos Nuevos* (New Times). The paintings are oil, in black, white, gray, and red, and faithfully reproduce famous photos of Fidel, mostly from the time of the revolution, but within contemporary commercial contexts, in which Fidel appears to be promoting products and businesses. There is a painting of Fidel astride a horse (a well-known photo of the revolution) with the Marlboro symbol beneath him. There is a painting of Fidel and Che trawling off a sportfishing boat, with the words MARINA HEMINGWAY (an existing tourist marina) in one corner. There is a painting of Fidel smiling, eating Chinese food with a large bottle of Coca-Cola beside it and, underneath, the words, LAS COSAS VAN MEJOR CON COCA-COLA (Things go better with Coke).

Toirac was about to have an exhibition when he was told that he couldn't display images of Fidel in those contexts, so he painted new paintings for the exhibition, substituting his wife in a uniform, smoking a cigar, for every image of Fidel. He shows us one of the paintings in which the image of his wife appears. He is not allowed to export any of the paintings showing Fidel, either.

We ask him about the painting of his we saw at Galería Vasquez.

'That has no advertisement with it. It is not part of the series. It is not considered ... ironic, though some may consider it ironic ...'

I. 40

Just as I have forgotten about the pig's head, I open the door of the most broken-down of our three refrigerators, a compact Minsk without shelves and with the internal freezer-compartment door broken off, so that everything in it stays only semifrozen.

There, on the floor of the Minsk, long-lashed eyes closed serenely, frost swirling around it, as if on some glacial altar, is our own little Lord of the Flies.

I. 41

Carlita is from Bayamo, which is on the other end of the island, near Santiago, but her mother's cousin, Davide, lives in Havana. Carlita stays with Davide on her days off and on the weekends. Carlita would like Nick and me to meet him. Carlita is, in fact, determined for us to meet Davide, though she won't explain why. She has been trying to get us to come to Davide's house for several weeks, but Nick has been busy.

Davide is a retired architect. He designed hotels before *el triunfo de la revolución*, he even designed a hotel for Lucky Luciano, but then he became a revolutionary. He went back to working as an architect after *el triunfo*, but he designed more modest buildings then.

Davide, who is in his sixties, and his girlfriend, who is in her thirties, live in Miramar in a small house he designed for himself. It is a square brick house with louvers for windows. The bedrooms are in the basement, for coolness, he says.

Davide is slim and well groomed, with a boyish face, and seems at once pleased and appalled to see us.

We sit on Danish modern sofas in the living room. Macramé plant holders hang in front of every window, and on the windowsills are blown-glass bottles holding sand in brightly colored layers, urchin figurines with humorous signs on them, and a terra-cotta Mexican donkey with tiny cacti growing out of a small planter on its back. A guitar leans in one corner. Paintings of Cuban landscapes are interspersed with paintings of clowns and paintings on velvet of bare-breasted Polynesian girls.

Carlita sits on the edge of one Danish modern sofa, looking back and forth, from Davide to us.

Nick asks Davide if he knows of any good *paladares*.

'*Paladares?*' Davide says, looking uncomfortable.

I had the feeling when I first walked into Davide's house – and now I know it for sure – that Davide is sitting in a room with card-carrying capitalists for the first time since 1962. I have not had this feeling meeting other Cubans, but I do have it with Davide.

Davide says he doesn't know of any *paladares* . . .

I ask Davide quickly if he would like us to bring him back anything from Europe or the United States.

'Architectural magazines,' Davide says emphatically, looking relieved. 'Anything about architecture . . .'

I tell Nick after we get outside that he shouldn't ask people like that about *paladares*.

'People like what?'

'*Nick.*'

I don't know whether it's my being a woman or my not being X—ian, or whether it's just that marriages must have their little surprises every day, for on another day, it would have been Nick sensing the vibes and me saying the wrong thing.

I. 42

The children and I will be leaving soon for the summer (Nick will join us when he can), but we still have a few weekends left.

There is a median strip on the Prado, which is in places still paved with smooth terrazzo. It is ideal for in-line skating. We have seen children – Cuban children – on Rollerblades there already. The Prado is a copy of the famous promenade, Las Ramblas, in Barcelona.

We park the car at the beginning of the Prado near the Malecón. The children seat themselves on a stone bench and put on Rollerblades. They have knee pads on, too, and wrist guards. They start to skate. We walk behind them. Jimmie skates briskly, but Thea skates listlessly. Old people sitting on the stone benches that are still intact, and children climbing on the remains of lampposts and stone lions, stare at us as we pass. We see a few other children with Rollerblades on, but none with wrist guards or knee pads. Our children's clothes are not exceptional, just shorts and T-shirts, but they look extra-ordinarily pressed and gleaming, compared with the other children's clothes; and with the wrist guards and knee pads, our children looked pressed, gleaming, and science fictional. Our clothes are not exceptional either, just jeans and T-shirts, but they look gleaming, too, and together as a family we are huge and gleaming and all but carrying a big sign that says LOOK AT US. Jimmie skates ahead; Thea skates more and more slowly, her shoulders ever more hunched. '*Dáme un chicle,*' ('Give me some chewing gum,') a boy Thea's age says to Thea. Thea speeds up past him, then flops down on a bench beyond him. I bring my face close to hers. 'I want to go home,' she mumbles. She starts to cry.

We hear honking. A crowd gathers at one side of the median strip, across from an ornate building. It is the Palacio de Matrimonios and it is Saturday afternoon. No one is looking at us anymore, for a two-tone Ford Galaxie convertible has rolled up to the *palacio*, with a woman in a wedding dress seated up on top of the backseat. Ladas and motorcycles with sidecars bearing wedding guests pull up behind her. '*Viva la esposa!*' the crowd shouts. The bride, white-tuxedo-clad groom, and wedding guests enter the *palacio*. They emerge a few minutes later, and the bride and groom take off in the Ford Galaxie under a handful of confetti, the guests after them, honking and shouting.

It's one convertible and one wedding party after another after that, every ten to fifteen minutes. Thea stands in her socks on a stone lion with Jimmie, holding on to our shoulders for balance. Nick and I hold their Rollerblades tightly in our arms. 'I still want to go home,' Thea says after the second wedding group has left, but we manage to watch through a third group, then go home.

I. 43

I am packing my bag.

Nick comes in. 'I know now how to tell real cigars from fake cigars,' Nick tells me, ripping the wrapping off a box of cigars he has bought from the repairman's brother-in-law's uncle's second wife's present husband. 'If it's real, it bends but doesn't break.'

He bends a cigar. It breaks immediately, dry cigar flakes showering his hands.

'Pig penis,' Nick says in X——ian, crushing the cigar to pieces and throwing the box against the wall.

The Second
School Year

II. 1

The first thing Nick wants to do after I get back with the children from summer vacation is to take me to a good *paladar* and introduce me to some interesting people he has met over the summer: Natalia Bolivar and Reynaldo González.

Natalia Bolivar is an anthropologist, an expert on Santeria. Nick had Natalia over a couple of times during the summer. She sat with him on the veranda, drinking *mojitos* and talking about the old days. She is from a wealthy, conservative background and she told Nick her mother used to call the police, just as a matter of course, whenever she saw an unknown black person walking on the street in front of their house. As a teenager, Natalia became a revolutionary. She had used a machine gun and been arrested and tortured by Batista.

Reynaldo is the director of the Cuban Film Archives. In the evenings, he and his boyfriend, Eddie, run the *paladar* we are going to. It is the best *paladar* Nick has been to so far.

Reynaldo greets us as we enter. He is of average height, balding, with a cast to one eye. Eddie, much younger than he and with a very sweet face, does the cooking. Reynaldo is said to be the model for the gay guy in *Strawberry and Chocolate*.

There is an *apagón* (blackout) when we get there, so we spend most of the evening with candles. Natalia is in her late fifties or early sixties, statuesque, with white hair pinned up in a casual chignon and a mass of necklaces around her throat, most of them descending halfway down her chest. They shine dully in the candlelight. They are made of shells, beads (presumably in the colors of her chosen *orishas*, or Afro-Cuban Santeria gods), metal, and stone, and of other materials that I cannot identify in the semidarkness. I ask a question about them, but Natalia answers me rapidly, speaking with a heavy Cuban accent. I cannot understand anything she is saying, but I don't want to slow down the conversation by asking her to repeat what she has just said. I am having a hard time understanding Reynaldo and Eddie, too. Nick, though, can understand everything, it seems: he's making comments in all the right places. He's made a lot of progress in Spanish and *cubano* over the summer, while my Spanish has deteriorated and my *cubano* has deteriorated even more.

I ask Nick later what they were talking about, and he tells me he didn't understand. He didn't understand a thing; he just liked them, that's all.

II. 2

I bring architectural magazines from the United States for Davide. We sit on the Danish modern sofas in his living room while he leafs through them eagerly. '*Mira eso, qué interesante, gracias,*' Davide says. He leafs through page after page, slapping the back of his hand down on images he likes. He pauses on some photographs of a spare clapboard neoclassical American house with a wide veranda painted pale blue and white. 'I *love* this,' he says, holding the image up for me hurriedly. 'Look, so plain. You don't *need* a lot of . . .' He looks at the magazine. A large American flag is hanging down from one of the beams of the veranda. It's the Fourth of July edition. He doesn't finish his sentence and turns the page.

'I have a *paladar* for you,' he says conspiratorially. He scribbles the name down on a piece of paper.

II. 3

Dance classes have ended at the community center. The community center is closing. The building is going to be made into offices for a foreign company, the *directora* tells us. There is not going to be a community center anymore in Siboney.

Thea beams.

The *directora* tells us the teacher will be giving classes in her apartment on Primera Avenida. We will have to pay for them, three dollars a time.

Thea looks at me, stricken.

I tell her to try them, just try them at the new place, for three times. If she doesn't like the classes after three times, if she *really* doesn't like them, she is not going to have to take dance anymore.

II. 4

'I itch, Mommy,' Thea says.

I take Thea into Nick's study, shine the desk light on her bare chest. Red blotches cover her chest, back, neck, and stomach. I pull down her pants. They cover her crotch, behind, and upper legs. They are not *agua mala*, for it is not the season, and besides, the blotches are flat and wide, not raised. 'They really *bother me*,' Thea says, crying.

I cover Thea in calamine lotion. The outer reaches of a hurricane are passing by outside, and the phone works only intermittently. Not long after our arrival in Cuba, someone had thrust the name of a pediatrician at me. I'm kicking myself now for not having made a courtesy call on the pediatrician the last school year, just to get acquainted. I don't know why I think this would have made it easier for me to get through to her on the telephone.

I spend the night with Thea on a towel-covered mattress, reapplying calamine lotion. I finally reach the pediatrician after twelve hours of calling her neighbor on our cellular phone and leaving message after message. José drives to pick her up. Thea stays home from school. The doctor arrives, a tall, thin, smiling woman with black hair. Dr. Silvia.

THE PEDIATRIC ALLEGRY CENTER is in the Vedado section. It was somebody's house, reduced now to brown rooms (you can't make out in the dim light whether they are painted brown or darkened by time) and snaking corridors lit by flickering fluorescent lights.

We get in a line of about ten seven- and eight-year-old boys and girls and their mothers. Dr. Silvia stands beside us. The center is for Cubans only, Dr. Silvia explains sotto voce to me in broken English so that the others in line can't understand. There are hospitals for foreigners to go to, but you have to pay, and it's ridiculous to pay fifty, sixty dollars, she says, for exactly the same service you get here. It's maybe even better here because the doctor we are going to see, Dr. Yamila Lawton, is *the* specialist in Cuba for pediatric allergies. She was Dr. Silvia's professor and she won't see foreigners in the center, but she is Dr. Silvia's friend, and Dr. Silvia called her and asked her to see us, just this once. Then afterward, if I want, I can give Dr. Yamila a little present – not money, but a little present. I can send it to her through Dr. Silvia. Food, some clothes maybe. Just a little thing. Foreigners pay in the foreigners' clinics, but the doctors who work there don't get any of it; the doctors still get their same three hundred pesos a month (about eleven dollars) no matter where they work. 'The rest of the money,' Dr. Silvia says, whispering very close to my ear and making the beard sign, 'goes you-know-where.'

The door opens. 'Next,' a nurse calls.

Dr. Silvia walks in first, talking rapidly in Cuban. Dr. Yamila Lawton, a small woman in her fifties with eyes magnified behind her glasses, sits on a stool in a tiny room with one weak overhead lightbulb. She is flanked by two younger doctors. She tells Thea to take off her clothes. The blotches are subsiding but still visible.

'Could be strawberries, could be chocolate, shellfish, milk, wheat, egg whites, dogs, grass . . . Try this.' Dr. Yamila Lawton scribbles a prescription on a piece of paper. 'If it doesn't work, come back and see me.'

'But . . .'

'Next!'

II. 5

The building on Primera Avenida where the dance classes are being held is a stuccoed, poured-cement six-story building built, it looks like, in the late fifties. The ground floor is an open carport and garage. High tides and sea spray have eroded much of the stucco and cement on the first three floors down to the rusted steel underneath. Thea and I look at the elevator and decide to walk to the fifth floor.

Thea is feeling fine now. The blotches went away in a couple of days, but since they were starting to go away anyway, we don't know if it had anything to do with the medicine, and she continues to eat everything she ate before.

The apartment is already crowded with the girls from the community center and their mothers. It is much cooler, though, in the apartment than it was at the community center. Sliding glass doors lead onto a corroding terrace facing the sea. Some picture windows on either side of the sliding doors are broken and boarded up with plywood. 'Hurricane Andrew,' one of the mothers explains to me, motioning with her head toward the plywood. The terrazzo floor is smooth and cool, but one class is leaving and another class is arriving, so that between the gesticulating mothers and the many limbs getting into and out of leotards, it is hard to find a place even to stand.

The teacher greets us, kissing us on both cheeks. She squeezes Thea's arm. 'Try, Thea, try . . .' she says.

The teacher explains that there are so many girls that they will have to take turns exercising. The first group starts. The girls, most of them the same age as Thea, but smaller than she, bend their bodies backward into perfect O's and do splits with nonchalance.

The Cuban girls listen to the teacher. They do what she tells them to do; they allow the teacher to bend them, bend them more. They concentrate in a manner far beyond their years, far beyond the concentration of any foreign girl. The mothers sit on the sidelines watching intently, straining their bodies in the directions their daughters bend, traveling with their daughters as they bend, spending a quarter to half of a month's salary for one lesson and traveling with their daughters, in their dreams, to Mexico City, to Toronto, to Paris, and to beautiful hotel rooms with bellboys bustling into them carrying flowers.

II. 6

Manuel gives the children a present after we have been back a few weeks. It is a dead tarantula in a jar. We leave the jar on a table in the upstairs hallway. The children show it off to friends who come home with them after school.

Nick says it bothers him, having it there in the upstairs

hallway, but we don't move it, and after a few days it becomes part of the decor.

II. 7

I am in the parking lot of the Diplo at three o'clock in the afternoon, walking as fast as I can to the car, for it is blazingly hot, when a fiftyish woman in a Lada with a swooping blond bouffant hairdo stops alongside me. She doesn't even ask me if I speak English; she just launches right in, in perfect and somewhat haughty British English: 'Excuse me. I make cakes. Devil's food. Sponge cakes. Meringue. Birthday cakes, wedding cakes, cakes for other occasions. Look.' She gestures with her hand toward the backseat. There, loose on a plate on the backseat, sliding toward the backrest, a bit of frosting already having smeared the backrest, is a cake with pink meringue icing on it. The icing, which has been whipped into waves, has a liquid sheen to it, and widening airholes, as if it is about to give way in the heat.

'Thank you for telling me about this, but we have a cook at home, and I don't think she'd like it so much, me coming home with other desserts.'

'I see. Well, ta-ta,' she says. She revs the Lada and streaks ahead to the next foreign woman she sees crossing the parking lot.

II. 8

At the recommendation of friends, we call on Saida Carrera, who is ninety-five, and her sister, Lilian, who is ninety-three. Saida and Lilian live in a medium-sized mansion in Vedado, built, we are told, by their father at the turn of the last century. It was their country house then. The neighborhood grew up around it. Some say the neighborhood is called Vedado (Forbidden) because blacks were not allowed to enter it; others say that is not *at all* why it is called Vedado but don't come up with another reason for its name. Still others say it is called Vedado because it was forbidden for anyone – black, white, Chinese, or *mulato* – to be out on the streets in Vedado after dark.

Vedado is younger as a neighborhood than Centro Habana,

but older than Miramar or Siboney or Cubanacán. It is cozier, too, than the newer neighborhoods because the houses are closer together. Greek Revival row houses exist on the humbler streets, sometimes whole blocks of them with perfectly aligned front porches framed by columns, so that you can stand in the middle of one porch and look all the way through successive porches to the cross street at the end. The effect is supremely pleasing. Grander streets sport freestanding small and medium-sized Greek Revival houses, with strips of garden on one side and driveways on the other leading to carriage houses in back. Some have cast-iron balconies. The newer houses, from the 1920s, are Spanish-style or art deco, with larger gardens, and there are a few houses from the fifties. Thick, dark ficus shade the streets. The streets look somnolent, melancholy, and American all at the same time, like some more heartrending version of New Orleans.

We step back, as we always do when coming to a big or medium-sized house where Cubans live, and double-check the street number to make sure we have the right place. Nick twists a bell placed waist-high on the massive front door.

Cuban friends have told us that in the first few weeks following *el triunfo de la revolución*, the first thing to change about Cuban houses was that outdoor furniture and pots were either removed from the front porches as a precaution or stolen. Later the window hardware broke. It was usually just a question of a latch or a spring, which could not be found at any hardware store. Storms came, unlatched windows were blown open and panes were broken. No glass could be found, so the broken pane or panes were boarded over. Still, the windows leaked in driving winds, letting in water, which caused floors to buckle and plaster on ceilings below to stain and crumble. Maids, butlers, cooks, and gardeners quit or were let go. Curtains left on windows mildewed and then rotted away. Paint peeled off window frames, causing them to leak more. Cement porches cracked, and weeds took root in the cracks, causing them to crack more. Cornices chipped, and plaster columns wore through, showing steel reinforcements.

A wizened four-foot-tall *mulata* in slippers stands in the gloom. She has been hauling on the door with two hands. Behind her stands a snow-white, very old woman in a crisp, ironed, black-and-white polka-dot dress. She is also wearing pearls, pearl earrings, and black-and-white spectator pumps, several sizes too big, Minnie Mouse–like on tiny feet at the ends of bird legs.

'Come in! Come in!' she says. Nick grabs hold of the doorknob and hauls up on the door to ease it over a bump in the floor. The doorknob comes off in his hands.

'That always happens,' she says.

Nick hands the doorknob to the *mulata*, who shuffles off with it, calling a man's name.

Saida takes Nick's hand, then mine, in both of hers. 'I am so pleased to meet you. I knew your predecessor. He was a darling person.'

We tour the house. It is nearly bare, except for a Louis XVI–style love seat in the living room, covered in white-on-white jacquard silk in an exuberant late art deco pattern of looping S's and spirals, and in the dining room, a massive oak table, with a drum-shaped hanging metal lamp, lined in shredded orange silk, over it. Flat shapes cut out of the metal depict running satyrs. In the dining room there are some odd chairs, a caoba (Cuban mahogany) sideboard, and on the walls, some platters depicting scenes of Old Havana that Saida tells us were made in England in the nineteenth century. We admire the platters. Saida says they and the few pieces of furniture she has left are the things she will never part with. Saida's sister, Lilian, who at ninety-three is two years younger than her sister, dozes in a chair in the dining room. 'She is not doing very well today,' Saida says loudly. She has already explained to us that her sister is deaf.

Nick places a bag of X—ian food products on the dining table – canned mushrooms, pâté, preserved plums, raspberry jam, crackers, some sparkling wine.

'But this is a marvel!' Saida says, picking up one can and one package after another and holding them close to her eyes. She pulls our faces down to hers and kisses us on both cheeks. She calls the *mulata* to come and have a look. 'We have enough to eat for *weeks*,' she says. The *mulata* starts shuttling the cans, jars, boxes, and bottles to the kitchen.

Saida opens a drawer in the sideboard and removes a wavy piece of paper. 'This is the only thing I have left that I am willing to part with!' she says. She puts it in Nick's hands. It is hard to see, by the strength of the twenty-five-watt bulb in the hanging metal lamp, what it is. Nick carries it to a leaded-glass window that is still intact. It is a study in sepia ink of two fat-thighed babies and an arm.

'One person who was here told me it might be by one of those *holandesas* (Dutchmen)!' Saida says loudly, we presume because she's used to speaking to her deaf sister. 'You know, the one who always painted *gorditas* (fatties) . . .'

'Reubens?'

'*Eso es,* – ' Saida says, though it doesn't look that old.

Nick and I sit on the love seat in the living room. Saida sits on a wooden box. Nick tries to get Saida to sit on the love seat, but she insists on sitting on the box. The *mulata*, who we have realized is a maid, shuffles between us, in a brown cardigan with holes in the elbows, serving us coffee and tiny biscuits.

The front door opens, a teenage girl in cutoff blue jeans greets us brightly and disappears into the back of the house. Saida does not introduce her or explain who she is.

Saida speaks of the trouble she has had with diplomats. 'I sold the wife of the ambassador of Bolivia so many things. A Chinese urn, some Syrian chairs inlaid with mother of pearl. She said she would send me the money. My son said not to trust her, but I did. She never sent the money.' Saida says she is not interested in selling to diplomats anymore. 'Many have been lovely, but one or two have been dishonest.' Saida has a son living in Puerto Rico who is seventy years old and comes to visit her regularly. 'He has tried to get me to move to Puerto Rico, but what would I do in Puerto Rico?'

A man walks down the stairs carrying a bicycle. Saida nods to him. 'My physician,' Saida says after he is out the door.

Saida was fifty-three at the time of *el triunfo de la revolución.* 'When we heard that there was a young lawyer in the mountains who was going to change everything, I said, 'But this is *una cosa maravillosa* (a marvelous thing).'' Saida clasps her hands together and closes her eyes. 'We – and by *we*, I mean people of my class, but who were for *justicia* (justice) – sent him money, so much money, for arms, for supplies. It was dangerous to do that. I sold an emerald bracelet. 'What do I need an emerald bracelet for,' I said to myself, 'when my people are starving, are being tortured? . . .'

A side door opens. Another man, in his thirties, in running pants and a bare torso, walks through an adjacent room, carrying a bag full of sweet potatoes. '*Hola, mi amor*' ('Hello, my love'), he calls to Saida. Saida nods but does not introduce him, either. Saida does not introduce anyone, we guess, because if you were to introduce all the people walking through this door and that door in large or medium-sized, seemingly abandoned Vedado mansions, you would never finish any story.

II. 9

We are in the Plaza de la Catedral. Various vendors are selling from their stalls. I am taking an executive from the home office around Old Havana. He wants to buy a black coral cross with a silver Christ figure on it to give as a Christmas present to his wife. The vendor wants twenty dollars. The executive is not sure if the coral and silver are real. We then go into an official shop. We see a similar cross, but with less silver, in a display window.

'How much?' we ask a boy with a badge on who is working there.

He says he doesn't know and goes to get a salesgirl, who opens the display case for us.

'How much?' we ask.

'One hundred twenty dollars,' the salesgirl says.

'But outside it's twenty dollars.'

'That's because it's not real coral and real silver.'

'Too expensive,' we say, and start to leave the shop.

The boy with the badge catches up to us on the threshold of the shop. 'Do not believe my colleague,' he says. He doesn't care whether anyone in the shop hears him. 'The crosses they sell in the shop are the same as the crosses they sell outside.'

We look back into the shop. The salesgirls are nodding in agreement at what the young man is saying. Even the salesgirl who helped us is nodding.

'Why such a difference, and why are you giving us the information?' the executive asks.

'This is a state shop. The state wants to make money. It doesn't care how it makes money. We are paid in pesos, and it is so little that it doesn't matter if we sell from the shop or not. It's the same if we tell you to shop on the outside.

Follow me; I'll take you to someone who sells good crosses.'

We cross the square with him to another vendor who shows us a cross of the same type, only smaller and with less silver.

'How much?' we ask his vendor.

'Thirty dollars,' his vendor says.

'But it's much smaller and much more expensive than the first one we saw,' we say to the young man.

'That's because it's better quality.'

We thank them and start to walk back to the original vendor.

The young man catches up with us. 'My friend can make a discount for you . . .'

We return to the original vendor and end up buying the cross for eighteen dollars.

II. 10

Thea lies facedown on her bed, unable to move.

'You don't have to go to dance class anymore if you don't want to.'

Thea looks at me in disbelief.

'You gave it a really good try, though, you really did . . .'

Thea jumps from the bed. She wraps her arms and legs around me and squeezes me tightly.

SEAMOS UN HAZ DE GENERACIONES. This one confuses us. It means either 'Let us be an ace of generations,' and the Spanish word *as* (meaning 'ace') is misspelled *haz,* or 'Let us be a bundle of generations.'

II. 11

I am becoming more skilled in the arts of *conseguir* and *resolver.* Rather than always going through the help, I try to break out on my own.

Returning from the bakery with Miguel, we see two spear-fishermen walking down the street. One has a long fish slung over his back. It's a *serrucho,* I think. They make excellent *escabeche* – the fish is filleted, breaded, fried with onions, then soaked in vinegar under a weight for at least a week, and eaten cold.

'That's a *serrucho,* isn't it?' I ask Miguel.

'Yes,' he says.

'Let's ask them how much it is.'

Miguel calls to them from across the street. They approach the car, still dripping.

'Is that a *serrucho*?' Miguel asks.

'It is.'

'How much do you want for it?'

'Ten dollars.'

It's a good deal. Fish is usually a dollar a pound, and this fish is more than ten pounds.

I pay them and they flip the fish into the car, onto the naked backseat.

'THIS IS NO *SERRUCHO*!' Lorena yells, waving the fish at me, the tail of which has already been cut off by Manuel, fried, and served to the children last night, Lorena's night off, for their dinner. 'This is *picua*! It can be toxic! You have to throw it away! People have died eating this fish!'

Concha, Danila, Manuel, and Miguel stand behind her, in a V formation, nodding in confirmation of this fact – Miguel, who helped me buy the fish, and Manuel, who fried it.

I could have killed my children, but there they are, nodding in a V formation, with only Lorena yelling about it.

'You've got to help me, you know,' I say to all of them. 'You have got to tell me when something is wrong.'

They keep nodding.

I SPEND A WEEK not sleeping much, playing one disaster-with-the-children scenario after another in my head. They are poisoned. They fall out of palm trees, out of mango trees, out of ceiba trees. They fall headfirst off the jungle gym at school. They are run over. They drown. They are eaten by sharks. They stray from a school group, wander into a military zone, and are shot. They are murdered by evil grown-ups. They are forgotten by Nick and me somewhere (because it slips our minds that we have children), and some other couple (kind, upstanding Cubans) find them so beautiful and intelligent that even though they live in reduced circumstances, they adopt them and give them the little that they have; Thea and Jimmie forget us, English, and X— ian and speak only *cubano*.

II. 12

I have found a gymnastics teacher for the children, Lety. Lety teaches the children two afternoons a week in a gym at the Hotel Tocororo. The Tocororo, we have found, has the least-squalid gym room, where the floor has no splinters in it, and the adjacent pool, where the children go after lessons, is relatively *jinetera*-and-sexual-tourist free. Lety is a retired professor of biology, but when she was young, before the revolution, she was a champion gymnast and competed in the United States and Puerto Rico. She also traveled often to the United States with her parents, just for the fun of it, because it was so easy to get there and so cheap. A round-trip airplane ticket to Key West cost ten dollars. She drove all the way up the East Coast to New York with her parents, *y le encantó de los* Luray Caverns of Virginia.

When the *periodo especial* started, Lety discovered she was making the equivalent of five dollars a month as a professor of biology, so she retired from the university and now uses her gymnastics experience and knowledge of English to teach gymnastics to foreign children.

Lety, who is in her early sixties, lives in an apartment in Siboney, not far from our house, and has been bicycling five miles uphill to the Tocororo, I discover after a few lessons, in the heat of midafternoon in order to meet us. I tell her she cannot do this. Nick, who is milling around nearby, cuts into our conversation and says that I can simply pick Lety up with the children on the way to the Tocororo, and I say to Lety, 'You see how he has a superior mind?' just to say something. It seems too good to be true, to be able to spend time twice a week with a likable English-speaking sixty-year-old Cuban, who probably isn't an informer, and in a car no less, where, it is popularly believed, there are no microphones.

II. 13

I am seated at a late-fall dinner next to a high-ranking member of the Foreign Relations Committee of Cuba's National Assembly. He is wearing an orange open-necked shirt and a polyester stretch-knit sports jacket.

The talk turns to Helms-Burton, the bill proposed in the U.S. Congress that would tighten the embargo against Cuba. He says

Helms-Burton is an expression of the extreme right wing of the United States, which includes the Cuban exiles of Miami, of course, and reflects the strategic importance of Florida in presidential elections.

I tell him you have that on the one hand, and on the other hand you have the apathy of the rest of the American public. Cuba isn't important to them.

He says it is amazing how uninformed the American public is and how uneducated *norteamericano* people are. Where is Cuba, where is Santo Domingo, where is Puerto Rico? you ask them, and they don't know. They are only interested in what directly concerns them.

I wait at this point for him to make some qualifying statement about how he is, of course, not talking about me, but he goes on to say it's tragic how the *norteamericano* people are becoming more brutelike every day. He shakes his head sadly. He tells me that just the other evening he saw a *norteamericano* program on television – this was made in *norteamerica*, by *norteamericanos* – and it showed a school where they train animals to have sex with humans, and hotels where people go to have sex with animals. He tells me that 40 percent of the *norteamericano* population have sex with animals. He says it's pitiful, really . . .

I make mistakes in Spanish. I speak with a really broad *norteamericano* accent. I make my *rs* really hard so that a mortified flush will come over his face when he realizes it's a *norteamericana* he's saying this to, so that I will then be able to say to him, *It's odd, I am a* norteamericana, *but since I have been in Cuba, I haven't found an animal that appeals to me yet. Of course, if a really handsome German shepherd were to come along . . .* , making him flush even more, but his expression remains exactly the same. I take away all the accents when I speak, and mix up the genders of nouns even worse than I usually do. Still nothing.

'You really know the United States well,' I finally say.

'I've never been there,' he says, 'but I read a lot.'

'Where are you from in La Yuma?' someone finally calls cheerily to me from across the living room, where we stand after dinner, drinking coffee.

I watch him out of the corner of my eye: still nothing.

LA YUMA, THE UNITED STATES is called, from the 1957 film *3:10 to*

Yuma, starring Glenn Ford and Van Heflin. It is not a pejorative term, as far as I can make out, just a term: '*Voy pa' la Yuma*' ('I am going to the Yuma').

II. 14

'*Señora*, I have to talk to you about something,' Lorena says, her voice lowered.

We go into the hallway.

'I can't work here anymore.' Her voice is shaking. Tears are starting to stream down her cheeks. 'I can't work with Concha. She is mean to me . . .'

Concha of the plucked eyebrows and the cigarette-hoarse voice, who bites the side of her thumb and whose two children have left Cuba.

'Everyone says I am a spy, but I am not a spy . . .'

'Who says you're a spy?'

'Everyone.'

'Well, no one has said it to me. And besides, even if you *were* a spy, what difference would it make?'

'I am *not* a *spy*.'

It's Muna, I'm sure. I told her what the wife of Nick's predecessor said, just so that she would watch what she said. I know now that was telling her too much.

'I know,' I say, 'but say if you *were* a spy . . .'

'I'm not a spy.'

'I know you're not, but just say you were, or . . . Miguel were . . .'

'Miguel has to make his reports . . .'

'OK, he's not a good example.'

'But he makes his reports . . .'

'But how is that spying if we know about it?'

Lorena considers this.

'Say if . . . *Danila* were a spy . . . what is there to report about? We are very boring people. We don't do anything worth talking about. 'The *señora* likes loose tea'? 'Yesterday she complained about the *apagón*'?'

Lorena stops crying. I hug her. She is round but very firm. 'Don't sink to Concha's level,' I say.

II. 15

Carlita has to do her *servicio social,* which all young Cubans must do if they do not do military service. For one year, Carlita will be teaching swimming not at the Escuela de Natación but at a big pool in a park not far from our house. I can take the children to the pool in the park and she can integrate them into her group. Carlita explains to José how to get there, then tells us that we should not go in the Land Cruiser with José but should follow him in the Mitsubishi, which I should drive. José will then drive past the pool and go home, and I will park a little distance from the pool so that my new car will not arouse suspicions. Carlita says I should drive there in the Mitsubishi every time and park a little distance away, just like I did at the Escuela de Natación.

I tell Carlita that I don't think it sounds like a very good arrangement, but Carlita says it will be fine.

II. 16

Jimmie has a high fever and diarrhea. Diarrhea medicine we brought from the last country works for a few hours; then the diarrhea comes back with a vengeance, liquid, dripping down the backs of his legs and along the floor as he runs, crying, with me after him, to the bathroom.

Dr. Silvia comes in the afternoon with medicine but says we'll have to get a *muestra* (stool sample), take it to the laboratory, and have a *coprocultivo* done. Dr. Silvia tells us that we must take the sample to the laboratory at a time when a friend of hers is there.

Nick ends up driving to the laboratory at 6 A.M. with Manuel to guide him, calling up at the windows of the laboratory until a woman with her hair in curlers and face cream on leans out of the window. Nick leaves her with the stool sample and a gift bag of X—ian products, for Dr. Silvia has said her friend won't take any money. It's too risky to take money, Dr. Silvia says, and what is there to buy in the stores, anyway?

IT'S SHIGELLA JIMMIE HAS, which is fatal if left untreated. It's a bacteria, usually picked up from water. It is curable, though, with the medicines we have brought from our last country. Dr.

104

Silvia says not to worry, though: medicine for shigella can be found in Cuba, too.

The diarrhea stops, but Jimmie has no appetite and drinks only oral rehydration salts in boiled water for the first two days. He has lost five pounds. On the third day, he eats an egg and rice. On the fourth day, boiled mashed malanga, boiled chicken, three bananas, an egg, some bread, boiled carrots, and a grated apple from Chile – one of four bought especially for him from the Diplo.

II. 17

Querido Vecino! (Dear Neighbor!) is from the former Eastern-bloc country of Z—. He lives a few doors away. He is very playful whenever we see him, so we have taken to calling one another Querido Vecino! like they used to in the Soviet Union, complete with an exclamation mark. He has been in Cuba five years. He speaks English, Spanish, and French with an accent like Bela Lugosi's, as well as German, Z—ian, and Russian. He lives with his wife, his twin sons, three dogs, three cats, three kittens, innumerable birds, and a small alligator, which is kept in the bathtub of the guest bathroom upstairs. He puts a hand on my hipbone whenever we kiss him hello – actually, right above my hipbone – and bears down and squeezes until the curved bone is isolated in his hand, so that I am never sure if it's a cheap feel or some kind of Georgia O'Keeffe–like veneration of pelvic bones.

Querido Vecino! and his wife go swimming every afternoon in the saltwater pool at the Hotel Comodoro before the salsa and the sexual tourists heat up and the *jineteras* come out in force to shake them down. Sometimes we pass them, doing the sidestroke, skirting floating objects. Sometimes we go home with them after swimming to drink *mojitos* and watch CNN.

Querido Vecino! collects animals, he says, because he doesn't have much else to do since the end of the 'special relationship' between Cuba and the Eastern bloc. Once, he was obliged to take care of a retired Z— ian cosmonaut who was mugged in Santiago de Cuba, but that's been about all. Nick says he is just being modest, he knows Querido Vecino! is a very significant triple agent. Querido Vecino! chuckles. Still, Querido Vecino!

says, six cats are too many and they would like to give some kittens away.

We go home with two of Querido Vecinos!'s kittens cupped in our hands, our hair still wet from the Comodoro. One is tiger-striped, and one is black with white patches.

We walk one block home in the orange dusk, rubber sandals flapping, tiny claws and teeth worrying our fingers, and feel for a few moments as if we are in some kind of ordinary surburbia in some kind of First World place, but then the guard, seeing us coming, flips a switch, and the wrought-iron gates open with a creak worthy of the rue Morgue.

II. 18

The first store to be refurbished on Calle San Rafael has been open for a few days. It was a peso store, selling, like all stores before the collapse of the Soviet Union, goods from Communist-bloc countries as well as goods made in Cuba. Following the collapse of the Soviet Union, it limped along for a few years selling (for pesos) goods made in Cuba, its display windows dispiriting, its salesgirls lolling on broken stools. Dollar stores selling quality imported goods to Cubans became possible following the legalization of the dollar in 1993, but it has taken such stores a while to get going. Expensive, isolated house-hold items in tourist stores, such as the Black & Decker sandwich maker we spotted in one store, it is finally explained to us, rep-resent a kind of 'transitional' period: they are meant to be bought by visiting Miami relatives for Cuban family members, or by sexual tourists for their *jineteras*. Expensive items such as the sand-wich maker can't be in dollar stores for Cubans yet, it is explained to us, because Cubans can't afford them, and seeing something so beyond their reach in the newly opened dollar stores (the Cuban friends who are explaining to us speculate) only depresses Cubans. Our Cuban friends remind us that they are talking only about entirely state-run stores. The *cuentapropista* stores, like the one in the old Woolworth, in which individuals rent spaces and sell what they are allowed to sell, are another category, as are the artisans and old-book vendors on the Malecón and in the Plaza de la Catedral.

Cubans line up in a short line outside the store on Calle San

Rafael and are let in one by one, while small support groups of friends and/or relatives wait outside, biting the corners of their thumbs and craning their necks around the heads of other people looking through the window.

Nick and I finally find a space to look between support-group members' shoulders. The store has clean bowfront windows, an aluminum-slat ceiling, and fluorescent lights. The shelves are nearly filled. Gillette shaving cream we see, Johnson's baby shampoo, Palmolive soap, packs of double-edged razor blades, baby socks, pastel-colored men's socks, an alarm clock, an extra-long shoehorn, three hairbrushes, boxes of toothpicks, cologne, nail polish, a folding, magnetized backgammon game for traveling, some airmail letter paper, a lone box of Tampax, a lone box of panty liners, some bedside lamps, some stonewashed jeans, some organza baby dresses and *guayaberas* hung up on a rack at the back of the store, an invalid's toilet suspended in an aluminum frame. Customers emerge smiling, clutching one or two things in a bag.

Farther down the street, a long line is forming in front of one of the few peso stores still open. The shelves in the window are bare but for a travel poster of Kraków. The line goes through the empty store to a barely lit counter in the back of the store.

'What's going on?' Nick asks one of the people waiting in line.

'They just got a shipment of talcum powder.'

II. 19

Lety says it was so beautiful after the triumph of the revolution. People were so happy. She was in Florida, in a gymnastics competition. 'When news came that Batista had fled, all the people who had left Cuba because of Batista were trying to get back. The ferries were full, the airplanes, everyone rushing to get back. *Estaban locos.*' She laughs. 'People were hiring fishing boats, people were hiring anything that floated, just to get back.'

II. 20

At a party I chat with Alex, a diplomat who lived in New York in the seventies. He wonders if Fidel loves men more than

women. He does hang out more with men than with women:
the diplomat wonders if I have noticed that. I say I haven't
noticed because I haven't seen Fidel yet, only on television and
once speeding down Quinta in the back of a black Mercedes.
Old hippies and the Fab Four do come to mind when you see
him, he says, but also gays in the West Village of Manhattan,
circa the late seventies, with the uniform stuff and the boots.

I cough from some drops of *mojito* that have gone down the
wrong way. 'But the untrimmed beard?'

'That's meant to put you off the track.'

II. 21

There is a school at the end of our block. Every morning you
can hear the children reciting:

Pioneros del comunismo,	(Pioneers of communism,
Seremos como el Che!	We will be like Che!)

The director of the school and an assistant come to our door
this morning. The director tells us they need detergent, rags for
cleaning the floor, disinfectant, a broom. There are little
children in the school. She and the teachers are afraid for their
health. They have had nothing to clean the school with for
months.

Concha says to just give them a little bit because no matter
how much you give them, they will always ask for more. I send
Concha to the school with some detergent, rags, and disinfectant. Concha says we can't send them a broom, though,
because we only have one and won't have any if ours breaks.

The director says she doesn't know how she can thank us –
then asks us if we have any lightbulbs.

II. 22

I spy a movement in the jar containing the tarantula.

I grab the jar and start running down the stairs.

The children run behind me. 'Mommy, why are you
running?'

'Creatures need air to live, they need food and water. The

108

tarantula has lived without air, food, or water for two weeks . . .'

We nail holes in the lid. We get some grains of hamburger and a cup of water. I throw the grains of hamburger in the jar and sprinkle water over the tarantula, which is moving animatedly now.

'Eat, Charlotte, eat!' the children and I tell him or her, whom we have decided to name after the spider in *Charlotte's Web*.

We raise the jar to be able to look at Charlotte's underside. Charlotte is squatting over the hamburger and stuffing hamburger into a masticating orifice with its two front legs.

'It's a miracle!' I say to Miguel and Lorena, who are watching us, bemused. 'Two weeks without air, food, or water.'

Miguel and Lorena shrug. '*Es una tarantula cubana.*'

II. 23

Lorena says she has to tell me something. She is telling me because she, José, Concha, Miguel – they are all concerned. She is telling me because she feels like a sister to me. 'Yes, like a sister,' she says, patting her chest. 'And the children, I feel like I am their aunt. I hope you don't mind me saying this . . .'

'On the contrary. I feel very complimented.'

'*Bueno.*' Lorena tells me I should not let the children take swimming lessons at the public pool in the park. They do not put enough chemicals in the pool. The children will become sick again. Jimmie has already been sick once – maybe he got it from the pool. There are too many rough children there, too. José has told them how other children jump in the pool, big boys, not looking where they are jumping. She and the others are afraid the children will be injured. Many Cuban mothers do not send their children to that pool anymore, nor to any public pool.

II. 24

The children and I go to the countryside with Miguel to get food to feed the swimming-pool construction workers.

Construction on our swimming pool will start soon. Cubalse, the state conglomerate, that's supposed to provide all construction materials and do all construction work (supplying workers who are paid the equivalent of two dollars a day) has given an estimate of $40,000 for the construction of a pool. An independent contractor has given an estimate of $11,000. We don't know how much the independent contractor is paying his workers, but he reduced the price by $1,000 when we told him that we would provide the workers with a good lunch every day.

We don't know if it is completely legal to do work with an independent contractor. It seems to be the kind of thing that you are not supposed to ask. We got the name of the contractor through a series of whispered conversations at the school gate and notes written back and forth between me and other families who have installed pools. The contractor talks to me sotto voce even in our own garden. Trucks slide in and out with materials, workers looking both ways past the gate as they move through it. Still, there is always a guard at the gate, provided, as all employees are provided, by a state agency. The help presumably continue to make their reports. Digging is going to involve jackhammers, which are not exactly discreet.

Building the pool means fifteen for lunch every day, counting the pool people, our regular help, and now Walter, an upholsterer who has moved in with his sewing machine and has been working in the attic on slipcovers and cushions for one month.

Miguel says that his neighbor, the plumber, doesn't have any more pigs. Miguel then tells us that his family has a farm near Matanzas and that we can get what we need for the lunches – pigs, chickens, lambs, turkeys – from them. Later, when the plumber is actually *at* our house, Manuel calls me aside and says that Miguel has *said* the plumber didn't have another pig, when the plumber actually *does* have a nice, fat pig. Manuel says he doesn't understand it. Cubans usually help one another . . .

LOS TIEMPOS DIFÍCILES REVELAN LO MEJOR DE CADA UNO (Difficult times bring out the best in people), reads a sign on the road to Miguel's family's farm.

I laugh. Miguel laughs, too.

Some have said that if we feed the workers, the work will go faster because they will not have to go out to look for lunch. Others have said that if we feed them, the work will go on longer, and the better the food is, the longer they will stay.

Nick asks Miguel the day before we are supposed to go if it is legal or illegal to go into the countryside and buy food directly from a family. Miguel says there is no problem. Nick says he wants to be sure that it isn't a problem with – he doesn't know who – the People's Power, the Committee for the Defense of the Revolution, the Martyrs of the Twenty-sixth of July ...

'There will be no problem. My cousin's father-in-law's brother's wife's uncle is a vice-secretary of the Communist Party of the region.'

It's been raining since we left Havana. The Toyota Land Cruiser dives into mud holes and out again with a sucking sound. Farmworkers file by under the rain, wearing garbage bags, the corners pointy on their heads.

We stop the car and remove the jar with Charlotte in it. We walk through a fallow field to a stand of trees and bushes. We open the lid, put the bottle on the ground. Charlotte remains in the bottle. We tilt the jar up. Charlotte slides out onto the dirt. She gazes at a tuft of waving grass and disappears around a large clod. 'Good-bye, Charlotte! Have a good life!' Thea and Jimmie and I call after her. We get back in the car.

From the windows of the Land Cruiser, we look into *guajiros'* (farmers') houses – dark rooms with curtains (which serve as doors) blowing into them, babies scrabbling on floors.

We pass through a provincial town, its elegant square ringed by colonnaded buildings, the stores under the colonnades empty, and at last come to the luxuriant hollow where the ten brothers and sisters of Miguel's family live, in scattered houses.

Kisses on both cheeks for the children and me in front of the first house we come to, from a blue-eyed, narrow-faced uncle, his wife, and three blue-eyed, narrow-faced teenage children.

Turquoise walls and a kitchen counter of powder blue and yellow tiles, a single cold-water tap. A 1950s refrigerator painted turquoise. In the living/dining room, a solid neo-Gothic caoba sideboard, a table with six chairs, and some rocking chairs, and off one bedroom, a bathroom with a real door.

The toilet has no seat, the lid is off the tank, and inside the tank there is no mechanism left, just a tin can covering a pipe end. Some paper napkins are produced to serve as toilet paper and are placed discreetly beside the toilet by one of Miguel's cousins before I shut the door. The lower part of the bathroom door has a lacework of holes in it made by termites, so that I can

111

peer through to the bedroom (from which all family members have withdrawn, to give me greater privacy) as I crouch over the seatless bowl.

My eyes fix on the paper napkins serving as toilet paper perched on the lid of a plastic trash can nearby. They are very good quality paper napkins – two ply, with tiny shells embossed in the corners. Delsey. They are the kind you can't find in Cuba. They are the kind we brought in our shipment from Southeast Asia.

I find myself wondering how Miguel, who is loath to drive his 1957 Buick to Guanabacoa (five miles outside of Havana), let alone to Matanzas (seventy-five miles away) or his family, who have no visible means of transportation, were able to get the napkins all the way from the *despensa* to here.

In the yard outside the house, pigs, chickens, lambs, ducks, turkeys, a garden of roses and mariposa lilies. Papaya, peanut, yucca, avocado. Our children follow Miguel's cousins on planks through the mud, play with sticks, chase chicks, and peer through the planks of a nearby shed at a black Canadian sow with twelve piglets at her teats. I sit in a rocker on the veranda, admiring meat on the hoof and claw. Nothing like paying through the nose at the Diplo for a scrawny chicken to make you look at a barnyard and drool.

It's too wet to kill a pig, they say. They have to boil water under a big pot outside to scald the pig after it's been killed, and it's too wet to build a fire. We agree on a lamb. Their chickens are too small. We will have to ask another uncle or aunt for chickens. Off we go in the Land Cruiser to ask at one house after another of blue-eyed, narrow-faced people, whose ancestors came from Asturias, in northwestern Spain. More houses with wonderful color sense, red coffee beans, sacks of unhusked rice, cherries and corn fermenting to make wine, peanut butter fudge from their own peanuts. The children, tired now, refuse to get out of the car, but the relatives keep pressing peanut butter fudge on us, so I pass the fudge to Thea and Jimmie through the car window. I am embarrassed by the children's inertia and by the size of the Land Cruiser. 'Must consume a lot of gas,' the relatives speculate. One cousin, a doctor, asks me how much a car like that costs. 'About twenty thousand dollars,' I lie. Another cousin, a very young engineer who is studying English, asks me if it is true that in the United States, people can do what they want to do.

'What exactly do you mean?' I ask.

'Anything. You can do anything. There is freedom . . .'

Ten pairs of blue eyes are on me.

'There are not the controls that there are here. But there is not the social safety net that there is here, either. In the United States, you are free to succeed, but you are also free to fail.'

The engineer considers this. There is an approving murmur around me.

We branch out in our search for chickens. We even go to a non–family member. 'Everyone takes their chickens to Varadero, to the tourist hotels,' it is explained to us. A man in an olive green uniform with red epaulets jumps behind a tree as we pass. I wonder if headlines in tomorrow's *Granma* will read EXECUTIVE'S YANKEE WIFE CAUGHT BUYING ILLEGAL CHICKENS. We find an aunt who has another fat lamb. The shuttling around works out perfectly because while we are away from the first uncle, they kill that lamb, and then, as we are returning to him, the aunt kills her lamb. The first uncle serves us lunch – one of the bigger chickens, black beans, rice, avocado, fried bananas. I serve Jimmie chicken. 'You mean they had to kill a chicken for our lunch?' Jimmie asks.

'I think they bought it in the supermarket,' I lie.

The headless lambs, as big as medium-sized dogs, are placed in black plastic garbage bags and stacked on the floor of the front seat, between Miguel and me. The children are too bored by the rain to be inquisitive. Peanuts, we take also, as well as avocados, limes, and yuccas; Miguel will return in two days for the chickens and a pig, after the weather has gotten better and the pig can be scalded and fat chickens located. The peanuts and other foods are piled on top of the lambs in the front seat because the children have taken over the space in the back, sprawled on cushions, listening to tapes. 'It's a big, big world,' their song goes. They sing along.

I think of how even though there is lamb in the *agropecuario*, it is out of the reach of most Cubans, and I wonder if when we serve lamb for the first swimming-pool construction workers' lunch, it will be the first time some of them will have eaten lamb in years. I don't know why I am enjoying planning the swimming-pool construction workers' menu so much. I don't know why it causes me so much pleasure, imagining the swimming-pool workers' reactions to the food we will serve them, but it does.

I think, also, of how much better off Miguel's family will be with the thirty-five dollars they have been paid for everything so far, and with the money they will be paid for the pig and the chickens, and about how much more prosperous they will probably always be than the *guajiros* in the houses we passed on the way here, because of connections, planning, coordination, and a solid family network.

I start to think, also, about the Delsey napkins showing up there beside the toilet, then decide not to think about them anymore.

II. 25

Alexis Esquivel lives in a small porticoed house in the Vedado with his *marinovia* (a Cuban word combining the word for spouse, *marido*, with *novia*, the word for fiancée, meaning a live-in girlfriend) María del Carmen, a psychologist, and her daughter, a psychology major at the university. Alexis looks to be in his late twenties. María del Carmen doesn't look over thirty, but her daughter is twenty-one, so María del Carmen has got to be at least in her late thirties. Alexis is a good-looking, light-skinned black man with dreadlocks, his girlfriend is even lighter, and her daughter, with straight blond hair and blue eyes, could be German. An old lady, entirely Spanish-looking, enters the house. 'This is my great-grandmother,' Maria del Carmen's daughter says. We sit in rocking chairs in a circle under a single fluorescent tube.

It is a jumble of colors, Cuba at its best, and of ages – copper-colored skin showing not a wrinkle, people having gone through the joy and pain of having children almost without a trace.

Hanging on the wall is a plaster bas-relief head of Fidel as a red Indian, smoking a cigar. All around the room there are paintings for an upcoming exhibition, *Hysteria del Arte*, to be shown at Vasquez's gallery-cum-*paladar*.

We wonder if Vasquez will be able to put the paintings up

without a problem. There's the Karl Marx–Groucho Marx painting again, back from the same gallery but returning to it. Another painting is of Marat, murdered this time in a baroque purple bathtub with IN GOD WE TRUST engraved on the side of it. Intravenous tubes come from his fallen arm, held by tiny, frolicking female nudes. Behind him, Robespierre talks on a cellular phone in a business suit, crowned by mystic symbols – the Masonic pyramid with an eye on top of it and the Star of David, among them. Marx hovers near them, in a lotus position.

Alexis shows us a folder of photos of earlier paintings. One shows Alexis as a newborn baby being looked at by Fidel (once again in Indian headdress), John Wayne, and Brezhnev. Its title is *The Adoration of the Magi*.

I ask Alexis, María del Carmen, and her daughter if there is a natural impulse among psychologists in Havana or in Cuba to analyze people in the government.

Alexis says young people are mainly interested in psychology because they feel crazy themselves these days. They were educated to believe one thing, and now there are many different messages coming at them. María del Carmen's daughter says that all their psychology texts used to be translations of Russian texts, but now they study the writings of the North American Carl Rogers. There is only one book per class. The whole class shares it.

II. 26

Work on the swimming pool begins. The workers set up a board on sawhorses in the garage for a dining table. We serve lamb for the first meal. One worker says he has not eaten lamb since Easter of 1958.

THE DIGGERS ARRIVE. The hole for the swimming pool will be dug by hand because the gate is too narrow to get heavy equipment through. Heavy equipment would also destroy the lawn.

The diggers are not how I thought they would be. I have been expecting four or five muscular young men – brown or white, like coiled springs – but instead I see only a pair of slender, elegant, jet-black men. There is something about their skin, too, that is not the way I thought it would be: it has a papery quality, and it sags a bit, under their shoulder blades and from their pectorals. A few sprigs of white hair on their chests, and many white sprigs on their heads. They are old, I realize. About fifty-five. It is strange for the engineer to have sent old guys when there are so many young men needing work.

I do not want to watch them work. I am afraid they will have heart attacks in the heat.

MUNA TELLS ME THAT Manuel has told her that one of the diggers – the shorter one – is seventy-two.

I am appalled: grandfathers jackhammering all day long under the sun in our backyard! I start planning the speech I will make to the contractor when he shows up. The estimated two weeks to finish digging is of course a complete lie.

I spy on them from my lookout post on the second floor as they work. They are very efficient. The hole now big enough for both of them to stand in, the taller one jackhammers a chunk of rock off like a piece of Parmesan cheese, and the shorter one shovels it out. A sewer line, a water line, and an electrical cable have been revealed. Rougher young men would have broken them.

The diggers sit in the shade, smoking cigars. The word *edad* (age) is mentioned – I don't know by whom. The shorter digger squints up at me in my lookout post. 'How old do you think I am?' he asks.

'Um . . fifty-five?'

'*Gracias,*' he says, 'I was born in 1921.'

The taller one says, 'And I was born in 1928.'

'*Felicidades,*' I say.

'*Gracias,*' they say.

Suddenly everything seems OK to me, I don't know why.

II. 27

There are two basic kinds of Negroes in Cuba, Lety tells me in a combination of English and Spanish: *negros de pasas* (Negroes with raisins) and *negros de pelo* (Negroes with hair). *Negros de pasas* are black people or brown people with kinky hair. *Negros de pelo* are black people or brown people with straight or wavy hair. To be *un negro de pelo* in Cuba is to get the best of both worlds. '*Ay, qué hermosa (o hermoso) es esta negra (o*

116

negro) de pelo' ('Oh, how beautiful is this negress [or negro] with hair'), people say, sighing. Foreigners, too, love *negras de pelo.* 'Italian and German men are *locos* for *negras y mulatas de pelo.* They are *locos* for them *una barbaridad* (a barbarity, meaning very much).' Lety says, shaking the fingers of one hand. 'They see them and they want to marry them and take them out of Cuba right away! They are fascinated by them. They look good in their apartments, in, *yo no sé* (I don't know) ... Frankfurt. *Los norteños* (men of the North), they can't get a tan, but they want to *look* at a tan. It's like having sunshine in their houses. *Ay,* being *una negra de pelo* in Cuba is as good as having a visa to Canada or western Europe, guaranteed. And being *una negra* with blue eyes' – Lety shakes her fingers again, like they have been scalded – 'when the girl turns fourteen, people say, *'El norteño* is coming, *chica,* pack your bags!'"

Then in addition to the *negros de pelo* and *negros de pasas* categories, Lety says, there are skin-color gradations: *Leche con una gota de café, leche con café, café con leche, café con una gota de leche, negro, muy negro, negro azul, negro trompudo, negro azul y trompudo* (milk with a drop of coffee, milk with coffee, coffee with milk, coffee with a drop of milk, black, very black, blue black, thick-lipped black, blue thick-lipped black), so that a medium-brown black person with kinky hair, for example, would be *un café con leche y pasas.*

There are two basic kinds of *blancos,* Lety says. *Un blanco* is a blond- or light-brown-haired person with blue or green or gray eyes. *'Pero* if a *blanco* has dark hair, or has dark eyes,' Lety says, grimacing slightly, bobbing her head, and holding one hand out in front of her, which she tilts one way, then the other, *'eso no es un blanco. Es un blanquito.'*

NICK COMES HOME with the news that a new person has been placed in charge of the council of plastic arts, a woman named Ruiz, who has issued a statement declaring that artists can no longer paint nudes, Fidel, or symbols of national sovereignty.

II. 28

Coming back from the *agro* on this November Sunday in our car, Manuel, who usually never says anything to me about his personal life, tells me that he and his *mujer* (woman or wife) have been living nearby, in the home of an elderly doctor, for more than fifteen years. Last year, the doctor died. The doctor, who had no family, left the house to them, but Manuel says that he is worried because the house is in a good neighborhood, and houses in good neighborhoods are often taken over by the government for the *nomenklatura*. Manuel says that when that happens, he will go to the United States.

Manuel is fifty-five.

I ask Manuel if he has any family in the United States. He says he doesn't.

I tell Manuel that life can be very difficult in the United States. It's hard to get a job, and there's no guaranteed universal health care, as there is in Cuba.

'But in the United States, there is liberty,' Manuel says.

Nick has told me to always be careful.

'There is liberty,' I say, 'but you could end up on the street, in the worst of cases.'

We arrive home. Manuel gets out of the car to open the gate.

II. 29

I park my car in Habana Vieja. I make sure to have only one dollar in my purse, as I am alone. A young man starts to follow me.

'Do you want to buy some cigars?'

'No, thank you.'

'Can I wash your car?'

'No.'

'Would you like to buy a T-shirt with Che on it?'

'No.'

'Can I have *una fula* (a dollar)?'

'No.'

'Do you want a boyfriend? Just for tonight, though . . .'

'*I do not want a boyfriend!*' I yell, standing on the curb. People at a nearby café turn and look at me. The young man scuttles away.

Lety says that *realmente* (really), for average Cubans, things were not so bad in the seventies and eighties. 'There was a lack of freedom, true, people couldn't travel, and there was Cuba's involvement in the internationalist campaigns, which no one understood. Still, on three hundred pesos a month, people could buy what they needed, they could go out a couple of times a week, they could take taxis. Each profession had its *círculo*, or club, with a tennis court, a swimming pool, a little bar. It was a limited life, but people were happy. There were not that many things available to buy, and there was no variety and not very good quality, but still, *no fue tan malo* (it wasn't so bad).'

WE GO TO ALEXIS'S exhibition at Vasquez's gallery-cum-*paladar*. The gallery has just been filmed by CNN for a special on Cuban *paladares*. The paintings we saw in Alexis's studio are now on the walls. We ask Vasquez if anything happened. In a quiet voice he tells us that someone from the Ministry of Culture appeared and 'invited' him to remove the paintings from the walls, but here they are, still on the walls. He says it was very good that CNN had been in the gallery a few days before.

TWO X—IAN COMMUNISTS come for dinner. They say they are shocked – *shocked* – by the condition of Havana, by the low level of intellect of many of the officials they have met, by their lack of information, by the outright senility of some of the older officials. They say that a dissident they met – a Communist who called for reform in the party – had his telephone disconnected immediately after their visit and was called in by the political police. They ask us what these people think they are trying to do.

We have watched Fidel earlier in the evening on CNN, wearing a dark blue, double-breasted business suit, having cocktails in New York with U.S. businessmen and journalists.

We tell the X—ians we don't know what these people are trying to do.

WE HEAR THAT VASQUEZ's gallery-cum-*paladar* has just been closed by the police.

II. 31

Moles are appearing on Thea's back and neck, and some of them growing quite large. There is one on the edge of her hand, too, which is very black.

Dr. Silvia says she can take us to the greatest skin doctor in Cuba, Dr. Millares Cao. Dr. Millares Cao is world renowned for treating for vitiligo and psoriasis. People come from all over the world to the clinic he runs. There are days for foreigners, who have to pay, and there are days for Cubans. We will go on one of the days for Cubans, of course: Dr. Silvia will use her pull. I tell Dr. Silvia we really don't mind paying, but she says there is absolutely no point in paying. We'll have to spend a little more time in the waiting room, that's all.

WE SPEND TWO AND a half hours in the waiting room, Thea, Dr. Silvia, and I, with Thea missing school and Silvia apologizing. We play hangman, 'I spy,' and twenty questions, and toss coins. We are finally ushered into the inner sanctum. Dr. Silvia moves ahead of us, talking about her pull and our pull.

Gnawed, stained, beige-gray wall-to-wall carpeting. Functioning air-conditioning. No natural light whatsoever, and lamps that are so dim that it takes us a while to make out the doctor, far off in a recess of the room, behind a big desk. A couple of people in white coats, flanking him. Some drooping rubber plants.

We approach the big desk. Dr. Millares Cao is scowling. Dr. Silvia called me after she called Dr. Millares Cao last night, and said that everything would be fine. Dr. Silvia is still talking, a barrage of words, about how important we all are. I feel like I am with my mother and I am twelve. At best, it's the people flanking him who are making Dr. Millares Cao scowl: Dr. Millares Cao *has* to look annoyed to be seeing foreigners on a Cuban day, in case one of the people in white coats should talk.

In my halting Spanish, I tell the doctor about the moles of Thea's that worry me.

Still seated behind his desk, he asks me to take off Thea's shirt.

I look for an examining table; I wait for a light to go on. No light goes on. The doctor stays seated behind his desk, about eight feet away from Thea, still in semidarkness.

I turn her back toward him, show him the constellation of moles there.

'*Normal*,' he says.

I turn her to face him, show him the moles on either side of her neck, just under her jaw.

'*Normal*.' He doesn't even lean forward in his seat.

I show him the fleshy part of her hand, where a mole, very black, is growing out of unpigmented skin. I say that I heard it was the kind to watch.

'*Normal*.'

We slink out of the office. Dr. Silvia is sheepish.

I tell Dr. Silvia that the next time we see a specialist, we have to try to do it in another way.

Dr. Silvia nods.

WE HAVE AN EXCELLENT dinner at Vasquez's gallery-cum-*paladar*. It's not closed at all. That was just a rumor, Vasquez explains.

II. 32

Miguel calls me on the intercom, asks to see me in the upstairs hall.

His wife has fallen down and broken her leg. Broken her leg in the place where the cyst was removed. His mother stands behind him, biting her lips. He must take his wife to the hospital.

I tell them they can both go home immediately.

II. 33

Embargo, who is female, and Bloqueo (Blockade), who is male, are now preadolescent. They are loping and rangy. I fear incest because of the babies they might produce, but most of all I fear them escaping to *jinetear* (cruise like a *jinetera*) on our *avenida* and getting run over by trucks.

Bloqueo is what the U.S. embargo is sometimes called on billboard-sized slogans: NO AL BLOQUEO ESTADOUNIDENSE (No to the United States blockade), though a blockade is really when ships from one country surround another country and prevent all goods from getting into or out of that country. There was a U.S.

blockade of Cuba, but it ended in 1962. Now there is just an embargo. Whatever it's called, we have named one cat Embargo and the other cat Bloqueo so we can say 'No!' to either one of them when they scratch on the furniture.

I don't know how it happened, but I have gotten to be in my mid-forties without ever having been involved in the neutering of any animal.

Once again, the Cubans we talk to, even though it's only about cats, are adamant about our never going to a actual *clinic*. We are supposed to go to a veterinarian who *works* in a clinic but then works after-hours in his home: these veterinarians are the ones who have access to medicines. The out-of-it, newly arrived foreigners who go to clinics, the Cubans we talk to say, are the same ones who buy five-dollar-a-pound tomatoes at the Diplo. I think of making the point that foreigners are more likely to walk off planes and buy tomatoes than they are to neuter cats, but I don't have the energy.

I make the rounds of veterinarians to find the most plausible one. One veterinarian lives in an apartment building on Calle 13 in Miramar in a three-room apartment he shares with his wife, daughter, and grandmother. He is taking a nap when we come in and wraps a chenille bedspread around himself for the interview. He shows us the room where he operates – the steel table is fairly clean looking, but there are bloodstains on the walls and on books in bookshelves lining other walls, which are festooned with cobwebs.

Another veterinarian lives in a spacious house in Lawton. He is a professor of veterinary medicine. He shows me the place where he will operate. It is in his living room, on a carved mahogany coffee table, next to a Louis XVI–style display case with porcelain lords and ladies in it. When I act surprised, he says he will cover the coffee table with a towel.

Another veterinarian works in a house not far from ours, with a front veranda that serves as a waiting room. There are other families waiting on the veranda, with pets. The veterinarian, it is explained to us, used to work in a state clinic but now works full-time on her own.

One patient after another is called. There is a consulting room and an operating room at the back of the house. The veterinarian greets us. She is a woman in her sixties, with tightly curled steel gray hair and glasses, wearing a white coat over a checked shirtwaist dress and light blue plastic clip-on earrings. She takes us into the operating room. The operating table is stainless steel and the room is clean. There are bottles of what look like disinfectant or medicine on the shelves. Syringes are sterilizing in a stainless-steel pan.

The door opens. In walks another woman in her sixties, with tightly curled steel gray hair, glasses of the same style, a white coat over a shirtwaist dress in the same checked pattern, and light blue plastic clip-on earrings.

'You are twins,' I say.

They nod together, smiling.

'And you're both veterinarians.'

'*Claro*,' they say in unison.

I tell them that I am new to neutering, but I have the notion that I don't want a lot of surgical violence being done on our cats.

They tell me – in unison – that the simplest thing would be to remove the womb of Embargo but leave her ovaries intact. That way she would still have her sexual desire . . .

I jump in without waiting for them to finish. 'And we should leave the . . .' – I search for the polite word – '*testiculos* of Bloqueo, and that way they can have sex together and won't need to go out on the street.'

They nod, smiling. '*Eso es.*'

We take Embargo and Bloqueo out of the laundry basket we have brought them in. The veterinarians say Embargo is too young yet and that I should wait to have her ovaries removed until after her first heat.

'How will I know when Embargo goes into heat?'

'You will know.'

II. 34

Ivan is the other Cuban I can relate to at the firm, besides our Elegguá. Ivan is in his early thirties, with a small red goatee and a receding hairline. He's called Ivan because he was born at a time when Russia was really popular. He lives with his parents and a son Jimmie's age, whom Jimmie and Thea play with sometimes. I don't know what happened to the son's mother. Ivan had the opportunity to go on his own to Miami, he said, but he couldn't leave his son. 'There is nothing more important to me than my child,' he said simply, which of course hooked me right away. I don't know why only he had the opportunity to go to Miami, and not his son.

Ivan speaks Spanish, X——ian, colloquial American, French, German, and Russian. In addition to being the *conseguidor* of material things, Ivan is also the firm's technical *resolvedor* – of computers, telephones, and appliances. In a country of no yellow pages (nor of any telephone books whatsoever), this means that he knows who to call to fix what and, more important, that he knows when to cajole Cubalse repairmen, when to threaten them, when to show up at their places demanding service, and when to dangle the possibilities of cash rewards, rum, or food in front of them, or in front of their bosses, in order to get them to show up, and when to not struggle and just hire independent *cuentapropista* repairmen. Keeping after Cubalse repairmen is an art, but still it seems beneath Ivan's capabilities. It is assumed, therefore, that Ivan is an informer.

Ivan and I spend a lot of time in cars, going to see repairmen and appliance dealers.

'Did you see that *jine?*'

'My God . . .'

'And no support garments.'

'No support garments whatsoever.'

'How do they keep them up?' I know, but I want to hear him explain it.

'It's latex spandex. It squeezes them so tight they have no place to go.'

'If they went around like that in X——ia, or even in the United States . . .'

'Oh, *señora*, you don't know the half of it . . .'

'It's sad,' I say after a while.

'Cuba is *very sad* . . .'

Ivan studied computers in East Germany, but that's the only foreign place he says he's ever been. He has lots of foreign friends, though, he says. That's how he is able to speak so many languages and see Cuba with more . . .

'Detachment?' I ask, completing Ivan's sentence.

'*Eso es.* Detachment.'

I want to believe, but I know it's impossible, that Ivan learned so many languages and his detachment simply from talking to foreign friends.

II. 35

We are invited to the opening of the terminal for the first cruise ship to enter Havana harbor in thirty-eight years. The ship, of the Italian cruise-ship line Costa, is due tomorrow.

We drive to one of three terminals at which ferries from Miami and Key West used to dock. All three terminals were completely dilapidated. Costa restored the terminal to which its cruise ship will arrive tomorrow in only six months; the other two are still dilapidated. It has been renamed the Sierra Maestra, after the mountains from which Fidel began the revolution. On the outside, the terminal is a faithful restoration of early-twentieth-century Spanish-style industrial architecture. The inside of the terminal, however, has been made serviceable with aluminum-slat ceilings, rolled-on imitation parquet flooring, and cast-iron columns sheathed in ready-made aluminum tubes. Looking at the inside, it is easy to see how the restoration was accomplished in six months.

The *nomenklatura* – military, this time – stand before us in their uniforms and small paunches. Fidel has declared that tourism must be developed. Fidel is in China. Raúl is not here, either. Speeches are made. Plaques are presented. The military men stand staring straight ahead, moving only to make a speech or to present or receive a plaque.

THE SEVEN-HUNDRED-FOOT-LONG cruise ship sits at the terminal with every porthole and window lit. Festoons of lights have been strung from its central funnels to the bow and stern. In the streets and buildings around it are only feeble and occasional bits of light. People crowd the shore. It's as if the Magic Kingdom has been air-dropped in their midst.

Nick and I are reminded that what we first notice about the First World when we go back for our summer breaks and for quick shopping jaunts to Miami are all the *lights*.

We drive one block from the restored cruise-ship terminal to the newly restored church of San Francisco for a concert given

125

in honor of the arrival of the cruise ship. The concert is to be followed by a dinner aboard the cruise ship.

The restored church sits in a restored plaza. A cruise ship's arrival means a restored terminal; a restored terminal means a restored plaza for tourists to walk to along restored streets. One restored plaza means more restored streets leading to a second restored plaza, and so on.

In Havana, *restored* usually means everything made nice on the outside. It means drainage and plumbing, reinstalled cobblestones, roofing, facades remade faithful to history, but interiors made serviceable (we assume because of cost restraints) with only the cheapest European materials. A restored building may be a seventeenth-century Spanish colonial baroque palace or an early-twentieth-century McKim, Mead, and White Renaissance-revival office building, bank, or club on the outside; but inside it usually looks like a low-rent office or apartment building in the suburbs of Milan.

It also means few Cuban tenants. They are removed when a building is restored and are generally not permitted to move back in again. To this end, the buildings are usually restored not as living spaces but as boutiques selling items Cubans can't afford and foreigners can buy cheaper and better at home, or bleak, expensive, empty bars, or bad, expensive restaurants, or offices for the joint-venture foreign capitalists the government thinks will come, lured by 51-percent-for-the-Cuban-government, 49-percent-for-them deals. Most restored offices so far are empty. The effect is one of a stage set depicting a central business district, but without businesses – real businesses, of the kind that compete with one another and with a local middle class being allowed.

It also means Eusebio Leal. Now in his fifties, Eusebio Leal is the self-taught *historiador de la Ciudad de La Habana*. First known for his compelling historical television lectures using Havana buildings or neighborhoods as his starting point, Leal awakened average Cubans to the beauty and significance of the architecture of their pre-*triunfo* urban heritage and (it is said) single-handedly convinced Fidel of the importance of not letting Habana Vieja rot into the ground. Before the emergence of Leal, there was a tendency to portray whole stretches of Cuba's pre-*triunfo* past as a kind of dark ages, in which nothing of cultural significance was achieved. So inspiring and effective was Leal that he was permitted to found an entire corporation for the restoration of Old Havana, Habaguanex, which he runs with the assistance of various foreign partners; and if some of the buildings are tacky on the inside, if the streets are sterile, and if it's suspected, at least in Miami, that Leal has gotten rich restoring Old Havana, he is at least doing *something*.

Eusebio Leal wears a blue *guayabera* during the day, but at night he wears a black suit, with a black tie, as if in mourning. He has worn a black suit and tie for years, he says, and will wear it for many years more.

A miniskirted all-girl Cuban chamber-music group, the Camerata Romeu – all of them very young and very good looking – stride like panthers onto the stage of the seventeenth-century Church of San Francisco. The deconsecrated church, with its elongated Catalan vaults permitting a wide nave, is well suited to concert music. The sacristy was destroyed in the eighteenth century by the English, who used the church as a powder magazine during the brief period they occupied Havana. The domed sacristy has not been rebuilt, but its interior is tastefully depicted in trompe l'oeil on the church's back wall. Unlike other buildings restored by Habaguanex, deconsecrated churches and convents are generally well restored on the inside as well as on the outside. A dull terra-cotta tile floor is in perfect keeping with the church's austere elegance.

The musicians are followed by their conductor, Zenaida Castro Romeu, very young also, miniskirted, with buzz-cut hair. All the music we will hear, Ms. Romeu announces, is by Cuban composers. The first two pieces are played well, but it is hard to tell that there is anything Cuban about them. The last two pieces, though, one by Lecuona and one by Lopez-Gavilan, really swing. In the Lopez-Gavilan piece, the players drum an Afro-Cuban beat on the backs of the violins and bass. The crowd applauds mightily. The group plays many encores. I find myself missing friends, wishing they could all be with me in the Church of San Francisco, listening, too. I find myself thinking, too, about how little there is in Cuba that is just so-so: it's either totally dispiriting, or just so wonderful that I want to have all our friends from all over the world instantly at our side: *Listen to this! Look at this! Smell this!*

ABOARD THE CRUISE SHIP, Mrs. Costa, the wife of the owner of the Costa line, approaches our dinner table, which is dotted with empty places, and with a perplexed and embarrassed air explains sotto voce to Nick and me that she is sorry, but that many Cuban officials did not say whether they were coming or not, even though 'RSVP' was clearly written on the invitations. Then, to the whole table, Mrs. Costa says in an apologetic voice that she would like to move us to another table, to fill it.

In his speech, Mr. Costa refers to today's date, December 2, the date of the disembarkation of Fidel from the boat *Granma* (now in its own special house behind the Museum of the Revolution – a reproduction, for the original one fell apart – *Granma* was sold to Fidel in Mexico by an American who was evidently fond of his grandmother) onto the island of Cuba to begin the decisive struggle against Batista (the Cubans make approving noises), as a propitious date for the arrival of the first cruise ship to Havana in thirty-eight years (more approving mumbles).

At the end of the dinner, the waiter circulates, taking orders for coffee. We have just given the order at our table when the minister of transportation rises and starts shaking hands. All the other Cubans rise, as if on cue, and start shaking hands. 'They're leaving *now*? Before we've had our *coffee*?' Mrs. Costa says under her breath. They file past us, a blur of tight green uniforms. Mrs. Costa, who is sitting in their path, pushes herself in her chair as close to the table as she can get in order to let them get by. She looks at us wide-eyed, holding her breath.

'Keep them dogies movin', *rawhide!*' a middle-aged Canadian businessman sings.

II. 36

The opening of the seventeenth annual New Latin American Film Festival at Karl Marx Theater. There's a red carpet in front of the main entrance. Two doormen in white uniforms with gold braid on their shoulders open the doors of the cars of the arriving guests, while celebrity watchers gape behind velvet ropes. In the lobby, a television anchorman interviews celebrities as they arrive. This is simultaneously shown on a TV screen in the theater. The cavernous theater, however, is poorly lit and smelly, and the red carpet and the red plush on the seats are worn in most places to dull black. A Chinese diplomat dozes on my shoulder. The dim lights dim further. There is a ballet skit. People in turn-of-the-century costumes. They dance here and there, eventually settling into some turn-of-the-century theater seats. A small screen descends. A silent movie is projected onto the screen. It shows scenes of Havana in about 1915. We see a bustling neighborhood of elegant shops and well-dressed people. There are electric streetcars and lots of automobiles. We wonder what the organizers of the film festival are trying to do, showing a spiffy Havana.

Alfredo Guevara (no relation to Che), head of the Instituto Cubano del Arte y de la Industria Cinematográfica, or Cuban Film Institute, a soft, pale, fragile-looking man, addresses the audience. He hails the festival as a Dionysian and Apollonian event.

People in the audience lean forward, their faces straining. I wonder if it's because they are trying, as I am, to remember what *Dionysian* and *Apollonian* mean. I wonder, too, if it's because they are trying to figure out, as I am, what *it* means, someone close to Fidel giving a speech about opposing Greek gods.

The film – *Put Your Thought in Me* – is the first work by a young filmmaker whom Guevara is said to be in love with. It is a story of Jesus in a kind of semi-Renaissance time into which the modern age intrudes in the form of bicycles, eyeglasses, guys in Batista-era white linen suits and two-tone shoes. There are borrowings from Fellini, from Buñuel, from Terry Gilliam. Suddenly, Christ is in a motorcade and is shot, like Kennedy.

After the film, Nick and I say to some Cuban acquaintances, who are walking with us to the same parking lot, that we probably would have appreciated the film more if we were Cuban and were able to understand all the references, but the Cubans say they thought the film was very bad, too.

We'd like to know what the films of the film festival will be, where they will be shown, and when, but the organizers of the film festival cannot publish an accurate schedule more than a day ahead of time because they are never sure whether a film they have ordered will arrive in time, or at all, and then, even after the schedule is published, there are always changes at the last minute and unscheduled blackouts.

On a slow evening in early December, Nick and I escape the children and go downtown to a *paladar* that we were shown by a roving *paladar* guide the week before. We have gotten used to it by now, being led by young men down dark alleys. This one is a *paladar* we think visitors will like because you have to go through a garage to get to it, but before we take anyone there, we want to check out the food.

A guide tells us that he thinks the *paladar* is closed. We cannot believe him. *Paladares* are always open. He knocks on the door. The owner appears. The *paladar* is closed, he says, because the two children of a couple who worked there have been murdered, strangled by a maniac in Pinar del Río (a city more than a hundred miles to the west of Havana) and left in a restaurant refrigerator along with the bodies of four other children, who were also strangled. The couple had left the children in Pinar del Río with their grandparents and had come to work in Havana to make some money.

Nick and I don't feel like eating anymore, but we don't feel like going home, either. We end up standing outside a state-run restaurant that calls itself an Arab restaurant. It is in a lovely colonial building with a cool, beautiful courtyard, and there is a menu outside with the words *hummus* and *tabbouleh* and *falafel* written on it, and there *are* forty thousand people in Cuba who consider themselves of Syrian or Lebanese origin – *Turcos*, they are called, because their forebears immigrated to Cuba when the Ottoman Empire still existed.

They have no hummus. The tabbouleh, when it comes to the table, consists of carrots, peas, and potatoes. The falafel turns out to be hamburger and fried chicken. The main course is supposed to be meat, but it is unidentifiable. There are some Egyptian paintings on the walls and a couple of dirty rugs on the floor. A belly dancer comes out and shakes some bells on her waist, disconsolately, to canned music.

IN GRANMA, AN ARTICLE describes how six children were found dead in a refrigerator, but there is no mention of a maniac or strangling.

II. 38

We go to see an Italian movie, part of the film festival. We are invited by the Italian ambassador and his American wife, Carey.

The director of the film and an actor in the film get up and talk before the show. The movie is called *The School* and the director says, very sheepishly, that unlike Cuban schools, Italian schools have a lot of problems and the film is about that.

Carey tells me about letters her husband receives from Italian men in Cuban prisons: 'Mr. Ambassador, I am being unjustly imprisoned. True, I knew she was fourteen, but I had a business relationship with her aunt . . .' She tells me about Italian wives who call or write the embassy from Italy. 'I thought I knew my husband. We have been happily married for eighteen years, or so I thought, but my husband went on a business trip to Cuba, saying he would return in two weeks. That was two months ago, and he still hasn't returned. Every time I call him and ask him when he will be returning, he is evasive . . .'

In the film there's a reference to Italian students making a long-distance call to Fidel Castro with a message of support.

Carey says the problem with a lot of the male Italian tourists is that they fall in love. They fall in love and throw themselves heart and soul into getting Italian visas to remove Cuban girls from Cuba, a country they purportedly admire, but with a crusading vigor spurred (the men sometimes confess) by a desire to 'save' the girls from Cuba. It's confusing. Carey says you can see the girls they fall in love with standing on the median strip in front of the embassy every morning – stacked heels on the ends of pacing, endless legs have destroyed the grass and carved a kind of bowl in the dirt – with striving Italian men of all ages next to them in Che Guevara T-shirts.

Carey says the problem is that a lot of the male tourists are ready to fall in love before they even get to Cuba: all Cuban girls have to do is nudge them over the edge.

II. 39

A directive has been issued to all ministries, banning Christmas trees in all government offices. It's a pagan tradition, the directive says. Then, confusingly, the directive also says it's a way for the church to assert its power.

It's a fight, it is generally agreed, between the orthodox and the not-so-orthodox while Fidel is in China.

I ASK LETY ABOUT the Tienda de los Novios (the Store of the Fiancés). Nick and I have passed one on Avenida Galliano many times, and we have seen others around the city. Lety explains that engaged couples are allowed to shop in the Tienda de los Novios between the time of their application for a marriage license and the wedding ceremony. They are given a *papelito* (little paper) allowing them to buy from the *tienda*, for half price, basic home items, many of which are often not available in regular stores. They are allowed to buy two sheets and two pillowcases; two towels; an electric fan; glasses, plates, bowls, cups, and saucers for four; assorted pots and pans; a set of kitchen spoons; a spatula; two night tables; a broom; a dust mop; and some brushes.

Then the engaged couple can go with another *papelito* to the specialized *bodeguita* of their barrio (neighborhood) for bread for sandwiches, cake, beer, rum, ice, and soft drinks. They are also given, following their marriage, two free honeymoon nights in selected hotels.

Lety tells me engaged couples are given *tienda* and *bodeguita* privileges no matter how many times they may have been married before. Five, six, seven times, it doesn't matter – she doesn't know why. She says some *locos* get married just for the sheets, the beer, and the free honeymoon nights.

I ARRIVE BACK FROM a one-week trip to Miami with five suitcases packed with swimming-pool chemicals, fabric, thread, zippers, a Rubbermaid dish dryer, children's books, car parts, espresso-pot gaskets, kitchen utensils, stove-burner replacement parts, refrigerator replacement parts, shoes of every kind for us and for the help, plastic bags, medicines for us and for the help, and Christmas presents for Nick, the children, and everyone I can think to get Christmas presents for.

I have also brought back a bathing suit with a matching pareo for Carlita. I take it to her uncle's house, where she usually stays now. She is not there, so I leave it with her uncle's girlfriend.

It is a relief to get to Miami, but it is more of a relief, after one week in Miami, to be back in Havana.

* * *

IT IS DECEMBER 24. We have been given a pile of candies, so we contact the director of the school at the end of the block and ask if we can distribute candies in every class. Children, dressed in José Martí Pioneers outfits, meet us in the front hall. They do a show for us. One little girl sings a song from the movie *Aladdin*, in Spanish. Others do a dance number to U.S. rap music.

We visit the classrooms one by one and go from one desk to another, holding a tray of chocolates for the children to pick from. The director moves ahead of us, explaining in each classroom that we are distributing the chocolates '*para n—, para el nuevo año.*' Fortunately for her, *Navidad* (Christmas) and *nuevo año* (New Year) both start with the letter *n*. There are still quite a few chocolates left over after we have distributed one to each child, so we leave them with the teachers. The teachers and the director kiss us warmly as we leave. '*Feliz N—! Feliz nuevo año!*' they call to us.

WE ARE TOLD THAT when Christmas was abolished as a holiday in 1969, a holiday called Children's Day was established in September. It was established in September because there weren't any other holidays in September. It was a day on which children were supposed to receive a gift. The rationing of toys, which had already been in place for several years, was systemized further. Families were permitted, through ration books, to buy one 'basic' gift, one 'nonbasic' gift, and one 'additional' gift, for a total of three gifts per year, per child. One gift could be given on Children's Day, one on the child's birthday, and one on a day of the parents' choosing.

At first it was announced on television at which stores and at what times the toys could be bought, the result being that stores were besieged by customers and immediately cleaned out. A system was then devised for reserving by telephone a time for buying a basic, a nonbasic, and an additional toy.

The ultimate solution was a lottery system, conducted zone by zone within the city. Sale periods of six days were established. Lotteries were conducted in stores, bodegas, and local CDRs (Committees for the Defense of the Revolution – neighborhood watchdog groups), where parents went to be told what day, what hour, and in which store they could go to make their purchases. In this way, only those whose reservation was for the first hour of the first day of the sale period were able to buy a good basic toy such as a bicycle.

The system lasted until 1981; after that, people just bought whatever they could find, whenever and wherever they could find it.

II. 40

A loud noise wakes us up. I wonder, for an instant, if it's the *norteamericano* invasion some Cubans still think is coming. We have seen Cuban troops on a flat patch of land along the sea near Cojímar practicing for it. Sometimes I have an impulse to roll down the car window and call to them, '*Hay un yanqui por aquí!*' ('There's a Yankee over here!').

I lie there, waiting for more. Moonlight is slanting through the blinds, making white stripes on the tile floor. Our house is utterly screenless and yet, magically, no insects come inside, only the smell of night-blooming jasmine.

It starts again. It's like an old-fashioned siren, the one you crank. The *norteamericano* invasion siren, which they test once a month, sounds more high-tech. It's like moaning, too, and muezzin calling worshipers to prayer. Rising and falling, and at the end, snarl-moans and rustling bushes.

'Cats,' Nick says, rolling over. 'Embargo must be in heat.'

II. 41

I have not heard anything from Carlita yet about the bathing suit and matching pareo I brought her from Miami. I call Davide's house and leave a message for her to call me.

CARLITA NEVER GOT THE bathing suit. Davide's girlfriend, who received the bathing suit when I dropped it off, kept the bathing suit for herself. Carlita didn't know anything about the bathing suit until I called her. She asked Davide about it, Davide confronted his girlfriend, they had a big fight because of it, and the girlfriend moved out of his house.

'They broke up because of a *bathing suit?*'

134

'*Eso es.*'

Carlita tells me they had been living together for three years.

II. 42

Sunday. Manuel is nearly alone with us in the house. Only one maid is on Sunday shift, working upstairs in our room. Manuel says he would like to have a word with me.

We step onto the veranda. Manuel lowers his voice. Some of the help have been abusing their privileges, Manuel says. Concha has been seen taking small amounts of coffee and carrying it home in a plastic bag. She has also been seen taking cloths for cleaning the floor. Danila has been washing her personal things in the washing machine, with our detergent. Miguel is embarrassed because he is the one with the keys to the *despensa*. He is afraid I will think he is the one who has been taking things. But Danila and Concha know where I keep the keys to the *despensa* . . .

I SLEEP VERY BADLY, thinking about how I will have to speak to the help the following day. I decide to get it over with right away. I call everyone into the pantry. *Trust*, I looked up the night before in the Spanish-English dictionary while I was rehearsing; also, *to abuse*.

'Do not abuse my trust in you,' I say to everyone, trying to scan the range of faces as I speak. 'Taking a little or taking a lot, it's still the same thing. The washing machine and detergent are not for your personal use. I cannot live with people whom I cannot trust. If you have a material problem that is making your life difficult, speak to me openly about it, and you and I together can see what we can do to resolve your problem.'

Muna is hiding around the side of the refrigerator. I am wishing I were far away.

After my talk, Muna hands me Miguel's keys to the *despensa*. 'He does not want to keep them anymore,' Muna says.

I catch up to Miguel in the garden. 'Please keep the keys. I trust you,' I say, thinking that the Delsey napkins at his uncle's house, though really, *really* not available in Cuba, got to his uncle's house from some other source or (I now think) were perhaps taken from the *despensa* especially for our trip, Miguel

135

knowing the conditions at his uncle's house – a little stack of them, for traveling – and passed, shortly after our arrival at his uncle's house, to his cousin, who placed them, as invisibly as a fairy would, next to the toilet before I entered the bathroom.

He takes the keys. 'Thank you,' he says.

II. 43

Nicoletta, a half-X—ian, half-Cuban woman, based in Sweden, who is working temporarily in Cuba, comes for dinner. She describes a visit her firm made to Fidel a few days ago. They wanted to discuss the $3 million deal her firm was interested in making – to start a string of Laundromats throughout Cuba – while all Fidel wanted to discuss was China. He kept them standing, nine executives and their wives, for forty-five minutes while he talked. Finally, one of the wives said, 'I don't know about anyone else, but I would like to sit down.' Aides stood tensely nearby. One of the executives tried to bring up the subject of the Laundromats. Fidel said, 'All problems will be resolved,' and went back to talking about China. They went into another room and were offered *mojitos* and coffee. More talk of China. Fidel held his right hand by the wrist or kept it behind his back the whole time they were with him, Nicoletta tells us. At the end of the session, Fidel insisted on kissing each of the women in the group. Nicoletta says his eyes were heavy-lidded and unfocused as he went from one woman to another, muttering, '*Dáme un besito, dámelo, dámelo* . . .' ('Give me a little kiss, give it to me, give it to me . . .').

Some say Fidel had a ministroke in Japan, which is why he stayed an extra day there on his way to China. They say that the 'cold' he was supposed to have had in Japan was really that.

II. 44

A February cold wave in the eastern United States means temperatures in the fifties in Havana. '*Frío, frío,*' people say, walking around hunched over, holding their elbows if they don't have a sweater, or if they do, walking stiffly, unused to the bulk.

Concha runs to open the gate, her arms bare.

136

I ask Muna if Concha owns a sweater. Muna says she doesn't. I have Manuel and Miguel bring down trunks of heavy and less-heavy clothes from the attic. I find a blue sweatshirt for Concha. I find pants, sweaters, and sweatshirts for the other people at the house, too.

II. 45

Cool weather means more cocktail parties, art openings, and Americans. I meet U.S. congressional staffers at a party. Republicans and Democrats. Most of them tell me right away that they think the embargo is an obsolete policy. An aide to a Republican congressman says to me, 'It's too bad we can't put Fidel and Jesse Helms and Jorge Mas Canosa in a boat and push them out to sea.' He says any calls Cuban Americans make to him begin with their telling him how much money they contribute to the Republican Party.

It is beginning to look more and more like Helms-Burton won't pass.

One of the staffers, a woman, tells me about a strange thing that happened during a photo session with Fidel following a meeting with him that afternoon. Fidel insisted on being surrounded only by women staffers and kept his hands rigidly at his sides as the women were being grouped around him, and as the shot was being taken, Fidel called out to his aides, 'See? I'm not touching them!' which was translated to the group as, 'I don't want to crowd them.'

It was funny, she says, how the phrase was translated. It was also funny that the translator thought the phrase should be translated at all, because after meeting them, the translator had realized that all of them spoke Spanish and had given up translating after the first few exchanges.

ON THE WAY TO AN art opening, our Elegguá recounts a recent story involving one of the last surviving men from the disembarkation of the *Granma*, whose nom de guerre was Comandante Universo. Comandante Universo, a retired general, raised pigs. Because of his connections, Comandante Universo had access to better-quality slops – slops from the army's agricultural projects, slops from hotel restaurants (many hotels are run by retired generals). Even more important, he had enough gasoline to drive around to pick the slops up. One day there was a load of milk, which either couldn't make it to the processing plant or was on the verge of going bad. Comandante Universo was somehow able to get hold of it and gave it to his pigs.

This was too much for Comandante Universo's neighbor, who denounced him to his local CDR. Comandante Universo took a gun and shot his neighbor dead in front of a lot of people. He then gathered all the guns in his house in a pile on his front porch and sat in a rocking chair on his front porch until the police arrived. 'Here are my guns,' he said, gesturing toward the pile of them. 'Do with me what you will.' Comandante Universo was sentenced to thirty years in prison.

'But the neighbor was very stupid,' Nick says. 'The neighbor was an idiot.'

'A complete idiot,' our Elegguá agrees.

WE MEET THE STEPMOTHER of Che Guevara at the Argentinian ambassador's house.

Ana María Guevara is on her way to Europe to promote a miniseries on Che's adolescent years. With her is a slight young man who looks fourteen but is actually twenty. As Ana María (who looks to be about fifty-five) talks, we wonder, *Could this really be Che's stepmother? If the boy is her son, does this mean that we are then looking at Che's half brother?* There is something delicate and Che-like about him. Finally it is explained. Ana María was forty years younger than Che's father. When she met Che's father, who had separated from Che's mother, Che was already in Cuba. She herself never met Che. Che, if he were alive, would be sixty-six. The boy is indeed Che's half brother, the youngest of three children she had by the father of Che. Che, if he had lived, would have been forty-six when his little brother was born.

There is silence as we contemplate the span of reproductive years of the healthy human male.

I HAVE LUNCH WITH an American group making an art tour sponsored by the Center for Cuban Studies. The Center for Cuban Studies, based in New York, hosts various educational tours for Americans. It is run by Sandra Levinson, who came to

Cuba on journalistic assignment in the sixties. She injured herself while cutting cane, and Fidel Castro himself, who happened to be nearby, picked her up in his arms and carried her out of the cane field. She swears she never had sex with him, though – not even once. 'Everybody says to me, 'Come on, Sandra, we know you did,' but I didn't, I swear!'

I ask some of the Americans I know how the art they have seen so far has been.

'Well . . . ,' the Americans say to me.

I take some of the Americans to visit Antonio Nuñez. Antonio's paintings look like wallpaper, with one or two small elements in them repeated many times. One painting shows alligators (Cuba) fighting with bulls (Spain), one shows alligators fighting with bears (Russia), one shows alligators fighting with eagles (guess who), and one shows the alligators chasing their own tails.

WE GO TO REYNALDO and Eddie's. Eddie opens the gate. He looks stricken. 'The *paladar* is closing for always.'

'Why?'

'Because . . .' Eddie twists his hand in the air as he walks into the back of the house to get Reynaldo.

Reynaldo appears. We sit in rocking chairs in the living room. All the tables and chairs are pushed to the wall.

It's the new law, Reynaldo says. Every *paladar* is going to have to pay $300 plus 400 pesos a month for a 'license,' as well as a portion of its earnings in taxes if the *paladar* makes more than $3,000 in a year.

'But who can pay that?'

'No one.'

Reynaldo tells us that there is another new law, too, that people who run *paladares* from now on are going to have to show police the receipts from whoever sold them their food. The only legal receipts are those from the Diplomercado and the *agropecuario*.

'But who can run a *paladar* and pay the prices they ask at the Diplo and the *agro*?'

'No one.'

'*CAMARONES, LANGOSTAS, FRESAS, queso blanco*' ('Shrimps, lobster, strawberries, fresh cheese'), thin brown men murmur all day long outside the Diplo, the market on Forty-second Street, and the *agro* on Calle A in Vedado. You murmur back to them. They disappear around a corner and appear within a few minutes with battered gym bags.

II. 46

We have a new swimming teacher, Gonzalo. Carlita found him for us. We stopped going to the pool in the park after a few times there, and it was too complicated, after our own pool was finished, for Carlita to come here.

II. 47

Manuel brings things to the house that he thinks might interest us. He brings us a photo of a gathering of Bacardi employees in Santiago de Cuba in the 1940s. The men wear linen suits and two-tone shoes.

We know that Manuel managed part of a farm outside Camagüey before the revolution, for a man whose family is now living in Miami. The man had a big farm, but he spent most of his time in Havana. We ask Manuel now what else the man who had the big farm did.

'He was the chief of police under Batista.'

'Oh.' We change the subject.

'Did he really say that?' I ask Nick later.

'That's what he said.'

CONCHA BRINGS MAIL to me in my writing room. She clears her throat. '*Con su permiso . . . ,*' she says.

'Yes?'

Concha asks me if I would like to buy a Stradivarius violin.

'*What?*'

Concha says she has a friend who has a friend who has a Stradivarius that he would like to sell.

'*But they cost hundreds of thousands of dollars!*'

Concha says the violin is worth $3 million, actually, but the man she knows will sell it for $2 million. She says it's not stolen, that it belonged to his great-grandfather, that he has papers from that town in Italy, Crema, Croma . . .

'*Cremona?*'

'That's it.'

'I'll have to ask my husband about it,' I say.

I'll have to ask my husband about it is a phrase that still works very well in Cuba.

AT DINNER, NICK TELLS ME that he has heard that Muhammad Ali, when he was in Cuba recently delivering humanitarian aid, had dinner with a woman, a former Black Panther, who is wanted for murder in the United States.

I ask Nick if he could pass the hot sauce.

Nick asks me if I don't think that's shocking and revolting.

'What?'

'Cassius Clay, one of the greatest American athletes who ever lived, in Cuba on a humanitarian mission, having dinner with a fugitive from American justice, a murderer . . .'

I shrug. 'I don't think we know all the details,' I say, but I can see Nick's expression darkening.

'We're just not communicating,' Nick says. 'We're having a communication gap.' The chair grinds back. He starts to leave the table.

'Ni-ick . . . I'm not saying I *condone murder* – of course I think it's revolting, if indeed she did murder someone.' This seems to be the right thing to say, for I can see him softening somewhat. 'I'm just saying I'm . . . not surprised, knowing how things work in the United States. Besides, maybe he is trying to get her to give herself up.'

I'm happy I can come up with something, but Nick, too, should make allowances for a little moral laxity on my part, for after all, our maid (who, when I brought her a $4.95 rain jacket from the United States, acted like it was the crown jewels) just this morning tried to sell me a Stradivarius for $2 million.

II. 48

We go to see a movie, the first Cuban movie ever made, about transvestites in Havana. It's a movie about how, yes, they had to struggle, with society and with their parents, but now society

141

accepts them, and their parents love them no matter what. (The most heartrending part of the movie is when it shows how transvestites make false eyelashes out of carbon paper, which is toxic, and wear them, risking their eyesight.)

If it were a movie made and shown in the United States, France, or Mexico, for example, you'd say, 'Big deal,' about the whole thing, but the movie theater is packed, people shout and cry all through the movie, and at the end, there is a standing ovation.

II. 49

I descend the steps of the Meliá Cohiba Hotel, ready for beggars, male *jineteros*, or freelance car watchers, but surprisingly, no one approaches me.

My eye falls on an object on the sidewalk. It is a watch. I look to see if there is anyone nearby who looks as if he has lost something. There are some regular hard-up-looking people around, but they are at a distance and strangely distracted. I pick up the watch and slip it into my bag. Still no one looks my way.

Once in the car, I take the watch out of my bag and look at it. It is a man's gold watch. If I were in a normal country, I would turn it in at the hotel desk, but here the desk clerk would probably keep it for himself. I will give it to a Cuban who doesn't have a hotel job. I put it in my bag and start the car. Still no one approaches, and a newish car, revving up outside a hotel is always a magnet for someone needing something. It is as if there is a force field around me, causing time to stand still and keeping other humans away from me and semiparalyzed, allowing me to pick up the watch, examine the watch, think of whom to give the watch to, making me woozy from the strangeness of it.

II. 50

I take a field trip with the children to visit a newspaper.

All newspapers – *Granma, Juventud Rebelde* (Rebel Youth), *Trabajadores* (Workers) – are in one building, behind the Plaza de la Revolución. All newspaper production has been cut back since the beginning of the *periodo especial. Granma* is still published daily, but it is just a few pages. *Trabajadores* and *Juventud Rebelde* are published once a week.

A newspaperman greets us at the entrance and takes us up unswept stairs to the offices of *Juventud Rebelde*. We see the newsroom, which consists of fifteen desks with manual typewriters on them. Only three desks have people working at them; the other desks are absolutely bare but for the typewriters, which look about forty years old. Dead malanga plants serve as decoration.

'Please speak slowly and clearly,' the teacher leading the field trip says to the newspaperman. 'The children are very small.'

We visit the pasteup room, the corrections room, the room where the pasteup is fed into a computer, the telex room. These rooms are smaller and have more activity. One man sits at a desk reading *Time* magazine, a Spanish-English dictionary beside him. Some of the children start getting restless. We walk upstairs to see where the printing plates are made. The rooms are nearly abandoned. Two fluorescent lights still working out of a line of ten barely illuminate the dark hall. A tall, elderly *negro de pasas* pulls a large black barrel on a dolly, his face grim. He pauses in midstride to let the children pass. The toes of his shoes have been cut away to give his feet room. He stays frozen in midstride even after the children have passed.

Nobody else in the hallway seems to notice the catatonia and carry on as if it's normal to see him frozen like that.

It's very active in Cuba, this random time-standing-still, people-being-paralyzed thing. It's like in fairy tales: some people frozen or turned to stone, others very much alive among the statues.

I look back: still frozen.

We enter a cavernous room where the printing and folding presses are, twelve of them lined up in a row. Only one is working. We look inside the machine where pages are being printed and folded. A long conveyor belt carries them out, folded, to the floor above. The printer gives each child a copy. They are pages of an English textbook. The newspaperman explains to us that now that not as many newspapers are being produced, the presses are being used for other jobs.

We go back down the unswept stairs, under sunlight that filters weakly through unwashed windows, to the main floor, where there is a model of the building we are in, on display in honor of its tenth birthday. The building is modern, just recently built, but without the model and the sign underneath it, it would be impossible to know this.

I RETURN TO THE house earlier than I said I would, to find Danila, dressed in street clothes, ready to leave for the day. Beside her on the curb is a container of green liquid. She stumbles over the curb when she sees me. Miguel and Concha are near her, watching.

'Hello, everyone,' I say, then go into the house.

The container of green liquid doesn't look like something we have in the *despensa*, but I am not entirely sure.

II. 51

The next day, Danila comes up to me and starts mumbling. 'I'm sorry I left early yesterday,' I manage to make out.

'If you would tell me ahead of time when you have to leave early, then you would never have to apologize,' I say, surprising myself, for I sound as if I am taking the situation coolly in hand, or as if I have spent the last eighteen hours thinking about how Danila left early, when in fact I haven't been thinking about it at all.

I don't work up the nerve to ask her about the green liquid.

THAT NIGHT, AT A dinner party at which there are no Cubans, someone mentions a Stradivarius for sale.

'Oh, that old Stradivarius. It's been around for years,' someone else says.

II. 52

NUESTRA FORTALEZA ESTÁ EN LA BASE DE LA SUPERVIVENCIA DE LA PATRIA Y DE LA REVOLUCIÓN SOCIALISTA (Our strength is the basis for the survival of the country and of the socialist revolution), reads the slogan on a billboard placed in front of the parking lot at the Diplomercado. Underneath the words are images of children in military uniforms, lifting Cuban flags. One child holds a sign on which is written ¡VIVA LA REVOLUCIÓN SOCIALISTA!

The billboard is placed next to two other billboards, one for

Adidas and one for Bagley S.A., which is, I believe, a biscuit manufacturer.

I'm pretty much inured to big slogans by now, but some of them still manage to catch my eye.

II. 53

My brother Sam is here. He is six foot one and weighs 220 pounds. His friend Bill, who is six foot four and probably weighs about the same, is here with him. I never take my purse to Old Havana, or if I do, I take it with just a few dollars in it and nothing else, but today I would like to stop on the way home and pay for a painting that I have bought for Nick for $650. I have Sam and Bill with me to protect me, and I know Sam and Bill won't mind my stopping for a moment on our way home to pick the painting up.

We make a reservation for lunch at Galería Vasquez. Bill and Sam are impressed, I can tell, by my savoir faire as we enter the foul, dark hallway, the kind of place where you would be sure to be mugged in the States but in Havana never are, and climb up a winding outdoor staircase in a courtyard full of dripping pipes, screaming children, tomato plants in coffee cans with eggshells in them to ward off the evil eye, broken birdcages, bicycle parts, shreds of clothes drying in the wind. Squid guts are splattered over the last flight of stairs.

Cultivated, gentle Arquitecto Vasquez takes our order for lunch, which we will return for in a few hours. We go down the stairs again and into the Plaza de la Catedral. A gaggle of people trail behind us as we cruise the vendors. They are asking to be our guide, trying to sell us cigars or PPG, an anti-impotence medicine. When they get to be too insistent, I turn to them: '*Sí, somos extranjeros, pero que culpa tenemos nosotros? Si no pueden dejarnos en paz, voy a llamar a un policia*' ('Yes, we are foreigners, but what fault is that of ours? If you can't leave us in peace, I am going to call the police'). They scatter before I am able to finish. We tour the Plaza de Armas and enter the Palacio de los Capitanes Generales to see the Basura de la Historia, or 'dustbin of history' – a room in which busts of past Cuban presidents are scattered at random on the floor. There is also a broken headless eagle from the top of the monument to the USS *Maine*,

145

and a case of Coca-Cola placed underneath a Spanish colonial armchair as if it were a chamber pot. An ornate ivory telephone on a table by the side of the armchair is mysteriously off the hook. On the wall is a death announcement for Fulgencio Batista.

We continue to the Plaza Vieja, where the first slave market was, which became, around the turn of the last century, the Jewish wholesale section. So busy was it that an underground parking lot was installed in 1946, creating an ugly cement platform where the square had been. It is now being smashed by the army with pneumatic drills. We gaze at the porticoed colonial buildings (some restored and devoid of Cubans, others with a hundred people living in them, in buildings no bigger than generous three-story town houses) and at the deeply funky Palacio Viena, an art nouveau hotel built in 1912, divided infinitely into teeming living spaces.

Everywhere on the street, there are poor *negros* and poor *blancos* and poor *mulatos*. (In Cuba, technically everyone is poor, but in Siboney, where we live, people on the whole manage to look and act less poor.)

We turn on Calle Cuba and start heading for the Church of La Merced. There are fewer people on the street now, and I am no longer walking between Sam and Bill, but to the left of them. 'Isn't it relaxing,' I say to Sam and Bill, ' – how you can walk down a street like this and not feel any kind of menace?' Just then I feel a gentle unburdening, and I am thinking about how light I feel, how relaxed, when the next thing I know, I'm looking at a familiar shoulder strap, trailing gaily from the hand of a thin young man who is running past us. I wonder what my shoulder strap is doing, trailing along in front of us, and then I realize it's trailing from my purse, which is in the hand of the boy running in front of us, my purse with the $650 inside it and a latch attaching the strap to the purse that you can undo with a flick of the finger. I was insane to take a purse with a strap like that to Habana Vieja.

I start running. 'What the hell?' Sam and Bill say, and they start running, too. I am trying to think of the word for 'thief' in Spanish as precious seconds tick by. Finally it comes to me: *ladrón*. '*Ladrón!*' I start yelling. '*Ladrón!*' The thief turns up a deserted street. We follow. An old man lunges at the boy, but the boy easily skirts him. A woman leans out of a coffee shop. '*Cógelo!*' ('Get him!') she yells. There's supposed to be a policeman or an undercover agent on every corner, and they *were* there near the *catedral*, but now there is no one. Bill moves ahead of us and is gaining on him. Bill has very long legs, but he's fifty years old. '*Ladrón!*' I scream every time I have breath.

The thief turns another corner. The street is fuller now – children, people lolling in doorways. They will catch him now for sure. He is moving away from Bill. '*Ladrón!*' There are some able-bodied people, but they do not move from their lolling positions. I am aware of how *blanco* we are, how touristy in our baggy clothes and enormous, stark white jogging shoes – I was of course aware of it before, but now I *really* am. Bill and the thief are so far ahead of Sam and me now that we can't see them anymore. I stop, panting.

Little children crowd around me. 'Were you robbed?'

Sam returns. Between pants, Bill says that the thief had a friend on a bicycle waiting for him about halfway down the block. The thief jumped on the back of the bicycle, and together they rode off in the direction of the waterfront.

A little boy guides us to the police station several blocks away. Sam puts his arm around me as we walk. 'Poor sweet pea,' he says.

'Better me than you,' I say.

Bill tips the boy one dollar. 'That's a lot of money – ' I say before I can stop myself.

We are led upstairs to a room where there are two plainclothesmen sitting at ancient typewriters. I sit down in front of one of the plainclothesmen. '*Un momento,*' he says. He is working on an earlier report. Sam and Bill sit nearby, in low-slung vinyl-covered chairs with stuffing coming out of them. Sam grins tenderly. 'Poor sweet pea,' he says again.

The plainclothesman introduces himself. His name is Orestes. I tell Orestes what happened.

'Was it a *negrito?*' Orestes asks. He himself is a *negro de pelo*, slightly *chinito*.

'He was not very black.'

'Was he like him?' Typing, he gestures with his head toward a medium-brown man sitting in front of the other desk. The man turns and looks at us indifferently.

147

'Like him.'

'*Mulato*,' he says while typing.

Orestes asks me if I can describe the thief. I say I only saw the back of him. Orestes gives me a stack of about seventy-five mug shots to look through – all black or *mulato* boys between the ages of thirteen and twenty-five, looking like deer caught in headlights. He asks me if I would be able to identify the thief in a lineup. I shake my head no. I translate Bill's description of the clothes the thief was wearing. Orestes asks me to describe the contents of my purse. I have to tell him that there was $650 in it. There were credit cards in it, too, and a driver's license and some mementos. Keeping U.S. credit cards, which cannot be used in Cuba, in my purse is further evidence of my staggering lack of judgment.

'Sweet pea . . .'

'Hey, it could have been worse . . .' I say breezily, while thinking painfully of the mementos in my wallet, which are now gone, too – blood-type cards for the children made after they were born (the blood that was tested drawn from their tiny heels), the fortune from the first Chinese restaurant I went to with Nick, a two-dollar bill.

I took a purse with that kind of strap and with $650 in it to Habana Vieja, I realize, because Sam is my big brother.

Orestes has to type the report twice because he does not have any carbon paper. It takes about an hour.

When Orestes has finished typing, he tells us he wants to return with us to the scene of the crime. We are led back down the stairs to where there is a dented Lada police car, its trunk held down with twine.

I ask Orestes if we can take photos of my brother and Bill in front of the police car, then of my brother and me. Orestes says we can, as if to show how relaxed he is. We pose, grinning broadly.

A tall, pockmarked uniformed policeman pushes himself off a backless kitchen chair, propped against a wall under the shade of a *yagruma* tree, where he has been dozing. He ambles toward us. He is going to be our driver. We ask this uniformed policeman if we can take a photo of him, too, in front of the police car, but he refuses sternly and sidles away.

Bill sits in the front seat of the Lada with his knees under his chin. I scoot forward in the middle of the backseat to give Sam and Orestes more room, but still the backseat of the Lada is so small that I am practically in Orestes' lap. 'Can you believe this?' Sam and Bill say to each other for about the twentieth time.

I tell Orestes the robbery occurred between the Convent of Santa Clara and the Church of La Merced. I had wanted to show Sam and Bill the Church of La Merced's dim baroque interior. We stop in the middle of the block, get out, and start to walk.

'Here?'

'No.'

'Here?'

'No.'

At the intersection, just before the Church of La Merced, I see the street with the long, blank wall running along it. It's where the thief chose to turn because there were few people on it. Bill, Sam, and I reenact the scene for Orestes. Orestes looks for a doorway where there might have been witnesses. He approaches a take-out *paladar*. 'Oh, it's you *señora*,' the vendor says, noticing me behind Orestes. 'Yes, I saw it all.' Orestes has made contact. It is a tiny ray of hope. He says to the witness that he will return.

He offers to drive us anywhere we would like to go. I ask him to take us back near the cathedral so that we can continue our tour of Old Havana.

I shake Orestes' hand as we get out of the Lada. I have gone from feeling angry and trying to feel cheerful back to feeling foolish and ashamed. *Orestes is a good man: he will help me.* I imagine our children's newborn feet, miniature bendable bananas, in Orestes' thin hands: Orestes will save the memory of their feet from the bottom of Havana harbor, along with my American Express gold card, which does not work in Cuba anyway.

'It's not the money – it's the cards and papers that are the most important to me,' I say earnestly as I shake hands with Orestes. Orestes nods with what looks like understanding, though we and Orestes and the uniformed policeman all know what Orestes (whose extreme thinness gives him and other Cubans the air of unwitting ascetics) would choose.

Sam and Bill and I eat an excellent lunch at the gallery-cum-*paladar*. Sam has to pay, for I have no money.

We walk to the Prado. Children ask us for money. I tell them my money has all been stolen.

'Really?' they say. 'You don't have any money? Any money *at all?*'

'*Mira.*' I turn my pockets inside out and spread the lining out for them to see.

The children crowd around me. The boldest children finger the empty lining, then carry the message to children waiting at the back of the crowd: 'It's true! She has *no money*!'

II. 54

Sam and a Canadian friend of mine, Marianne, and I go to the airport to fly to Santiago. Sam's friend Bill flew back to the United States yesterday. Our plane to Santiago is delayed three hours. We drive home, have a sandwich, and drive back. The plane is a Russian Tupolev, with wires dangling inside the cabin, seats and armrests missing, and steam emerging from under the seats and fogging the cabin.

We are met in Santiago by a man who can only communicate with us in grunts and hand signs. We refuse to go anywhere with him, until finally an airport official appears who assures us that the man is indeed from the travel agency, which was contacted before our arrival. He drives us to a hideous modern hotel on the outskirts of Santiago, but it is too late at night to complain, and anyway, it turns out the driver is also deaf.

II. 55

Today's driver can speak and hear. We tour Santiago. It's a kind of Jerusalem of the New World, so much started here. It's also a relay point between two worlds, or three worlds if you count the Arab world, too, Santiago having been founded just a decade after the Arabs left Granada.

We visit the main square and the house of Governor Velazquez, with its *mosharabia* – Arab trelliswork in place of windows – and a gold smelter built right into the house. In addition to being much older than Havana, Santiago is also more dramatic and more Caribbean, with its hills turning into mountains, its heat, and its black majority. We see the balcony from which Fidel gave his first major address following the liberation of Santiago.

We visit the Moncada barracks, which Fidel and his companions assaulted in 1953. The wide bullet holes scarring the face of the building were repaired after the assault. The scars were put back in after the *triunfo*. We visit San Juan Hill. Its summit is studded with monuments. We read about the charge of San Juan Hill from a 1953 Baedecker I bought in Havana. There are statues of soldiers with mustaches and hats that are pinned up in the front, and plaques in Spanish. There is one statue of a soldier without a mustache, with a hat pinned up on the side instead of the front, whose profile is like Grace Kelly's. There is no plaque, only four screw holes where a plaque used to be.

We return to the main square. We sit on the wide front porch of the Hotel Casa Granda, overlooking the square, and drink *mojitos*. A guard with his arms outstretched keeps dolled-up young Cubans of both sexes off the steps leading from the street to the porch. The young Cubans crane their necks around the guard, marking which foreigner to approach the moment he or she leaves the balcony.

We find a *paladar*. It seems to be the only one in Santiago. Sam drinks too many *mojitos* and goes back to the hotel after dinner. Marianne and I ask the driver to let us off a few blocks from the Casa de la Trova, or concert space for the promotion of traditional music, in downtown Santiago. We saw Cubans hanging on the bars of the windows of the Casa de la Trova earlier in the evening. They are still hanging on the bars. We slip down the street unnoticed, pay, and enter a brightly lit room. There are few people actually in the audience. The musicians are wearing jeans and straw cowboy hats. They are playing *son* – traditional country music for three voices with guitar, bass, and drums. It is plaintive, sweet, and charming. Marianne and I would be happy to sit there all night, listening to Eliades Ochoa and his group, but after a few songs, they announce that they will continue playing in an adjacent bar. Most of the audience leaves, but a few people move to the entrance to the bar.

Two Cuban men in their thirties approach Marianne and me. 'Can we go into the bar with you?' they ask.

151

We don't know what to say to them. They do not seem like *jineteros*, but it has been so relaxing, slipping down the street and having no one attach themselves to us, relaxing being ignored, the way middle-aged women generally are, the world over.

They follow closely behind us and sit at our table. Finally one of the men says, 'We have to sit with you because we have to look like we are your friends. Otherwise, we can't get into the bar.'

We look around. It is true: there are no Cubans in the bar, just one or two others, trying to seem like they are with groups of foreigners.

'Ah, tourist apartheid,' I say.

'Shhhhhhh!' they say.

Nick and I have heard of tourist apartheid, but this is the first time one of us has been so thoroughly on tour.

Marianne and I buy them beers. Before Marianne and I leave, an hour later, one of the men writes a poem for us on the back of the evening's program.

THE ROAD TO BARACOA from Santiago is the most dramatic in Cuba, winding through steep mountains and virgin forest. Boys wait at scenic turnouts selling *mamey* (a fruit the shape and consistency of an avocado but orange-fleshed and sweet), *guayaba* (guava), and strings of small bananas warm from the sun.

Telephone reservations were made by Nick's firm at the hotel where we are supposed to stay; confirming faxes were exhanged; but when we get there, they have never heard of us. Even so, the desk clerk manages to find rooms for us.

The hotel is in a converted Spanish fort overlooking the town. Its windows are sealed now, and air-conditioning units have been installed, seemingly in the middle of each window.

Once in our room, I climb on the bed and push back the curtains: a rectangular hole *has* been cut in the center of the window and an air-conditioning unit set into the hole, then sealed with brown stuff, which (I touch it with my finger) is still gooey.

BARACOA IS THE NEAREST town to the beach where Columbus landed in 1492, where he said, as his ship approached the shore, 'Never have human eyes beheld anything so beautiful.' In the church of Baracoa, there are the remains of what is believed to be the cross planted by Columbus. The oldest house in the New World, the original home of Governor Velazquez, built circa 1510, is here also. Baracoa was not connected by road to the rest of Cuba until 1971. It was reachable only by boat, and it still has the feeling of a place that is alone and floating, an island at the edge of an island. If Cuba were a regular country, Baracoa would have been discovered in the sixties and have become a Kathmandu or a Goa or a Maui or a Cadaqués, and then a Majorca or a Patmos or a Borocay. It has the right elements: the beaches are vast, deserted, and clean; four utterly clear rivers flow for tens of kilometers through virgin-forested ravines to the sea; and the population is innocent but catching on fast. The architecture (apart from one Soviet-style apartment block) is in the requisite range from adorable to impressive – Victorian houses in the 'newer' part, with verandas, around miniature squares; squat, massively thick walled churches and other build-ings in the colonial part; thatched huts on the outskirts with packed-dirt yards, which are direct imports from Africa; a lower Spanish fort and an upper Spanish fort. All would be real estate opportunities, if Cuba were a regular country. As it stands now, though, Baracoa is one of the poorest towns in Cuba. There is no commercial life, as far as we can make out. Stores are absolutely empty. Gaunt people shuffle down the road and mill in the squares. We have seen papayas and bananas growing on the outskirts of town, but where they are sold is a mystery.

We are told that a shipment of 150 dresses made in India arrived the other day in a truck that stopped in front of an empty store. The dresses were sold right out of the truck. One dress at a time was simply thrown from the back of the truck to pairs of upraised arms. Money was balled up and thrown back into the truck – $5, or 150 pesos, for each dress. When they ran out of dresses, some women who hadn't managed to buy dresses got violent. Police were called.

TOMÁS, A LAWYER WHO lives in Baracoa, is a relative of a friend we have in Havana. He takes us to a community settlement on a beach at the mouth of the Doaba River. One sandy road leads between board huts with thatched roofs. Naked children and a few old people sit on sagging verandas. At the end of the road is the most substantial house. Its veranda does not sag, and the yard and steps and windows are filled with flowering plants in coffee cans and jars. Colorful compositions made of glass and seashells and driftwood, depicting human faces and animals and Santeria gods, dot the house's weathered clapboards. The house belongs to Gloria and her husband.

Gloria is a mixture of black, Indian, and Spanish. In Baracoa, because of its isolation, some Indian blood has been able to survive. She is tall and has almond-shaped eyes, an aquiline nose, reddish brown skin, and wavy gray hair pulled back in a bun. Her husband is shorter than she is, wiry, totally *gallego*, with bright blue eyes. Her house has several rooms. We walk through them, admiring the intense colors of the decor, to her backyard, which faces the sea. We sit on a bench and lean our backs against the boards of the house. A vast, empty beach stretches before us. She serves us homemade wine, made from papaya, coconut, and raw coffee beans. It is very good, not too sweet. She offers us some *dulce de coco*. We compliment her on the sweet.

'We have lots to eat,' she and her husband say. They have chickens, geese, and rabbits in cages. Her husband shows us his trap for catching crabs and his net for catching tiny eels in the lagoon at the end of the sandy road. They have a lime tree and coconuts, and they trade eggs, rabbits, crabs, eels, and fish for whatever else they need. Gloria shows us her handiwork. She has taken plastic bags – the mesh kind, for potatoes and onions – and shredded them into long filaments and then crocheted them. She makes scratchy placemats, doilies, handbags, table runners. The colors depend on the color of bag she is able to find – some of her pieces are beige, some yellow, some white, and some blue. We select several items and pay her fifteen dollars. She takes the money, smiling broadly.

We ask Tomás as we walk back to the car why it is that Gloria seems to be doing so much better than her neighbors.

'She is more intelligent,' he says simply.

We go at night with another relative of our Havana friend to a peso bar at the Hotel La Rusa. This relative is an architect, and his name is Nelson Figueroa. Nelson is about four foot ten and has a beard growing to the middle of his chest.

La Rusa was a Russian émigré who came to Baracoa in the 1920s and opened a hotel. She fled the Russian Revolution but ended up supporting the Cuban Revolution. She had affairs with famous men, including Fidel, even though she was older than he. She died in the 1970s. Portraits of her in 1920s finery adorn the lobby. The bar has a back porch that looks out onto the beach. Nelson is greeted heartily when we step onto the porch. He leaves us and starts making rounds.

There seems to be no tourist apartheid at La Rusa – the clientele is mainly Cuban, with a few foreigners. Tourists can go where Cubans are, but Cubans can't go where tourists are – that's the usual deal. Still, even the hardiest tourists (and quite a few Cubans) decide not to go to the peso places because of the dim lighting, grimy tabletops, flies, and inedible food. La Rusa, though, is pleasant and full of animated people who are not on the make. If there is filth, we don't see it.

A rock band called El Ruso is playing. The lead singer is one of La Rusa's great-nephews. He is blond. We sit down where there is a free space. Marianne, Sam, and I start talking to the other people at the table – two brothers in their fifties. One is a heart surgeon who works in Santiago; the other owns a Cuban restaurant in Miami. The restaurant owner has lots of gold chains around his neck and wrist; the doctor is in a threadbare plaid shirt. They are from Baracoa. The restaurant owner tries to get back to Cuba once a year. They offer us beers. Nelson Figueroa takes over the microphone. He sings Cuban rap in a raspy voice. People start yelling, waving beers around. '*Arriba Nelson!*' No one cares if we are foreigners or not. Cubans come to our table, kiss the doctor and his brother, and kiss us. We dance between the tables with Cubans and with one another. The doctor's brother calls to Sam, Marianne, and me in English over the music, 'This is a nice place, isn't it?' Nelson climbs up on one of the tables. He is so short that, like a child, he has to climb fully up onto a chair before climbing onto the table. Someone hands him the microphone. He wiggles his hips and sings more rap, screaming to the audience. We have more beers. The doctor's brother buys two cassettes of El Ruso at the bar and gives them to Marianne and me as presents. We thank him, we tell him he shouldn't have done that, but he raises his hand. 'Baracoa is a beautiful place, isn't it?' he calls, shouting to us in English over the music. 'My God, it is a beautiful place.'

II. 56

Our guidebook describes one of the two hotels open to tourists in Camagüey as 'a Soviet-built monstrosity' with 'the surliest staff in the entire socialist world,' so we opt to stay at the Gran Hotel Camagüey, in the center of town. Our guidebook tells us that the plumbing of the Gran Hotel Camagüey is 'problematic,' but a bronze statue of a toga-clad girl holding a lighted globe at the foot of a mahogany staircase in the lobby convinces us that we have come to the right place.

Our guidebook does not tell us that there is no water in the hotel *at all.* This we discover only after we have unpacked in our rooms. There was only cold water in Baracoa, and the weather has not been warm, so we have not showered for three days.

The desk clerk tells us that there is water, but only cold water, and only from 6:30 to 7:30 every morning. Our rooms cost forty dollars a night. The desk clerk has gleaming, waist-length hair. I ask her how she washes *her* hair.

'I stand in a basin in the courtyard in back of our house in the middle of the day when it is warmest, and my sister pours buckets of water over my hair. It is water we have saved from when the tank truck comes to our barrio, in a cistern.'

We eat the only thing available on the menu in the only restaurant open in town, which is the hotel dining room: a quarter chicken with spaghetti on the side. On top of the spaghetti are pickles and a dollop of mayonnaise.

MARIANNE AND I LIE awake from 5:30 A.M. on, waiting for the water to arrive, our redolent armpits secreted under the covers.

At 6:30 precisely, it arrives in a rush, roaring out of the sink faucet and showerhead (after turning handles all over the bathroom when we first arrived, we couldn't tell which way was off anymore), making puddles in the bathroom and in the room, and causing the toilet to flush, ceaselessly, for an hour.

II. 57

We watch it on CNN: the aftermath of the shooting down of the two Hermanos al Rescate (Brothers to the Rescue) airplanes. We learn about how the Hermanos, ostensibly looking for rafters, were warned previously by Cuba and by the United

States not to penetrate Cuban airspace. They had dropped leaflets on other occasions over the island of Cuba. '*No compañeros, hermanos*' ('Not comrades, brothers'), one set of leaflets said. We see various American officials on CNN asserting that the Miami-based pilots were in international airspace. We see various Cuban officials on Cuban TV asserting they were in Cuban airspace. We see the face of the informer, Juan Pablo Roque. We learn about his disappearance from Florida and reappearance, hours later, in Cuba. We see the face of his baffled wife in Miami. We see the faces of the four pilots who were shot down. We see the face of the Hermanos leader, José Basulto, who was in another plane nearby and was not shot down.

We hear the recording. 'We got them in the balls!' one of the Cuban pilots shouted after shooting one plane down.

We see Madeleine Albright at the UN, talking about balls.

We see Roberto Robaina, the Cuban foreign minister, addressing Madeleine Albright about balls.

We hear about how the Cuban pilots were going to be decorated in a public ceremony and how the ceremony was canceled.

AT A DINNER PARTY we are attending (no Cubans present), the talk turns to Cuban officials' feelings. It is agreed that what is driving Cuban policy in general is the protection of Cuban officials' feelings. They cannot have their pride offended: that is the most important thing.

One ambassador says it's impressive, when you read history, to discover how often it is driven by trivialities.

II. 58

It doesn't seem to be working out so well, the remove-the-womb-but-leave-the-ovaries idea. Embargo goes into heat frequently – it seems about once a month. Bloqueo stands beside her, nuzzling, as if to say, *I'd like to help you out, but* . . . The twin veterinarians tell me cats learn how to have sex by watching other cats.

There is a bloodcurdling yowl from under the curving marble stairs of the front hall. I jump up from my position in front of CNN with the only weapon I have in hand, a yellow sweatshirt, which I snap, stamping and cursing, at a black tom-cat who is locked in combat with Bloqueo. Virgin Bloqueo, attacked in his own home.

We *conseguir* chicken wire and put it under the gate and in all places where there is a gap. Still we see strange cats sashaying *tranquilamente* on our side of the fence, and Embargo and Bloqueo sashaying *tranquilamente* on the other side, inches from traffic.

II. 59

Raúl Castro speaks for five hours about actions and papers published by certain government-run study centers calling for reform. He calls it a 'democratic infection.'

Ascui, the head of the Center for Studies on the Americas, has a fatal heart attack the day after Raúl's speech.

His funeral is seen as the largest protest by Communist intellectuals in years.

II. 60

Lola is determined to have us for dinner, so since her kitchen is torn up to make still more improvements, she is going to have us at her daughter's house. She has prepared the dinner; her daughter is providing the house.

Lola shows us her torn-up kitchen before we take off for her daughter's house. Polished green marble countertops, it will have, *conseguido*ed from a friend of theirs in the marble industry. Hot and cold running water, *conseguido*ed from a relative who has access to water heaters. Hot and cold running water is harder to find in Cuba than green marble. New terrazzo floor tiles stacked neatly in the yard, *conseguido*ed from Cubalse. Her husband, an engineer, makes three hundred pesos a month (about thirteen dollars), but she sells her linens and other things, and they have a house in Guanabo that they rent to foreigners.

We drive to her daughter's house. It is neo-Gothic, built in the twenties, and pristine. Her husband is an agronomist and makes, Lola tells us, around ten dollars a month. We are led onto a terrace wedged between her house and the neighbor's.

There, in a tiny space between her house, her neighbor's house, and the piece of her house in back, is a swimming pool. It has been built up instead of excavated, so that you have to climb up a ladder to get to the edge of it. It is made of undulating cement, like a false grotto. A filter hums comfortingly. A shiny Jacuzzi ladder leads into it.

'Something tells me he's going to go this year,' Margarita, an antique-dealing partner of Lola's, whispers to me as Lola and Nick talk. She strokes her chin.

'Who?' I say.

'Him.' She strokes her chin again.

'But how?'

'The army is dying of starvation.'

'Hm . . . ,' I say.

'How long have you been here?' she asks.

'We're into our second year.'

'How much longer will you be here?'

'Probably two more years.'

'I'm sure you will be here for his departure.'

We eat lobster salad, boneless chicken breasts, and a boneless leg of pork marinated in bitter orange and pan-roasted slowly with malt. French wine is served.

Margarita's husband speaks. 'A foreign journalist said to me that the problem with Cubans is that they think the world spends all its time thinking about Cuba, but the world really does not think about Cuba very much. We think Cuba is important, but Cuba is not a very important country. Isn't that so?'

'Is this cold wave we're having good for the mango crop?' Nick asks.

II. 61

More and more foreign firms are moving into Cuba. They take long leases from the government on mansions on Quinta Avenida and put up signs in front of them. They are buying shares in agricultural properties. Mansions in Cubanacán are being offered for sale, too, to any foreigner willing to put up a few million dollars.

II. 62

Our tour of Pinar del Río, the capital of Cuba's westernmost province, begins near the main hospital. Near the entrance to the hospital, there is a big hole with steam shovels beside it. It is a project of tunnels and underground bunkers for Fidel and his commanders to hide in, in the event of a U.S. invasion. It is said that there are tunnels going all the way from Pinar del Río to Havana, 150 miles away.

The subject of the tunnels comes up. Are they to protect against Yankee aggression? I ask. Our Cuban guide confirms that they are. After a little while it comes up that I am *norteamericana*. It slips in very gently, though, and, as happens more often than not, causes not a ripple.

Felix, our Danish guide, whispers to me as we are walking – a little bit ahead of the Cubans – that he found no anti-*norteamericano* feeling in his work in Pinar del Río. He tells me that a local official told him that 40 percent of the population of Pinar del Río are *anexionistas*.

'*Anexionistas*?' I have never heard this term.

'In favor of annexation with the United States.'

I tell him I find that hard to believe, but he repeats to me that this is what a local official told him.

We visit a home of the Loynaz family, which is now a museum. Dulce María Loynaz is considered Cuba's greatest living lyric poet. She is in her late nineties and lives in Havana.

We visit a tobacco farm. It's the farmer's own family farm, from before *el triunfo*. He has been allowed to keep it. Tobacco farming requires great skill and care, so most tobacco farmers were able, following the nationalizations, to stay on their own farms. The farmer shows us the fields. He shows how they pick the leaves from the bottom first. He shows us the barns with the wrapping leaves. They are the most valuable. He stretches one over his hand. You can see his knuckles through it. It is like kid leather. He tells us that there is about $4 million worth of tobacco in the barn we are standing in, but he has to sell it for what the state tells him to sell it for. We go into his house to drink a coffee. It is a better *guajiro* house than most; the pine studs and boards of the six-foot partitions, which serve as walls, are new. His son is there, but he is a doctor and has no interest in keeping the farm.

We go to a *paladar* – the only one in Pinar del Río. The most important artist in Pinar del Río, Oliva, meets us there. He has a jutting jaw and a Mexican face. He shows us the art nouveau building he has been given by the government to have a gallery in, of *pinareño* artists. It will have an apartment for him, too, with his studio in back. He is optimistic; the cement on the walls of his new gallery space is smooth and new. He takes us to the studio where he has been working while the art nouveau building is being renovated. We see a painting he is working on, which is his response to *Guernica*: it is called *El Gran Apagón* (The Big Blackout).

We go to see other artists, then to the home of a man who I think is an artist, too, but when it comes to group movements and everyone is speaking X——ian, I am the last to know. The man is in his fifties, very *blanco*, with a refined, aquiline face; large, liquid eyes; long eyelashes; and abundant, slicked-down hair, like an actor of the 1930s. He is dressed entirely in white. Framed photos of him, in various lights and at various ages, dot a bureau and other surfaces.

The man asks us where we would like to be, in the living room or in the bedroom. I think he is going to show us some paintings, but then someone says, 'Let's go into the bedroom.'

In the bedroom is a small, low table with some statues and candles on it. He stands in front of the table, lights a cigar, takes a few puffs, puts it on the edge of the table, takes a swig from a bottle of rum, spits it in a corner. He kneels down and starts talking into the ground, lightning fast, unintelligible. He asks me if I would like to know anything.

'Anything what?' I ask.

'About the future, of course!' Felix, Nick, and our Cuban guide say exasperatedly, in unison.

Later, on the street, I tell the others that I needed to be prepared, that they were all talking before we got there, in X—ian, in Cuban, and I didn't know what was going on. I didn't know we were going to see a *babalao*. The guy starts babbling. Everybody's standing around me. I can't ask a question with everybody standing around me. If I'd known, I would have prepared myself. I would have made a list of questions. I would have made everybody except Nick leave the room.

We end our tour at the home of our Cuban guide. Our guide

lives with a female relative who is a dwarf. Our guide says that he has taken us to see many artists, but that he is an artist, too. He shows us his work – compositions of sand in fanlike grid patterns, like spiderwebs, which have been glued onto Masonite panels measuring about nine inches by eleven inches. The gluey smell and the designs are slightly sickening, like Spider-Man comics leafed through in unaired boys' rooms.

He wraps some panels in copies of *Juventud Rebelde* for us to take home. He puts the panels into my hands, presses my hands around them.

II. 63

There is a surprise tribute to Natalia Bolivar in Coyula Park, on the occasion of the launching of one of her new books on Santeria.

More police than people are here when we arrive. Loudspeakers are blaring disco at 10 A.M. The weather is already steamy, but trees have not put out their leaves yet, so there is little shade. We are greeted by a kind-faced female friend of Natalia's who seems to be the mistress of ceremonies. We are seated in velvet chairs along with a handful of old bohemians/revolutionaries – people in their sixties and seventies who became disillusioned years ago but have not gone to Miami and have become involved in fields that have nothing to do with politics, such as anthropology, botany, and music.

In front of us is a shelter of poured cement with trees and grass sprouting from its roof, the top layer peeling up from the bottom, like the sole of an old shoe. A distinguished-looking, well-dressed woman in her sixties arrives. 'Naty,' someone calls her. It is Naty Revuelta, ex-lover of Fidel and mother of his only daughter, Alina, who left for the United States and was joined later by her own teenage daughter, Naty's granddaughter. Naty and her then husband sheltered Fidel in their home in the early days of the revolution. I try not to stare, I am dying to tell Nick who she is, but I would have to raise my voice too much to be heard over the blaring disco music and she is too close to us. Her well-dressedness is a feast for the eyes in a sea of spandex, broken tennis shoes, cutoff plaid polyester dress pants, gauze-thin T-shirts, no bras, too tight *guayaberas,* and cowboy shirts with hairy tummies sticking through.

Naty looks angry. She approaches one of the officials of the Playa district, which is sponsoring the event: 'It's ten o'clock in the morning! We are old people here! This is not Cuban music – this could be anything! We can't converse . . .'

It's the first time I've heard a Cuban complain about the music – loud, blaring music in public places, designed to drive away anyone over twenty-five, except for besotted sexual tourists with their *jineteras.*

'But who loves this music?' I ask the official, emboldened.

'*I* certainly don't,' Naty says, 'and I'm going.' And off she goes, Indian dress swinging, stupendous tanned legs striding in bone-colored pumps.

Natalia Bolivar arrives and is greeted with flowers. She thought she was just going to give a talk on her new book today. She didn't know anything about the tribute.

The testimonials begin. The woman who first greeted us speaks into the microphone. She looks down at the ground as she speaks, moving a chair out of the way, and we wonder at first if she is testing the mike, then realize that she is in the process of making a speech and introducing the various speakers.

The microphone is then handed to a man in his sixties wearing a tight cowboy shirt. He speaks about Natalia's *vida clandestina* as a teenage revolutionary, when she wielded a machine gun and was tortured by Batista's police. He speaks about her contribution to the revolution and about her subsequent contributions to the anthropology of Cuba. The ambassador of Nigeria is here, his mouth framed with tribal scars.

The man speaks for a very long time. Natalia leans against a tree, looking at the ground. When she shifts, the mass of necklaces on her chest shift with her. I recognize the colors of Ochún, the *orisha* of femininity and of rivers. Natalia, who, though no longer young, is still very beautiful, has been married many times. She is not married now and lives in an apartment in Vedado – some say with eight cats, others say with twelve, and still others, twenty, as well as many dogs and a *majá* (a small boa constrictor native to Cuba) who disappears for months into the walls of her apartment and then, just as unceremoniously, reappears.

The man is still talking. Adolescent girls in biking shorts, popping gum, skate down the center aisle and up onto the platform, oblivious. Wizened elderly people shuffle by on the periphery. Four small *mulato* boys with shaved heads, one with black sores and lumps on his head, in cutoff pants with broken flies held up with string, take four chairs in front, swinging their legs.

Ex-revolutionaries tend to tiptoe among the young so that they won't be asked questions like, 'Hadn't you ever read *Animal Farm?*' This morning, though, they are not tiptoeing. They are telling us that they were involved, and I realize, as I watch them and listen to them, that *it is as hard to understand the fervor of another time as it is to understand Swahili in one day.*

A little boy burps. The man keeps talking. The hideous poured-cement structure, which he is wisely standing not under but rather in front of, in spite of the heat, looks like it is going to collapse at any minute. The sun is full on us now. Members of the audience pick their chairs up and move back, looking for new shade.

A NEWSCASTER DESCRIBES the massing of U.S. troops in Florida as a menacing act.

We sit up in our chairs, then remember: it's the shifting of the U.S. Southern Command to Florida.

II. 64

May Day. A quarter of a million people parade. Nick and I watch it on TV.

The head of the student union speaks, and our Cuban baby-sitter, a recent university graduate filling in for Muna, who has gone on a visit to Bangladesh, says, '*Qué horror*,' and runs from the room. Pedro Ross, the president of the Central de Trabajadores, or Cuban Workers' Union, speaks. The camera catches Fidel making a widemouthed yawn as Pedro Ross speaks.

A diplomat who was at the parade tells us it was impressive, how they mobilized marchers through their jobs: if you didn't go, you risked losing your job or being demoted. He says the placards were evenly distributed, a picture of a national hero every hundred people or so, an anti–Helms-Burton slogan every two hundred. They also put the army in it, in plainclothes.

II. 65

A man outside the *agro* asks Miguel if we would like to buy some eggs. He says they are $3.00 for a carton of thirty. In the Diplomercado, a carton of twelve costs $6.90. The man then indicates to Miguel the alley where we should meet him with the car.

We drive to the alley; Miguel gets out, walks to a high fence, stands on tiptoe, and whistles. The man with whom Miguel spoke and a woman emerge, carrying bags. We say we will buy four cartons. They ask if they can sit in the back of our car. Miguel starts the motor. 'We have to go somewhere else, because here . . . ,' Miguel says.

They open their bags and start removing eggs as we drive. They have pieces of egg cartons; we have a hatchback. Miguel says they can set them up on the shelf in the back of the hatchback. It is in full view of the window, but Miguel says it is no problem. We park on a shady side street. 'We've come all the way from Artemisa,' the woman says, pulling eggs out of their bag. Artemisa is seventy-five miles away. 'It was really difficult with all these eggs, riding in the back of a truck, trying to keep people from crushing them. The truck was stopped, but the police didn't look in our bags, *gracias a Dios.*'

Miguel keeps his eye on the rearview mirror. 'We have to keep moving,' he says.

They can see things that I can't, and yet they keep setting eggs – 120 of them – up on the shelf in back, right in plain view.

We pick up Miguel's wife from the asthma clinic on the way home. She walks on crutches because the bone, since she broke it, is not growing back, possibly because of a vitamin deficiency, Miguel says. His wife had to go to a clinic today because her asthma was so bad, and she needs to be picked up by us because there are no buses.

A CUBAN WHO COMES for lunch says that the general belief among physicians is that the true problem lies with Fidel's hypothalamus – hence the torrents of words, the illogical behavior.

165

II. 66

'If I see pole beans on my plate again, I'll scream,' I say.

'*Ay señora, disculpe*' ('Excuse me'), Lorena says, 'but we have no other vegetables in the *despensa.*'

Pole beans, carrots, cucumbers, and Swiss chard are the only vegetables you can count on in Cuba in the hot, tomatoless months, and it's living in Cuba that makes you realize how you really need more than four kinds of vegetables, day in, day out, to put some brightness in your day.

Tomatoes grow only six months of the year. You see them dwindling and becoming mottled and sickly from the middle of April until May, when they have disappeared from the *agro* entirely. By October I find myself dreaming of them. 'But they manage to grow tomatoes *in India* all year long,' I find myself saying baselessly, but only to myself or to Nick or to some receptive foreigner, for speaking of tomatolessness or other vegetablelessness to a Cuban doesn't help them any, and even to foreigners I can talk about it for only so long without being branded a weirdo or a bore. Back come the tomatoes in October, puny at first, then increasingly large and full, and the price comes down until, by December, you are dragging home ten pounds of tomatoes at a time from the *agro* and making soups and sauces and fresh tomato juice. Fat the world becomes again, moist, and I think about the whole winter ahead of us with onions in it, lettuce, cabbages, eggplants, beets, and leeks.

II. 67

A Cuban writer favored by the government comes with his secretary for dinner.

Bleh! and other sounds equivalent to 'Yuck!' our Cuban artist-and-writer-friends-not-favored-by-the-government said when we told them who was coming for dinner. One wiped his fingers, as if he were trying to remove some viscous substance from them. Our friends said the writer and his secretary would level a wearying litany, especially at me. That is what they are told to do when they go to a foreigner's house.

In the garden after dinner, the secretary tells me about how things were before the revolution. 'No black girls were allowed in our school, but there was one, almost white, adopted by a white lady. She went to the hairdresser regularly, so they were able to keep her hair under control. Since she was a very religious girl, our Catholic club in school voted for her to play the Virgin Mary in our Christmas pageant, but the Spanish priest we had vetoed it. 'The Virgin was a white girl,' he told us, and he put in the role of the Virgin a silly girl who wasn't religious at all, just because she had long blond hair.'

Racism, our friends said they would talk about, as if in 1959 this was news.

She goes on: 'Ninety percent of the population was analphabetic, and I don't mean to offend, but you can't imagine how *terrible* the Americans were here, walking around like they owned the place.'

'I am sure they were terrible,' I say.

She smiles sheepishly. 'I am sorry to be saying this, because *you* are an American.'

Analphabetism, our friends said they would talk about, and they would say it was 90 percent, when the real figure was 30 percent. Everyone knows pre-*triunfo* analphabetism was 30 percent, our friends said, but still they say 90, as if no one knows anything.

I shrug. 'When you travel as much as I have, you get used to hearing how terrible Americans were, or are.'

She is silent. I wait for her to start reciting pre- versus post-*triunfo* infant mortality statistics, which is the other subject our friends said they would bring up, but she seems blocked. I know I should try to get her on some other subject – cooking, grandchildren, giant pandas – but instead I repeat, 'I am sure they were terrible. And seeing the problems that are here now and what people put up with – it makes someone like me understand how bad things must have been under Batista . . .'

She sits up, recharged. 'That's not why we put up with the situation we have now. We put up with it because what alternative do we have? To become like Puerto Rico? To let the Miami exiles come back? Have you seen what Miami is like? They are all mafiosos there.'

They would refer to the Miami exiles as mafiosos. They can't leave a party, our friends said, without calling them that.

'But isn't there an alternative?' I ask. 'Does it have to be only a choice between the way it is now and a mafioso-run state?'

167

She is silent and shifts in her seat.

'Can't you imagine something different?'

She mumbles something, shifts in her seat.

'What would you like to see here?'

'People being able to determine their own future. People being able to preserve their identity. To be able to live with dignity.'

LORENA ASKS ME TO translate from English the instructions on the back of a box of hair straightener. I haltingly translate the big letters at the top of the instructions: THIS PRODUCT CONTAINS STRONG CHEMICALS, WHICH, IF USED IMPROPERLY, CAN CAUSE BURNS, EYE DAMAGE, EAR DAMAGE, AND OTHER INJURIES. PLEASE READ THE INSTRUCTIONS CAREFULLY. IF PRODUCT SHOULD COME IN CONTACT WITH EYES, WASH EYES IMMEDIATELY UNDER RUNNING WATER FOR NO LESS THAN FIVE MINUTES. IF PRODUCT SHOULD ENTER EARS, FLUSH WITH WATER REPEATEDLY, USING BULBED SYRINGE OR WASHED TURKEY BASTER . . .

'This is a violence you are doing to yourself, Lorena.'

'It's a strong product.'

I am silent for a minute, then say, 'There is an expression in English in the United States: 'Black is beautiful.''

'I have heard this expression!' Lorena says. Lorena speaks a little English, and her pronunciation is good.

'You don't have to do this, you know, because you are beautiful.'

'Thank you,' Lorena says.

'The world may be dominated by one standard of beauty, but this is changing.'

'*Sí, señora.*' Lorena smiles indulgently at me, waiting for me to continue translating the instructions.

'I always wanted to have curly hair,' I say untruthfully. 'One is never happy with what one has.'

'This is true!' Lorena says, shrugging indulgently and raising her eyebrows. 'One always wants to be something else!'

II. 68

In the Diplo, a seventeen-dollar cabbage.

The Third
School Year

III. 1

'How are you, Manuel?' we ask him upon entering the house after summer vacation.

'Not very well.'

'Why?'

'Because someone entered the garage and stole the spare tire out of *la señora*'s car . . .'

'What about the guard in front? What was he doing?'

'The thief climbed over the fence in the back.'

'With all the things there are to steal here, why would he choose that?'

'It was the easiest thing to get at.'

LOLA'S BROTHER'S NEIGHBOR'S father-in-law has been kicked to death for his car. He was a man in his sixties, a retired orthopedic surgeon, who drove his car as a taxi in the evenings to make money. He waited for customers in the evenings just off the Plaza de la Revolución.

III. 2

Coming back from trips to the United States is almost 'fun' in the beginning. The seven in help. The swimming pool. The lime tree. The avocado tree, which has not yet borne fruit. The papaya tree. Embargo and Bloqueo. The first dinner outside in the night breeze. Six suitcases bursting with much-needed basics. The sense of novelty, relief, and security as each item is taken out of the bursting suitcases and put where it belongs. The delight of the help as they are handed the things they have asked me to find for them – medicines, dresses, shoes, shirts, support stockings, underwear, car-engine parts. The first visits to the *agro* and the Diplo. Seeing what is there and what is not, and trying to infer larger meanings from what is there and what is not. The delight to be had from finding an eggplant or some watercress in the sparse *agro* of September. The first visits to the antique dealers. Upholsterers, dressmakers, manicurists, and masseuses ministering to us at home. The roving fish vendors. The roving vegetable vendor and his sack full of avocados the size of footballs. The *jinetera* count on Quinta, on the Malecón.The artists and what's happened to them over the summer. Who is in jail. Who is out of jail. New laws and loopholes. The most recent live sightings of Fidel and of Raúl. Every scrap of gossip about everyone and everything, and reading into it as if the gossip were a novel composed solely of inferences, which one has put down and taken up again after several months. *Mojitos.* Daiquiris. Daiquiris *naturales.* A patch of *jinetera*-free beach. Sunsets over Havana viewed from the seaside bar just under the fortress of La Cabaña. Three whole hours of uninterrupted time every weekday when the children are in school, after I finish telling the help what to do and going to the *agro* and the Diplo. My well-lit writing room.

III. 3

Muna went to Bangladesh for a visit. She decided to stay there. It was too hard for her in Cuba. 'The climate is like Bangladesh,' she would say, 'but we don't have such broken-down houses,' or 'in Bangladesh, people work.' Muna was lonely, too, for other Bangladeshis. The total population of Bangladeshis in Cuba is six – two diplomats, one embassy secretary, and four Christian Bangladeshi women who met their Cuban husbands when they were students in Russia. One, who lived near Playa Girón, told Muna she cried every day.

We have started interviewing potential nannies. We have asked the help in our house and the staff at Nick's office to recommend women. One is a student, who comes for the interview in a halter top and short shorts with the cheeks of her behind peeking out below. One (very young) comes driving a brand-new Jeep with her name emblazoned in bold script across

172

the back. The Jeep was a present from her papa, she says. No one in Cuba has a new car. She wears a plaid miniskirt with matching purse and tam-o'-shanter and keeps tossing her hair and giggling during the interview. One barely speaks above a murmur, and another one, a psychologist, tells me that she will only be able to be here between appointments.

A VIOLENT RAINSTORM ERUPTS. Fine spray blows on our legs, but we are too full of food to move. We hear a crash, then scurrying in the vines climbing metal grillwork framing the veranda where we sit having dinner with friends from Argentina. A large rat swings headfirst through the grillwork and lands on the floor near our feet. It runs under the sideboard. We jump up. 'Get a cat, Manuel!'

Embargo is set down in front of the sideboard. She sniffs. There is a loud squeak. Embargo backs up. The rat, black, huge, with a pink tail, makes a dash for it, squeaking and baring its teeth, back out into the rainstorm. Embargo stays where she is, back arched, fur raised.

III. 4

Juana is thirty-six, married, with no children. She has a short, neat hairstyle and a lithe body and dresses modestly without being nerdy. This in itself is enough to put her ahead of all the other candidates, but Juana is also a former elementary school-teacher. She seems calm, responsible, and educated, and she seems to have other qualities that, if she were from another country, *would mean she came from a good family* – qualities that we are beginning to realize mean that in Cuba as well.

III. 5

Carlita comes to see me during the day, when the children are in school.

'I'm here to tell you that Gonzalo got married to a Canadian, he has gone to Canada, and he will not be able to teach the children anymore.'

We have seen Gonzalo since we have been back. He didn't say anything special to us, and the only thing different about him was that he had grown a goatee.

'But he left? He left since we saw him yesterday?'

'You saw Gonzalo? Gonzalo has been here?'

'Yes. He's been here twice since we've gotten back, to give the children swimming lessons.'

Carlita falls back against her seat with a crooked smile on her face. 'Ay, Gonzalo . . .'

'What is it?'

'Gonzalo called me in July. He said he had gotten married to a Canadian and he was going to Canada. He told me to let you know that he wasn't going to be able to teach the girls anymore.' She continues smiling her crooked smile. 'Ay, Gonzalo . . .' Carlita writes the number of the relative she is now staying with (she moved out of her uncle's house) on a piece of paper. 'The next time you see Gonzalo, tell him to call me.'

Cuba is a novel and a soap opera, too. Nothing of substance can be spoken about over the phone. People visit one another back and forth in order to say what they have to say. Just as on the soaps, if people didn't visit one another back and forth, if they said what they needed to say over the phone, there would hardly be any scenes to show. It keeps the action moving forward, the visiting back and forth, on multiple tracks.

I DON'T KNOW WHETHER he wore them the first few times he came, but Gonzalo, I notice now, has a large diamond ring on his wedding finger and a gold chain with a gold medallion on it around his neck. I hang around the pool, waiting for him to say something about a wedding, or a Canadian, or about the big ring on his finger, which flashes even in the late afternoon sun, but he says nothing about any of it.

III. 6

I find myself praying that Juana will take *us*.

I tell Nick, before Juana comes for her second interview, that offering her $200 isn't enough, but he goes ahead and offers her $200 anyway. Juana counters, saying she can't work for less than $300 per month. Nick says that is all right, but then asks her not to discuss her salary with anyone else at the house.

I can't sleep, wondering whether the children will be happy

with Juana and whether Juana will be happy with us. I worry that the $200 we offered Juana got us off to a bad start. Juana is more responsible and more dignified than I am, and she seems serene, too, and not desperate, as if in this land of no jobs she might find another job anytime she wanted to. I've seen the house she lives in, too: it's a nice house, with a banana grove in back of it and a late-model Lada in the carport.

III. 7

They have caught the boys who kicked Lola's brother's neighbor's father-in-law to death – two seventeen-year-old *orientales* (literally, Orientals, meaning people from the former Oriente province, on the eastern end of the island of Cuba, where the city of Santiago de Cuba is, or from any place east of Camagüey) have confessed.

'Take my car!' the *orientales* said the old man said to them. 'You don't have to kill me.'

The *orientales* told the police they killed him because 'the dead don't talk.'

A FROG NO BIGGER than a nickle is found, alive, in the middle of Thea's high, old-fashioned, neatly made bed at 2 P.M. on a school day. I ask the help if they put it there, as a present to Thea when she came home from school, but they look just as surprised as I do to see it there.

THE SEVENTEEN-YEAR-OLD *orientales* who kicked Lola's brother's neighbor's father-in-law to death have been executed by firing squad.

III. 8

Nick and I go with Nicoletta to visit Bibi Sebaya. Bibi Sebaya is one of the few surviving residents of the Country Club area – all elderly women now – who never left Cuba and have held on to their houses.

The Cyclone fence is rusty, but the grass is mowed and the trees are clipped. The spacious rooms, spreading out in a V from the entrance, are long and low, paneled in dark wood, with brand-new upholstery on the furniture, all of it covered with clear plastic. A short, stout lady greets us speaking rapid Cuban. I think she's trying to tell us that her husband has died three months ago. I turn to Nicoletta to ask for help, and the lady breaks out in perfect American – she attended the Spence School in New York City.

It's just a tad funkier than a normal rich person's house. A bent-over maid shuffles by in a housedress. The floor could be cleaner, the outdoor furniture brighter, but still the effect is making me forget where I am. Bibi is like some rich friend of my mother's except for the enormous portrait of her young self in strapless tulle on an easel smack-dab in the middle of the living room: my mother's friends' portaits were usually over the mantel.

Her tale comes in fits and starts, but you can tell that she never tires of telling it.

She had two children with her first husband, then fell in love with a revolutionary, a rich boy who was with Fidel in the Sierra Maestra. He stopped being a revolutionary when Fidel became a Communist. He spent two years in prison on the Isle of Pines. She went with him to the Isle of Pines. She went through almost everything you can go through in a revolution. The revolutionaries looted everything. 'This house, that house.' She gestures with her hand around the Country Club compound. 'There was one. A nigger named Manolo. Took the car of the old ladies across the street. 'You rich people are fat. A revolutionary has to be thin,' he told me. I took my daughter to the doctor a few years later, and I saw him in the waiting room. He had a big belly, and his wife, a nigger in a red knit dress, was fat, too. '*Qué tal, Manolo?*' I said. 'You said a revolutionary was supposed to be thin, but look at you! You've become fat! What happened? And the car you stole from the old ladies, I saw it outside. You really wrecked it. And your wife's fat, too!'' Her grandson had been with her in the house but went with his mother (Bibi's daughter) to Canada. The boy was scared of his mother. His mother speaks four languages but works as a house cleaner in Canada. 'She's a terrible girl,' Bibi says. She doesn't have good relationships with her daughters, who have characters like their father. One of her daughters denounced her second husband. Said he was CIA. They spent five days going through her house.

He was sentenced to twenty years. Bibi wrote Fidel that he was falsely accused, and he got out the next day. She has had an account at a bank in New York ever since she was at Spence. The U.S. government won't let her touch it, though, because she lives in Cuba. She transferred as much as she could to Switzerland. Her mother lived in Rome for fifteen years. She shows us a picture of her with her mother in Rome. 'My friends said I wouldn't recognize Rome anymore. It's full of niggers.' She's had cataract surgery. Even so, she can see only shadows. She loves her cats, especially her Siamese, which was given to her by the Lebanese ambassador next door. Every day, when her husband was dying, the cat would come and sit on the edge of the bed and stare at him. And the cat had never sat on the bed before. Bibi got diabetes late in life. Because of stress. Stress because of her other neighbor, the Finnish ambassador. She always got along so well with her neighbors. They were always lovely to her. She was great friends with the previous Finnish ambassador and his wife, but then they left, and Bibi says the ambassador's wife told her, "I would introduce you to the new ambassador and his wife, but I'm not going to do that because they're just horrible.' The new ambassador's wife kept trying to be friends with me, but I avoided her, saying, 'My husband's just gotten out of jail and it wouldn't be right, to go to an ambassador's house.' She got more and more angry with me, until finally she was climbing up in the tree with a pair of binoculars, spying on me. She denounced me to the police.'

'Why?'

'For having geese. I had a flock of lovely geese. She said they made too much noise. They had never bothered anyone before. The police came and said they were going to cut off their heads. That sent me to bed with my first diabetes. I finally found a farm in the countryside to keep them, but we had to go every day to feed them. But I got my own back. I got that Finnish ambassador fired. My husband and I were in Switzerland, and in Geneva we met the Finnish foreign vice-minister and I told him what they had done, and he said his ministry would look into how they were behaving over there. They sent inspectors there, found all kinds of abuses, and the Cuban police caught them trying to smuggle five sets of silverware out of the country. They weren't just transferred; he was fired! And I got his little secretary fired, too – a fairy who used to have masked balls with all the other fairies.'

We are in a *paladar* by now, so good that we eat *escabeche* and roast pork. Bibi has fish and saves a piece for herself, wrapped in aluminum to take home.

Geese, fairies, and niggers, I think in my bed as I try to digest the *escabeche,* the roast pork, and the disturbing terms that Bibi used in English, and I find myself wondering if the word *negrito* really was as breezy as all that.

III. 9

Juana starts, but it is an unusual day, for there is the twice-monthly Polar Bar, a kind of open-house barbecue at the Canadian Embassy where children eat hamburgers and swim and chase one another around on the tennis court. Cubans are not allowed at the Polar Bar. Juana comes for an hour before the children go. I cop another mom at the Polar Bar to look after the kids there and drive them home to Juana, who will be waiting for them. We have to go to five events – two cocktail parties, an art opening, a dinner, and a dance concert.

When we come home, Juana is watching TV with Thea and Jimmie, who are both so tired from the Polar Bar that they won't go to bed. Juana looks at a loss. 'This is not a typical night,' I whisper to Juana as I carry Jimmie upstairs.

Jimmie and Thea sprawl on beanbag chairs in their rooms, nightshirts hiked up above their waists, private parts challenging me in grim judgment as I demonstrate to Juana the telling of a bedtime story.

III. 10

The allergist who saw Thea last year for her skin blotches, Dr. Yamila Lawton, calls me over the weekend to say she wants to see me.

Now she sits with me on the veranda. We speak about Thea. I tell her about the findings of the specialist we saw in New York. She compliments me on my Spanish. There is a pause. Her eyes, magnified by her glasses, look sheepish. 'I suppose you're wondering why I am here.'

178

'Of course . . .'

'I have something to ask you.'

'That's all right.'

'I feel ashamed . . .'

'You can tell me.'

'You know the situation in this country . . .'

'Of course.'

'My son has just graduated from medical school. Look.' She reaches into her bag and pulls out a photocopy of the diploma. 'This is gold,' she says, tapping a medallion shape, black on the photocopy, at a corner of the diploma with her finger. 'They only give the gold medallion to the best students. He worked so hard. I want to give him something, a present for his diploma, but . . .' Her voice breaks. 'I feel so bad.' She opens her pocket-book, pulls out a handkerchief, blows her nose. 'I'm sorry.'

'It's all right. Tell me.'

'You know how it is here.'

'I know.'

'What he would like more than anything, he says, is a radio–cassette player. They are so expensive for Cubans, but foreigners, I know, can get a discount.'

I tell her I will try to get a discount at the electronics department of the Diplomercado. It will have to be included with the purchase of other electronic items from the Diplo so that it doesn't look suspicious, but we do need an iron. Then I think again and tell her I can pick one up when I go to Orlando in two weeks. I say I also have to think about the weight they allow me to carry onto the plane in Miami. I ask her how large she would like the cassette player to be.

She says it doesn't have to be big at all, just as long as it has room for two cassettes.

'No problem.'

More tears, openings and closings of the pocketbook.

After she leaves, I realize that it hasn't been established whether I am supposed to pay for the cassette player or whether she is going to reimburse me. I have to wait and see what happens, I guess.

'But really, not that many people ask me for things,' I say to Nick later at the dinner table.

'That's because they don't know you well enough yet.'

179

III. 11

Ivan, the one Cuban at the firm I can relate to besides our Eleggúa (who is not really Cuban) has just been fired for stealing firm property – Ivan, who said nothing was more important than a child, and whose son, Eduardo, a cheerful seven-year-old, came here sometimes to play.

Nick says that it began because Bernard, Nick's second assistant, saw Ivan loading plumbing pipes belonging to the firm into his car. The number two assistant asked him who had authorized him to take the pipes. Ivan named Fritz, the number one assistant, who was on vacation. Bernard told Ivan to put the pipes back and wait for the return of Fritz. When Fritz returned, he said that he had never authorized Ivan to take any pipes. Quietly, Bernard started to make other investigations and discovered missing plumbing fixtures, too, and a bathroom mirror.

'Ivan must be doing over the bathroom at his family's house,' I say to Nick, serving myself a few more *tostones*.

Nick looks at me darkly.

'I mean, here we always thought he was a spy, and it turns out he was just a thief.'

I add that it's a pity Eduardo won't be able to play with Thea and Jimmie anymore. Eduardo was the only Cuban child they played with, apart from Yolanda at school.

III. 12

We go to see an artist, Saidel Brito, at the Instituto Superior del Arte. Saidel Brito is the same artist who, at a show in the spring, presented a painting of the underside of a horse, four times larger than life, suspended from the ceiling, its testicles coming at you like two bombs. Underneath it, hung waist-high, was a burlap sling full of actual horseshit.

El Caballo, Fidel is called, but you can still paint a horse.

This time Saidel Brito has made a painted terra-cotta statue of a goat lying on his back on a lawn chair. *Caribbean Man*, Saidel calls it. The goat is wearing sunglasses and an undershirt, one leg is crossed over the other, its balls lolling formlessly on the chaise.

III. 13

Juana is the Rolls-Royce of nannies, as far as we can make out. She has gotten the children to speak Spanish. '*Cómo? No quieres hablar español conMIGO?*' ('What? You don't want to speak Spanish with ME?'), Juana says, rolling her eyes and tickling them until they speak Spanish without realizing that they are speaking Spanish. She is tireless. She plays Ping-Pong, hide-and-seek, capture the flag, handball, badminton without a net, checkers, cards, Spanish word games. She settles down with them on big pillows and reads with them or to them. She builds forts with them out of pillows, tables, and chairs and sits with them with a flashlight under blankets, telling them stories. She teaches them chess, how to read palms, and Cuban children's songs.

I get Juana's personal story in snatches, for we are not together much. She comes to the house for a few hours in the afternoon after the children are home from school, then stays on if we have to go out in the evening. If we come home very late, she calls her husband, Hernando, to come and get her in their car. Otherwise she walks home.

Juana's grandfather on her mother's side came to Cuba as a fifteen-year-old immigrant from Spain in the early twentieth century. He started sweeping out stores, and eventually owned a chain of stores in Cuba. He married a Cuban woman. They had several children. He sent all his children to study in the United States.

Juana's father worked for an American oil company but then became a revolutionary. Juana's parents already had three children at the time of the revolution, Juana being the youngest of the three. Juana's grandparents moved to Spain when the stores were appropriated. Juana's mother left her husband and Cuba and went to Spain, too, taking the three children with her. Juana's father persuaded Che Guevara himself to let him travel to Spain to try to persuade Juana's mother to return. Juana's mother returned to Cuba out of love for Juana's father and had three more children.

The family's house was appropriated while Juana's mother was in Spain. They had to move into a smaller house next door to it and look every day at the big house they used to live in. It was cramped with six children in the little house, but they built two new rooms on the terrace. They would go to Santa María del Mar for weekends, the two parents and six children, Juana tells me, all crammed into one Lada car. One child would be in front, on Juana's mother's lap, and the other five would be in the backseat. Juana tells me her father used to say he wished he had a mechanical hand mounted on the back of the driver's seat that would move on a kind of track, slapping Juana and her brothers and sister as they squirmed on the backseat, the hand going back and forth unceasingly. Juana's grandfather died, but Juana's grandmother, who is in her nineties, still lives in Spain. Juana's father died in 1985. Juana's sister now lives in Chile, and one of her brothers lives in Texas. Three other brothers live in Cuba.

Juana drives Jimmie and Thea to the Copacabana and teaches them how to snorkel in the hotel's saltwater pool. She takes them to the beach. She takes them with her own family to the beach and introduces them to her nieces and nephews.

Though she has tried everything, even going to a *babalao* and having half a pumpkin rubbed on her stomach, Juana is not able to have children.

A FIST-SIZED OBJECT falls into the pool, not far from Nick, while we are swimming with the children. At first I think it is a large seedpod from a tree (it is windy), but then Nick says, 'It's a stone.'

Nick picks it up off the bottom of the pool. It's a piece of cement block. I look up at the edge of the roof above us, but all I see are red tiles and white stucco. Quietly it dawns on me that it is a stone that someone has *thrown*.

'It was some kid,' I say.

Nick says he saw it coming out of the corner of his eye. It came from the side street. Our house is on a corner. Nick says the thrower had to have been back from the fence a considerable distance – in the middle of the street, or better yet, in the bushes in the empty lot across the street, out of sight of the guard (who is supposed to cover both streets but is often dozing) – and had to have thrown hard. He must have been an adult or a big boy.

There's a bus stop at the side of the house where the rock came from. Six-foot-tall metal sheets line the chain-link fence around our house to keep people from looking in, but between the fence and the low cement wall it is set in, there is a four-inch gap, and the low wall provides a nice toehold, so one can either stoop and look through the gap under the fence, or step on the cement wall and look over it to see us having a nice swim. We often see the ocher color of high school uniforms through the gap, and sometimes lips on raw teenage faces yelling, '*Puta!*' ('Whore!') and '*Maricón!*' ('Faggot!').

III. 14

Fidel, appearing on television, says Hurricane Lili, which is supposed to hit Havana tonight, will be the greatest challenge to the Cuban people since the beginning of the *periodo especial.*

Fidel's stomach is sucked in, and he looks clear-eyed and energized as he explains in detail, with the aid of maps and charts, the emergency evacuation plans.

In the part of the house where we all sleep, there is a way of closing three doors between ourselves and the outside, at least on the side nearest the sea. The children get in our bed. The wind mounts. Fight-or-flight hormones keep me awake all night, but Nick and the children are soon snoring. The wind wails in the palm trees as if toward some crescendo. The crescendo never comes, and at seven, I go bleary-eyed to the TV room. A guy with a pointer, a Magic Marker, and a big piece of paper on an easel is explaining that the eye passed near Matanzas.

First we hear thirty-six buildings were destroyed, then two thousand, then six thousand. No one in Cuba was killed, however, while in Puerto Rico three hundred people died. The absence of fatalities, it is explained on television, is due to the constant review and perfection of Cuba's emergency evacuation procedures.

III. 15

Dr. Yamila Lawton is thrilled with the cassette player I bring her from Orlando. She makes a halfhearted attempt to offer to repay me, but I tell her not to think of it. She opens her pocketbook, closes it, opens it, and cries.

NEW STEEL PANELS ARE welded in place over the gap at the bottom of the fence and at the top of the fence, next to the barbed wire.

II. 16

Nick and other executives and diplomats get back from a two-day bus trip to tour the destruction left by Hurricane Lili. The Foreign Ministry tried to persuade countries and companies to give special aid by showing them a videotape of the destruction, but the executives and diplomats said they had to see the real thing.

In two days, they saw a flooded orange grove, two banana plantations with wind damage, and a refugee shelter. On the way, they saw many small *guajiro* houses with roofs blown off and mattresses outside drying in the sun. Nick talked to one woman whose income was 79 pesos a month (about $3.50).

Nick says the hurricane's happening to them was like stealing ten cents from someone who has twenty-five, and it looked like all they needed to restore their miserable lives to the miserable lives they had before was nails. Nick says, laughing, that in the refugee shelter were spanking-clean mattresses that hadn't been slept in. There were no sheets, no bundles, no clothes lying around – just a handful of women and children who definitely looked as if they had been planted there. Nick says the scene at the refugee shelter was so fake that the diplomats and executives – who had been on the bus for two days – didn't know whether to laugh, be angry, or feel pity.

III. 17

Cocktail party. Reny is there, aka the White Rabbit. He is called that because he has a white goatee and, like the White Rabbit in *Alice in Wonderland*, is a running theme. Reny is about sixty, and one of his assignments (one doesn't know if it is from the Foreign Ministry, the Ministry of Culture, or the Ministry of the Interior) is to look after foreign wives.

Reny, who is the height of the average foreigner's wife and understands that I am still learning Spanish, speaks Spanish slowly and distinctly to me, pausing between one word and the next, inches from my face. He speaks about the next opera, the next ballet of Alicia Alonso. It is not unpleasant (Reny uses a good-quality mouthwash), and if you can withstand his first few efforts to get you to go to operas and ballets you are not interested in, he doesn't insist.

Another of Reny's assignments is to look after Mme. Voisin. Mme. Voisin is the widow of a leading French expert on grazing grasses who wrote extensively on the subject in the 1950s. Fidel avidly read the works of M.Voisin in the first few years following the *triunfo*. Fidel invited M. and Mme.Voisin to Cuba, met them at the airport, and escorted them personally to model farms, to dairies, and to schools. M. Voisin died a few days after his arrival in Cuba, of a heart attack. Mme. Voisin was given a standing invitation to visit Cuba anytime she wanted and has done so every winter since his death. Reny is allowed to visit her in Paris every spring.

Yet another of Reny's assignments is to dabble in antiques. Reny has dabbled on behalf of the Carrera sisters, and he continues to dabble in antiques on behalf of other elderly women who have opted to stay on. He lowers his voice when he talks about antiques, pretends that he is acting on his own, but seems to stay on good terms with the Carreras and other elderly women, even with the ones who have children who live abroad and return regularly to Cuba to check on them, so perhaps the government's cut is not all that onerous.

Reny sports a different look at every party. Tonight he's wearing a green silk Russian peasant blouse, buttoned on the side, and a silver peace medallion. His pants are tucked into knee-high boots.

'Make love, not war, Reny!' I call to him, flashing the peace sign.

Reny takes my hand and kisses it, beaming with satisfaction.

III. 18

I am taken to meet Alfonse, aka El Ingles (the Englishman) because his father was an East Indian from Jamaica. Alfonse is a handsome *negro de pelo* who has been allowed to cultivate a rubble-strewn empty lot on the outskirts of Siboney. He started with two helpers and three hoes and has been clearing the land by hand, removing the rubble and extracting from the soil shards of *dientes de perro* (literally, dog's teeth – sharp volcanic rock), which he is using to make raised beds.

Alfonse is also, through some new law or loophole, allowed to sell what he produces to members of his 'club.' For five dollars each time you attend the 'club' you receive a *jaba* full of vegetables.

Pole beans I see, carrots, cucumbers, and Swiss chard, but foreigners also bring Alfonse seed packets of plants he has only heard of and seen only in pictures on the backs of the packets. The foreigners translate the instructions on the backs of the seed packets for him.

'*Mira, señora*,' Alfonse says. He leads us to a raised bed in a corner of the garden. He pulls an empty seed packet off a stack. 'Do you know this vegetable?'

I tell Alfonse zucchini are very well known in the United States and in Europe.

Alfonse kneels, brushes other leaves aside, and shows me a mound out of which zucchini tendrils and leaves are beginning to unfold.

Memories of the taste and smell of zucchini come flooding back, even though I was in a country in which zucchini were readily available just a few weeks before. Memories of the tastes and smells of other vegetables you can't get fresh in Cuba come flooding back, too – of broccoli and asparagus and fat celery.

III. 19

It is Saturday morning. The children sit in the *despacho* in the morning, watching cartoons. I am in the kitchen, peering into the refrigerator, trying to figure out what to tell Lorena to fix for lunch for the help and for us.

Concha comes into the kitchen. '*Señora, me da pena* (it pains me), but I have to tell you that someone has been urinating in the wastebasket in the *despacho* (den), and I'm worried about it because it's near the electrical cords.'

'*What?*' I think it's my Spanish.

She repeats slowly. 'The wastebasket in the *despacho*. Urine in it. Electrical cords.'

'How many times has this happened?'

'Four times.'

186

'*Four times!*' It's Jimmie, of course, not wanting to miss a cartoon, or being afraid of going into the dark powder room, but at the moment, I'm trying to deal with an even greater strangeness: 'Why didn't you tell me about it before?'

'Because *me da pena*, I didn't want to get little Jimmie in trouble . . .'

'Concha,' I say, nearly dumbstruck, but knowing I have to go on, 'we adults have to be *united* in what we expect from the children.'

Danila stands beside her, nodding with recognition.

'You must not accept from the children behavior that you would not accept in your own house! It's not fair to them!'

'But *señora*, Jimmie, he has such a *carácter*, I didn't want you to get mad at him.'

'But Concha, *por favor*, we can't let the children think they can behave one way in front of one adult and another way in front of another adult. It will only confuse them. They will start to play on this.'

Danila keeps nodding. She looks relieved. Concha's face turns pink.

'The children live in a big house with a lot of people to help them, but they are children just the same.' On I go, trying to make sensible points, Danila nodding, Concha flushing. I am feeling shaken by how little I can trust them to do the sensible thing, and by how Concha was able to go on for so long, dealing with shit's near equivalent, and not make a peep.

I follow Concha into the *despacho*. She holds up the square wooden wastebasket with the urine sloshing inside it. It sits behind an armchair with a high back, against the wall. I didn't know six-year-olds could be so sly.

'Gross!' Thea says.

'Did you know about this?' I ask Thea.

'Gross! No!'

Jimmie holds a blanket up to his face and cries. I turn off the TV. He turns out of my arms, runs upstairs, and shuts himself in the bathroom.

'Jimmie, it's not *terrible*, what you did,' I say at the door.

From the bathroom, a furious squeal.

THERE IS A CRITICAL mass you reach in terms of numbers of help in the non–First World countries where you can have them. Four in help is fine, but with more than four, in most cases, confusion mounts geometrically: the number of help you have becomes inversely proportional to the actual amount of 'help' you receive. This I say to Nick at night when he is back from work and can concentrate, but we agree that we can't, we absolutely can't, deprive Danila, Concha, or anyone who is used to getting eighty-five dollars a month from those eighty-five dollars.

I TELL JUANA ABOUT Jimmie and the wastebasket, Danila, and Concha, and I tell her how we need her very badly.

WE HIRE MORE HELP. After two years of showing visitors the Plaza de la Catedral, Plaza de Armas, Palacio de los Capitanes Generales, churches of San Francisco and La Merced, Plaza Vieja, Museo de la Revolución, *Granma*, and Castillos del Morro y La Cabaña and finishing with a drink at El Floridita, I decide that I just can't take it anymore. I need a chauffeur for visitors. I go to Lola. She recommends her nephew, Roberto, who is working as a night manager at the Hotel Caribe and making ten dollars a month.

Roberto is a twenty-eight-year-old *blanco* with dark circles under his blue eyes. I tell Roberto it will be very irregular work, chauffeuring only when I have visitors, and I don't know how many visitors we will have. I tell him we may have many visitors in a row, then none for who knows how long. I go away in the summer, and then there will be no visitors. I tell him I will pay him ten dollars for a half day and twenty dollars for a whole day's work.

Roberto scoots to the edge of the chair and volunteers that for him a whole day means twenty-four hours. He speaks before the words are completely out of my mouth, struggling to keep his tone even. I say that some months he may make a good amount of money, but other months he may make nothing.

He says, jumping in again, that his health is more important than anything. His job as a night manager is ruining his health. He needs sleep. And besides, the Caribe is going to close – he is sure of it. Foreigners who check in without looking at the rooms usually check out within minutes, or the next day. It's going to be closed, taken over by a foreign chain, and redone, he is sure of it.

He will drive me and two American *señoras* to Cienfuegos next week. He will call in sick to the Caribe. Then after Christmas he will quit his job and start working for me.

I say I feel worried that he will be leaving something secure.

'*Señora*, it's ten dollars a month . . .'

III. 20

There's a fifty-person line snaking down some side steps at the *agro* in Vedado.

I ask Miguel to find out what it is they are lining up for.

Miguel comes back to me. 'It's for turkeys,' Miguel says.

'*Qué raro*,' I say. I have never heard of turkeys at the *agro* before.

'Years ago, before *el triunfo*,' Miguel tells me, 'people used to eat turkeys at this time of the year.'

Today is November 22.

III. 21

Opening of the eighteenth annual New Latin American Film Festival at the Karl Marx Theater.

More lights have burned out in the theater since last year's film festival, shiny black patches on the carpet and plush seats have expanded and in many places worn through, and the same smell is still there. I can define the smell now: it's the between-the-toes smell of adolescents, five hundred of them in a closed room.

There are interviews with the French director of *Indochine*, with some Brazilian guy, and with the Nicaraguan star of a Scottish movie as we wait two hours for the surprise film of the evening to be shown. The interviews are interspersed with advertisements shown on a small screen. It is the first time the festival has had sponsors.

The audience makes sounds that range from aghast to pleased as the advertisements are shown. One is a spot for Popular cigarettes. '*Soy cubana, soy Popular*,' says a lady with a chignon in a long, white off-the-shoulder dress, her neck full of jewelry. *Popular* in Spanish means 'known, famous,' but also 'traditional, folk, of the people.' Many people in the audience sit on the edge of their seats, as people here seem to do when confronted by an image of anyone or anything bourgeois. At the end of the interviews and advertisements is a cascade of all the names of all the joint-venture companies who are sponsoring the event, all of them with amalgamated, dissonant names like Etecsa and Suchel.

Alfredo Guevara's speech this year praises socialism and extols Fidel as the seeker of justice for mankind. Alfredo's voice is shrill and tremulous. Delicate hands grip the paper. There was no mention of socialism, nor of Him, in the speech he gave last year. Alfredo has high blood pressure.

People look sideways at one another. Legs move, kicking ankles.

'Cuba is the leader of the world in social justice,' Alfredo reads.

III. 22

No fish for many weeks. Some kind of crackdown. Just as I am getting ready to go to the one place that sells fish (frozen only) to Cubans, in La Lisa, fish comes – red snapper and crab claws stuffed in the hollowed-out seat of our favorite fish vendor's motorbike. We buy the ten pounds of snapper and crab that he has managed to stuff into the seat. He returns half an hour later with another twelve pounds stuffed into his seat.

III. 23

We go to the opening of the fifth annual Italian Film Festival, which is held in conjunction with the New Latin American Film Festival. The director Vivarelli is there. He looks older than he probably is, with a large potbelly, and chain-smokes. He is the only foreign member of the Cuban Communist Party.

Vivarelli warns the audience that the film we are about to see is a hard film but, mercifully, a short film.

Practically the first shot is a close-up of a woman's unshaved armpit. It fills the screen. The audience guffaws.

What's admirable, bordering on the miraculous, is that

no matter how much Cubans don't have soap or hot water, no matter how much they don't have even *running* water, no matter how hard it is to find even a dull, shaggy razor blade, Cubans still manage to be clean, and Cuban women always have shaved armpits.

The film is one close-up after another of women's armpits after that. When it's not showing armpits, it's showing good-looking, sullen young Europeans flopping around in Comme des Garçons gray and midnight blue outfits in an impersonal, devolved, squalid, back-to-the-future–type basement, or groping one another in Armani and Calvin Klein underwear.

The audience laughs and hoots all through the film. Many leave.

III. 24

Alfredo Guevara is placed next to me at a dinner. I tell him the person on the other side of me is from La Yuma, from New York.

'I was in New York once,' he says, chuckling. 'I was in prison on Ellis Island before my expulsion.'

'But it closed as an immigration center in nineteen twenty-four . . .' For some reason I know this.

'They still kept a prison there, for those trying to enter the United States illegally. It was in nineteen forty-nine. I was a student activist.'

'Have you never been able to visit New York itself?'

'I went again once, with the U.N. They said I could visit New York, but I had to stay with Cuban diplomats. I didn't want to go around New York with Cuban diplomats. I wanted to see the Village. I went to visit a journalist, and from there I managed to get out on my own, and so finally I saw the Village.'

'I'm glad. I was having an image of you sneaking out the window of the Cuban mission, like Audrey Hepburn in *Roman Holiday*.'

He smiles at this, then leans back in his chair. 'Cuba is a lot like North America, don't you think?'

'Yes,' I say immediately, surprising myself. 'I know some Mediterranean countries, and I would say it's closer to North America than it is to a Mediterranean country. There is no siesta here. That is very North American, to work all day long, eat just a sandwich, and leave work at five o'clock.'

It's a chance: he's supposed to be one of the least *duro* (hard-line) of all the *nomenklatura*, and he is wanting to show me and my *yumese* friend that he's not like the recent *duro* speech he made (which he was obliged to give, Nick and I have speculated, because the speech he made the year before was so un-*duro*, and because of the advertisements and the cascade of joint-venture company names shown at the festival this year), but instead all I say is, 'In North America, one of the worst things you can do is park your car on a sidewalk, or park facing the wrong way on a one-way street, or cut in front of someone else in a line. To do any of those things would be unthinkable. In Mediterranean countries, it's regarded as normal (even necessary) behavior. In North America, though, a crazy person can buy a gun and kill lots of people. In the Mediterranean, what's most important is life inside the home. In North America, because of the tremendous amount of social mobility, there hasn't been much of a chance to develop home life and its refinements.'

Alfredo Guevara smiles with recognition. 'I'm trying to give my son a sense of home life.'

'You have a *son?*' I repeat, trying not to sound too surprised. He is so very gay.

'I have a son who has a wife and a child, and they all live with me. But my son is always on the street. 'Why don't you stay at home?' I say. 'Eat with us, at least.' But no. He comes in, has a little snack, goes out again. There's no regularity to his life.'

What chance, I am now thinking. *Chance for what? Chance to say to Alfredo, who looks dispirited enough as it is, 'It's like North America on the outside, but it's like Spain a gazillion years ago on the inside. It's like an Arab country, even, the way people relate to power'?*

'I had to fight so much against my parents,' Alfredo Guevara says after a pause.

Alfredo Guevara was a leader of the student movement against Batista at the University of Havana. Like Fidel, Che Guevara, and most of the original revolutionaries, he was the child of conservative, middle-class parents who supported the status quo.

Well, you won, didn't you? I want to say, but instead all I say is 'Hmmm . . .'

III. 25

Alfonse says he showed the zucchini to an old man who remembered seeing them before *el triunfo de la revolución*. He told Alfonse they called them *calabazin*.

Alfonse gives me five four-inch-long zucchini to take home. He says he has to save the other six he has been able to grow for other customers. He doesn't know how much more the plant will be able to produce. Already the farthest tendrils are drying up and the leaves, which never grew larger than a hand, are curling. It must be the quality of the soil, Alfonse says.

I lay them on the kitchen table.

'*Mira eso*,' Lorena says, putting her face close to them and inspecting them from all sides.

The help file past the prone zucchini, stroking their stiff fur.

They are like cucumbers, Miguel declares, but they are also like squash, only with thinner skin.

Manuel, who is nearly sixty, says they may have been in Cuba before *el triunfo*, but he never saw them.

Deliverymen and repairmen put on their glasses, bend over them, prod them. '*Qué curioso*,' they say to Lorena. One then takes off his glasses. '*Qué grande es el mundo, verdad?* ('How large the world is, isn't that true?').

III. 26

There are no direct flights from Miami to Havana since the Hermanos al Rescate were shot down last year. Instead of flying directly, charter planes are now touching down in Nassau, resting on the runway, then taking off again after about forty-five minutes. This seems to satisfy whoever it is who needs to be satisfied.

As we are sitting on the runway in Nassau, a representative of the charter company announces that we will not be able to proceed to Havana in this plane. We will have to deplane. An airplane belonging to Cubana de Aviación is flying to Nassau to take us the rest of the way.

There is a scream on the plane, and agitated mumbling. People take charter planes to avoid Cubana de Aviación. It will be a Tupolev, we know, which is the same kind of airplane that crashed in Russia a week before. The passengers have already been broken by five hours of waiting in Miami, though, and Christmas is in two days. I am sweating. I am thinking of going back to Miami and trying to get to Cuba through Cancún. I am thinking of doing this, but I have five suitcases full of presents. I am thinking of suing the charter company for misrepresenting its service.

In the Tupolev steam rises as usual from beneath the seats and fills the cabin with drifting clouds. One habit of travelers to Cuba, apart from having on average one hundred pounds of overweight luggage, is to wear four or five hats stacked on their heads. This is the easiest way to make sure that they won't get crushed. Between the hats and the carry-ons, there is not an inch of extra space on board. The stewardess begins her pre-takeoff announcements. I am in the second row of seats. A twenty-year-old girl ahead of me suddenly reaches around and inserts a half-eaten hot dog, with mustard on it, in the net bag on the back of the seat, facing me.

'But what are you *doing*?' I say to her.

'The stewardess said to get rid of the trash, and here in the front seat there is no place.'

'But you don't—' I start, but there are so many miles to go with the girl I just take my last piece of Kleenex, wrap the still-warm hot dog in the Kleenex, and give it to the stewardess, wiping mustard from my hands onto my pants.

The Tupolev rumbles tentatively down the runway. The steam increases. Passengers cross themselves. Compartments containing oxygen bags flip open over the bumps, spilling oxygen bags and tubes. Passengers lean forward, pumping. Panels, armrests, hats, and carry-on bags shake loose, fall in the aisle, and are retrieved by darting stewardesses. Bottles roll. I am thinking of the five pieces of luggage for every passenger, the Christmas average, in the belly of the plane. We strain into the air. It's an hour and a half more to Havana, an hour and a half of shrieks and groans and cries of, '*Coño!*' ('Cunt!') and '*Dios mío!*' ('My God!') with every shake and strange noise of the plane.

'Cuba! I see Cuba!' a passenger near me shouts.

'Thank God,' his companion says. 'Now at least we won't die in the sea.'

III. 27

We've had houseguests solid for the past three weeks. I would like to use Roberto for every waking moment, even to have *mojitos* with the guests on the veranda. It's not that I don't like them, but my life is slipping by. The scary part is that sometimes I find myself beyond anxiety and in some kind of state of dumb happiness, which comes from having a swimming pool and from the deterioration of brain cells – several thousand of them controlling anxiety, located at the center of the brain, deteriorate when you are in your forties – and I find myself feeling like it doesn't matter whether I write or not.

Houseguests on my back, houseguests in my pockets and cuffs, so that I cannot crawl to the word processor. Then, in my mind, I play the alternate scenario, of never having met Nick and therefore having married or had kids or lived in strange places, the alternate scenario a linear progression from the moment of my big revelation (obvious for some, but for me a big revelation) that it was better to be alone than to be with the wrong man: the scenario of me alone in a prewar doorman building in Greenwich Village, leading an ordered, quiet life with good cheeses and plenty of time to write. Plenty of time to write and remember all my nieces' and nephews' birthdays. Plenty of time to write, but making myself do it for three hours every morning, followed by twenty-five laps at the New York Health and Racquet Club.

There is a ghost me that steps out of me and leads that life in snippets.

III. 28

Nick and I visit the westernmost part of Cuba. It is the first time we have been on a trip by ourselves, without the children, since Muna left more than a year ago. We spend the first night at Los Jazmines, a hotel built in a traditional style in the first few years following *el triunfo*. It is the first time Nick and I have been alone together in a hotel in Cuba. We enter the room, put down our bags, and open the French doors leading onto the balcony.

The setting of Los Jazmines is breathtaking, overlooking the *mogotes* of the Viñales Valley – massive, verdant rock formations, caused by erosion, that rise out of valley floors, like those in

Chinese landscape paintings, and exist only in China, Cuba, and a few other places in the world. In the valley grow corn, tobacco, yucca, lettuce, cucumbers, beans, horses, cows, sheep, pigs. The sun is setting, turning everything bluish green. We will return with the children, we say; we will ask about horseback riding.

In the dining room, a trio is playing 'The Pennsylvania Polka' very loudly to a group of elderly French tourists. They move on to 'Never on Sunday,' 'La Cucaracha,' and 'Guantanamera.' We ask the waitress if she can ask the trio to make the music a little softer. Our dinner is a shriveled quarter of a chicken, some dry rice and beans, some greasy and very tired sliced potatoes, then potatoes again in the form of canned cubed potatoes with canned carrots, and peas. The meal costs nine dollars per person.

Anita, who introduces herself as the head of public relations for the hotel, stops by our table. Anita is about twenty-five years old and very pretty. 'The waitress tells me that you don't like the music.'

'It's fine,' we say.

'No, really, she said you didn't like it.'

'It's fine . . . just a little loud.'

'I think it's about time we stopped the music.'

She signals to the musicians, who pick up their instruments and leave.

'And how is the food?'

'Do you really want to know?'

'May I sit down? I do really want to know.'

'Why, when we are in such a rich agricultural area, do you serve tired canned vegetables from Europe?'

She nods knowingly. 'This is something everyone complains about . . .'

'If everyone complains, why do you keep on serving them?'

'Because we are only allowed to buy vegetables from the entity that sells food to tourist establishments, and this is what has been available recently.'

'And why do you care what we think?'

'I just do. Maybe it's because I am young and have just started this job.'

III. 29

We drive the Cordillera de Guaniguanico the next day. It is not just Viñales that is full of *mogotes*; it is the entire *cordillera* (mountain chain), which runs eighty kilometers from Minas de Matahambre to Guanes. Minas de Matahambre (Hungerkiller Mines) is a tropical Wild West. We drive up and down hills topped by rusting nineteenth-century mining machinery. From then on, it's a high plain, wending its way between *mogotes*, full of caves and rivers that snake in and out of the caves and porous bases of the *mogotes*. Some of the caves are nearly hidden by thick vines. On the plain, tobacco, beans, rice, zebu cattle, *guajiro* houses with palm-thatched roofs, and corroding bridges. In eighty kilometers on this main road, we see neither bodega nor store, nor state-run restaurant, nor *paladar*, nor filling station, nor any sign of commercial life. The only signs of modern life are corroding steel bridges with wooden boards laid across them that shift precariously as we cross. It could be a dream of a place for kayaking, hiking, horseback riding, for sleeping in simple bungalow-style hotels with wide verandas, no electricity, and mosquito nets.

The *mogotes* end at Guane. From Guane to Mantua are pine-forested hills. Some of the pines are hung with resin-collecting cans.

Mantua, the northwesternmost city in Cuba, is a town of twenty-three thousand people, who live for the most part in small wooden houses with porches. The straight streets have U.S.-style sidewalks of poured cement with lines drawn in them and U.S.-style fire hydrants placed at regular intervals. One area in Mantua looks as if it might have been a business district at one time, but now there is not a café nor a bodega nor an *agro* to be seen anywhere.

There is, however, a historical society, which is nearly bare inside. A custodian rises from the seat where she is dozing and kisses us on both cheeks. There is a reproduction of the table at which the victorious *mulato* Cuban general Antonio Maceo sat when Mantua's Spanish mayor ceded the town to Maceo's forces. It's a reproduction, the custodian explains, because the town was burned twice during the war of independence. There are a few arrowheads, some remnants of cooking pots and stirrups from the colonial period, a photo portrait (taken in

1920) of a lady who danced all night with Maceo in 1896. There is a photo of the high school band, taken in 1940: braided uniforms they had then, plumed hats, and a full complement of shiny musical instruments, including a tuba, and there were majorettes in tasseled white cowboy boots with batons. There are photos of martyrs of the revolution and a photo of the one boy from Mantua who died (of disease) in Angola.

'But the town was burned *after* Maceo arrived?' we ask. 'Who burned it?'

'It was burned by the Cubans themselves. The Spanish retook the town after it was ceded to Maceo's forces and were trying to fortify it. The Cubans burned it so it would not fall into Spanish hands.'

Maceo died in Mantua later in the same year, in a Spanish ambush.

A thin *blanco* in his sixties arrives. He is introduced to us as the city historian. He takes each of our hands in both of his hands and squeezes them. 'It is so good to have some visitors,' he says.

We catch sight of a small boy standing outside in the alley peering through the shutters at us. He slams the shutters shut when he sees us looking at him. 'My grandson,' the historian says.

The historian explains that it is generally believed that the city's name is the Spanish name for Mantova, a landlocked Italian city, because the duchy of Mantova, in Italy, became a Spanish protectorate in the sixteenth century following the Spanish invasion of northern Italy. A duke of Mantova, Gonzaga, himself of Spanish origin, was chief of Spanish shipbuilding for a time in the sixteenth century. This is the first explanation. After that, there are two slightly diverging explanations, both having to do with a Spanish ship named the *Mantua* or the *Mantova* and captained by one Anatolio Fiorenzana. One legend is that the ship, pursued by the English, sought refuge behind coral reefs off what is now Mantua, and its captain and crew decided to stay. The other legend is that the ship was wrecked on the reefs, and those who made it ashore decided to stay. There is no money, though, to look for the remains of the boat or the shipwreck on the coral reefs, and there are no written records. All that is left is oral tradition and the fact that a lot of people in the town have names that sound like Italian names. There is also a copy of the original sixteenth-century shield of the town, which has in it the image of a sinking ship. Finally, there is the Virgin in the church, the Virgen de las Nieves (Virgin of the Snows), which is also the Virgin in the cathedral of Mantova. The Virgin was saved from both fires. No one knows exactly how old she is, only that she is very old.

There has not been a priest in the church for a long time, the historian says, but more priests are being ordained now in Havana, and they have heard that one will be sent from Havana soon. The house facing the church has the key. We kiss old women rocking on the porch of the house facing the church, who raise their faces to us expectantly, and are handed the key.

Over the door of the church is the copied shield with the sinking ship on it. Above the altar is the ancient Virgin of the Snows. She has the small mouth and full chin of eighteenth-century-and-earlier beauty. Her robe is white satin, with large rhinestone snowflakes embroidered on it. She holds a white tobacco flower in one hand. The tobacco flower, of carved wood, was added in the last century, the historian explains, when she became, in this tobacco-growing region, the Virgen del Tabaco as well. Her shrine is carved from one piece of wood. She holds a tiny Jesus in her arms. Jesus is the size of a newborn but has the face of a crabby four-year-old.

At the end of Cuba, the Virgin of the Snows. The expression 'when it snows in Cuba' is the Cuban equivalent of 'when pigs have wings.' The silence on the street outside, the loneliness, is like that in some wintry place. We sit in the front pew, willing the Virgin's sweet face to reveal the mystery of her origin and tell us when snow will finally fall.

III. 30

The only place to spend the night is in the Laguna Grande Motel, about forty kilometers from Mantua. The one-star motel is a former *campismo popular*, where workers were sent on vacation. Its small bungalows are made to look like thatched huts. The interior walls of our bungalow are lined with patterned curtains. At first we think it's because someone has an enthusiasm for sewing, but when we look behind them we realize they are to cover sweat and mildew on the plaster walls. The pillows are thin mats with lumps. Large ants crawl on the floor of the shower.

I ask the receptionist who shows us to our room if there is hot water. In a toneless voice she says that there is none running from the taps, but if we would like some, it can be heated in the kitchen. I ask in what container, in what receptacle, the hot water could be put, but I'm not using the right word. What I am trying to find out is whether I have to take my body over to the kitchen and wash there, so I ask, 'If someone wants to take a shower, how do they do it?' She gets in the shower and, with the same bored expression on her face, takes the telephone-type showerhead off the hook and trains it over her body to illustrate. 'I know how to take a shower,' I say. 'I just want to know where you put the hot water.' She holds up a plastic bucket with a top. The room costs forty dollars per night.

We go into the dining room for dinner. There is no other place for seventy-five miles offering food of any kind.

The tablecloth and the napkin are gray, as if they have been used for dusting. 'Can I please have a napkin that is a little cleaner?' I ask. Paper napkins are produced. The waiter appears. 'There is no electricity in the kitchen,' he says, 'so we can't cook the food. There will be a delay.'

'Can we look at the menu?'

'There will be a delay.'

'How long?'

He seems confused.

'Can we look at the menu so that we can think about what we want to eat while we are waiting?'

He hesitates.

'They want to look at the menu,' Roberto barks.

It is finally produced.

'I don't see why they didn't want to at least bring a menu,' I whisper to Roberto. Usually I don't say anything, but there are still times here when bad service, delivered so unapologetically, feels like an aggression.

When we are alone in the car, Roberto criticizes nearly everything, with no prompting from us, heaping the greatest vitriol upon the Bearded One himself, but here in the restaurant, Roberto begins a loud sotto voce speech – like an operatic aside

– about how unprepared they are for tourism. It's for the benefit of the restaurant staff, and for the handful of Cuban 'guests' – chain-smoking men in tight polo shirts who sit, also without food, at another table. Roberto speaks about how difficult it is to get soap, about how one state agency will not provide another state agency with the product for making a decent soap, about how difficult it is to get running water and to heat it if there is little gas. Nick and I flatter ourselves that the men in tight polo shirts might be our tails.

'But before *el triunfo de la revolución*, there were water heaters,' I say to Roberto. 'People had hot water . . .'

'My family never had hot water.'

Nick kicks me in the ankle.

After dinner, Nick vomits into the plastic bucket the receptionist told us was meant for hot water. I spray the sides of the bucket with the telephone-type showerhead and dump it into the hibiscus bushes to the side of our bungalow.

'I don't see any point in staying here another night,' Nick says, his face gray atop the lumpy gray pillow.

Staying in less-than-two-star hotels in Cuba during the *periodo especial*, we realize, means passing below the rock bottom of comfort, to the point where involuntary abuse of guests begins.

III. 31

We drive back to Havana the next day, stopping at a beach we have heard about, Playa Las Canas. We drive about fifty kilometers, then drive another eight on a deeply rutted road through a cow pasture dotted with royal palms. We come upon another former *campismo popular*, only one that is really abandoned this time. It is much more attractive than the Laguna Grande probably ever was. It is made of real palm-thatched huts, about thirty of them, spread out along a bay with not much beach but with a view of islands strung out along its entrance, all of them uninhabited. The huts have cement floors, which have buckled and crumbled. It is puzzling how in Cuba, when they build huts, they never build them on stilts, with wooden floors, as they are built in other tropical countries, but rather pour cement floors right on the ground. The slip of beach goes on for several kilometers in both directions. Cows have eaten the grass behind the beach, so that it is like a lawn, dotted with dried cow patties. Shade trees arch conveniently over this lawn and over the beach as well, so that you can choose whether to picnic on shaded grass or on shaded sand.

Every place we hear of and then make an effort to see, we have been telling ourselves, is for future reference, for when friends come. We will take time, we have been telling ourselves; we will load the car with stuff; we will have a convoy, even. The future looks dimmer, though, with each unspoiled, unsqualid, *jinetera*-free place we find, as we contemplate the monumental effort involved in driving many hours and taking everything with us – gasoline, food, tent, grill, and a guard, or two guards, to spell each other – then spending at least two days (otherwise the monumental effort wouldn't be worth it) and in the end feeling ridiculous, with guards to watch our canned tuna, and lonely (we admit it now), even with friends.

Deserted places can be mysterious and exhilarating, or they can make you feel lonelier still; in Cuba, deserted places make you feel lonelier still. We have tried to feel exhilarated, coming to a gorgeous, deserted place, and proud of ourselves for having found it. 'Think of how so-and-so would love to be here,' we say to each other, but it falls flat.

A *guajiro* is living in one of the more substantial huts. He is muscular and weather-beaten, in an army jacket with the sleeves ripped off, no shirt, and army shoes worn to a kind of leather latticework on top. His son is with him. We ask him how long the huts have been abandoned. He says they have been abandoned since last year. We say it looks like they have been abandoned for longer than that, and he says that a few people had been there the summer before, living in the huts that were in better shape. He says he's only been here two weeks. He asked the local Consejo del Poder Popular (literally, Council of the People's Power, or local Communist Party council) if he could live here, and they said he could, but he doesn't know how long he can stand it. Water is a big problem. He's requested the tank truck three times, and they've only come once. He says it's just his son and himself. He's been alone, he tells us, with his son since his son was born. The son is about fifteen, willowy, with doe eyes and bad acne. I feel that we are in a Hemingway story. We give them some canned tuna and some chocolate and a bottle of water. We wish them good luck. They wave at us as we drive away. I know I will think about them and about Playa Las Canas long after it becomes a Club Méditerranée.

We drive to the nearby town of Dimas to see if we can find some food there – a *paladar* is too much to hope for, but we are hoping for an *agropecuario* or a stand selling *yucas rellenas*. We pass a low stucco building with RESTAURANTE written on the side of it with flourishes. I go in. A woman stands behind an empty display case. She looks at me suspiciously. 'Do you have any food?' I ask. 'We only sell cigarettes,' she says. We drive to the shore, turn right, drive to the end of the street. 'Let's get out and walk,' Nick says. 'But where?' I ask. There is a military post in front of us. In back of us is a dock leading to a building. A cluster of men stand at the entrance to the dock. One of them seems to be a guard.

'Let's walk on the dock,' Nick says.

'They probably won't let us.'

Nick approaches the one who seems to be a guard. 'Good morning. Can we take a walk on the dock?'

'*Es prohibido.*'

'*Ah, prohibido.* That is a word I hear very much in Cuba.'

The guard pushes himself up from the wall he's been resting on.

'What country are you from?'

'It is *prohibido* to tell you.'

'What country? Japan?'

I would like to stop, face him, and ask him if he really thinks we are from Japan or if he is kidding. Sometimes non-Asian people in really, really faraway places (once, in the mountains of Greece) have thought I was Asian because my eyes, though blue, are a little slanty and my hair, though brown, is dead straight. I want to ask him if he thinks people from Japan have blue eyes and brown hair, but Nick yells, '*Prohibido!*' over his shoulder at him as we move to the car.

III. 32

Danila comes into my little room. She asks me if she can leave early. She was robbed the night before. She has to go to the police.

They took knickknacks from her shelves, she tells me. They unplugged the stereo but they didn't take it. Danila then says darkly that her husband was in the house drinking with a friend while she was at her mother's.

DANILA SAYS THE ROBBERY was worse than she thought: they took her blender and her electric frying pan, too. Her voice is trembling. The police were at her house. They said it is odd that there was no sign of anyone forcing his way in. Her husband was in the house drinking with a friend when the things disappeared, she tells me again.

III. 33

Fidel gives a speech on television about the Clinton administration's recently published *Transition to Democracy* paper, which is a blueprint for Cuba's transition to a democratic system following the death or removal from office of the Castro brothers. Fidel calls Clinton an idiot for proposing it. Never in the history of the world, he says, has one country so blatantly meddled in the affairs of another country. He says the United States is the most racist, violent, discriminatory country in the world. 'It discriminates against blacks, against women, against Hispanics, against . . .' He looks at the camera, searching. 'Children,' he continues triumphantly.

A South American journalist sitting with us in the *despacho* bursts out laughing. 'He is *really* having fun,' the journalist says.

LO NUESTRO ES NUESTRO (What is ours is ours), reads the slogan on the billboard at the PabExpo traffic circle in Cubanacán.

III. 34

Tight-fitting knee-high boots along the Malecón after dark now, and in the shadows of the street in back of the Meliá Cohiba Hotel, male *jineteros* in cutoff hot pants with bare midriffs, emerging from among the dead appliances and potted plants on front patios to flash their wares – hot pants hiked high, seams cutting into balls – in the seconds it takes for our lone headlights to pass. The hair is stringier, the scene harder than it was when we first got here: they are becoming pros.

We have gone to a play, *Te Sigo, Esperando* ('I Follow You, Hoping,' which can also mean 'I Follow You, Waiting,' for the words for 'hoping' and 'waiting' are the same in Spanish). It is the first play we have seen about a real situation, not a - 'symbolic' play set in a vague time that the audience has to read things into and figure out. Here the only thing to figure out is how the play, written by a Cuban living in Cuba, got to be performed in the first place. The play is about families divided by emigration. It is about trying to get by on a minuscule salary and care for an aging parent. It is about how Cubans exploit and blackmail one another. It is about anger and boorishness, about broken elevators, about the contortions Cubans have to make to acquire enough food, about the lack even of rags to wipe the floor. The audience roars and claps with recognition at the site of a sopping T-shirt slapped down on the floor to clean it. It is about how a person who plays by the rules gets shafted.

Toward the end of the play, the protagonist, facing the audience, asks, 'And do you think that with so much paternalism and lack of discipline we can really construct socialism?' The audience roars again and stamps, hoots and whistles. We emerge from the play energized and drive home along the Malecón.

III. 35

Gonzalo, our swimming teacher, has stopped wearing his diamond ring, though he still wears his gold chain. He has started spending every weekend with his parents, his ex-wife, and their son, Olaznog (which is *Gonzalo* spelled backward), who all live near Trinidad. He always brings back five pounds of shrimp for us, and we pay him ten dollars. The shrimp is piling up in the freezer. After about the fifth week, I offer weakly that we have a lot of shrimp already, but he looks so crestfallen that I buy another five pounds, then another, until I am giving shrimp away to friends.

III. 36

Ana María Guevara, the stepmother of Che Guevara, whom we met last year at the Argentinian ambassador's, lives in a pleasant house in Miramar. It is nearly bare, with a shiny terrazzo floor and just a few pieces of worn Danish modern furniture. At the back is a room with many windows, which she uses as a studio. The windows look out on a thick grove of banana trees. When I compliment her on the trees, she shrugs and says, 'I find tropical a little boring. It's always the same, but what can I do?'

Mrs. Guevara is an artist who works mostly in collage. The pictures she makes are portraits of her state of mind, she says, and of the states of mind of other people she knows. She can read people, she says; she can tell what's on their minds. She teaches some art classes, and she says to her art students, 'You paint that way because you feel like this,' and they say to her, 'My God, how did you know?' Her work keeps her . . . she hesitates. 'Well . . . *balanced*,' she says. Her collages are pieces of faces or human bodies surrounded by dark fields of color. Some of the collages have little jail bars in them.

She has three children who are in the university here. She is battling now for the rights to one of Che's diaries so that she can at least get some money.

Later, Nick says, 'She didn't really have jail bars in them,' and I have to swear to him that they did.

III. 37

Gonzalo is missing. He told us he would be coming back after the school holidays were over. He didn't show up after the holidays. He didn't show up the week after that. In the middle of the second week, I asked Manuel to call Gonzalo's family's home near Trinidad. The man who answered said that Gonzalo's family no longer lived there and he didn't know where any of them were. I called Carlita. Carlita said he'd probably finally gone to Canada. She called Gonzalo's house, and the man who answered the phone said without hesitation that he was Gonzalo's father and that Gonzalo was in the country. Carlita said to give it a little more time, and if we still didn't hear from him, I should call her again and she would find out what really happened.

Lety says that it sounds like Gonzalo is getting ready to leave, if he hasn't left already. Lety says Gonzalo's Canadian wife has probably been in Canada all this time and has probably only now finally arranged for his visa and ticket, and Gonzalo is probably in the final stages of arranging for his passport, letter of invitation from his Canadian 'host' (in which she declares that she will be responsible for all his expenses), health certificate, and exit permit, a process that takes months. Lety says people often drop out of sight before they leave, or stay very, very quiet, because if people understand that you are leaving, someone who doesn't like you can always go to your local CDR and say you haven't been behaving yourself – you've been selling things secretly, or you have a child you haven't paid support for, or you owe money to someone, or you've been saying or doing the wrong things – and your CDR can keep you from getting a passport or an exit permit. Then, once you *have* a passport and an exit permit, and you're only waiting for your ticket or to do last-minute things, someone can still denounce you for something – any person with any little bit of power who doesn't like you – and can keep you from actually leaving.

III. 38

Our neighbor, the Argentinian ambassador, tells us that one of the guards at her residence stopped her as she was walking outside her gate the other evening. 'I am so hungry,' he said. He told her that they are given only one meal a day – lunch. For dinner they are given sugar, water, and bread.

NO MORE CRUISE SHIPS will be coming to Havana. The Costa cruise ship line has been bought by an American company, and American cruise ships are prohibited by the embargo from coming to Cuba.

Costa cruise ships coming to Havana lasted for less than a year.

GONZALO IS IN CANADA. Roberto stopped at Gonzalo's parents' house on his way through Trinidad with some American friends of friends we had sent off with him. When he returns, Roberto also tells us that Gonzalo's parents showed him a photo of Gonzalo's Canadian wife. We ask Roberto what Gonzalo's Canadian wife is like, on a scale of one to ten. Roberto says that she is a six.

'A *six*?'

Roberto blushes through his tan. 'Well ...,' he says, '*las canadienses* and the others from the North, they are not like Cuban girls. They are more ...' His face flushes a little pinker.

'Roberto, *por favor* ...'

'Dry. *Son más secas.* OK, I said it now. *Disculpe.*'

'And how are they in Cuba?'

'Now it's my turn to say *por favor.*'

'*Roberto* ...'

'OK.' He takes a breath. '*Las cubanas tienen más* ...' Roberto outlines two half-moons in front of him, shimmies with his upper body, and makes a little growling noise.

SOME VISITING FRIENDS of ours – a married couple and their fourteen-year-old daughter – go to the beach. A slender young girl approaches them in the water. Our friends think she could not have been more than eleven years old. 'Can I swim between your legs?' the girl asks the wife.

The wife thinks the girl is a forward child, but she spreads her legs in the water, and the girl swims between them.

She asks to swim through the husband's legs. He spreads his legs as well, but they are both feeling uncomfortable about it.

'Do your wife or daughter speak Spanish?' the young girl asks the husband after she has swum through his legs.

'No,' he says.

She then asks the husband if he wants to have sex with her.

'We don't need anything,' the husband says.

She excuses herself and moves to the next foreign couple.

III. 39

We drive to Jibacoa with the children. 'Do we *have* to go to the beach *again*?' the children ask. We search around town for some friends to go with them, but the friends are already too sunburned.

The beach is nearly deserted. It is bright but not hot. There is a couple making out at our favorite spot under an arching shade tree, but they move after a while and we have the spot to ourselves. The sun shining directly down on the water at noon makes it transparent. Nick and the children build a sand castle.

We don snorkels and take off toward the reef. Jimmie really has the snorkel thing down now. We cruise over the reef. 'But where's the beautiful part?' he asks. He means the deeper part, where there are valleys and holes and there is coral – some umbrella-shaped, like trees on an African savanna, some like burgundy-colored phalluses with bright purple heads, others like fans. Suddenly we find it: the magic valley.

Jimmie raises his head. He takes the tube out of his mouth. 'It's fantaculous,' he says.

I keep asking Jimmie if he is tired, but he wants to go on and on. We come upon some razor-thin iridescent blue fish and follow them through a valley. The razor-thin iridescent blue fish join a school of yellow polka-dot fish, thousands of them. We follow them, enraptured.

After another half an hour, we move back to the shore.

'I have found a dollar!' Thea yells, coming up for air.

She leads us to a spot in three feet of water where a dollar bill is plainly visible, one half of it buried in the sand, the other half waving like a sea anenome. We will carry it home, I say, and dry it, and when we get back to a place where we can have things framed, we will frame it. It will be known from now on as Thea's Magic Dollar.

We drive home in silence. The chilrdren are sleepy from the sun. When we are nearly home, Thea says, 'It *is* weird, though, isn't it, one of *us* finding the dollar.'

III. 40

Lola says that there's a new kind of Cyclone fence that has been appearing in town, made entirely of plastic. People have put them up in their yards because of all the robberies. There are now bathtubs made of plastic, too. It's up to Cubalse to sell them, of course, but people have been acquiring them in their own little ways. The new solution the government has come up with is not to go after the people who cause them to disappear from the warehouses, but to go with a truck and a crew directly to the yards where the fences have been put in, and unless the owner of the fence can produce a *papelito* proving he bought the fence legitimately, the crew rips the fence out of the ground. They go into your house, too, and if they see a bathtub made of plastic and you can't produce the *papelito*, they take it, too, ripping it from its pipes right then and there. It has been happening a lot on Ninetieth Street in Miramar, she says.

III. 41

Thea comes into our room at 10:45. She says she is so nervous, she can't sleep. I go back with her to her room and lie down beside her. I ask her what she is nervous about. Thea says she is nervous because every Thursday, when they stay late at school to have piano lessons, and Juana stays, too, she is afraid that Juana will start talking to Yolanda and make a play date and that she will have to go to Yolanda's house and play with her, and tonight is Wednesday . . . she starts to cry.

I told Juana that I wanted Thea to try to be friends with Yolanda because she was the only Cuban child in the school, and since Ivan was fired, there has not been another Cuban child in our lives, and you can't be a child and live in a country and never know children from that country. I told Juana about the dance classes and the attempts to bicycle in a park and Rollerblade in the Prado. Thea and Jimmie know Juana's nieces and nephews, but they are all older or younger.

Yolanda lives on the twelfth floor of an ex–luxury high-rise. The first time we went there, the elevator, a blasted shell, looked so precarious that we climbed the twelve stories to the apartment. The stairwell and hallway looked like war zones themselves, but I tried being breezy and unconcerned as we climbed the stairs, taking what I believed was a 'when in Havana' approach because Thea, I thought, was still not old enough to notice squalor. Yolanda's mother seemed like a perfectly reasonable mother, and the apartment itself was, by Cuban standards, outrageously well appointed – freshly painted, with well-stuffed sofas and chairs, a new Sony television in the corner, and a computer. Still, Thea called me one hour after I got home and asked when I was coming to pick her up. The second time I took her there, Thea wanted to leave almost as soon as we got there. Both times I managed to persuade her, speaking X—, to give it a try, at least for three hours.

Thea is crying hard now.

I tell Thea she does not have to play with anyone she does not want to play with.

III. 42

Juana says she understands why Thea doesn't like going to Yolanda's place. It is scary there, she says. The kids in the building ride the elevator up and down by themselves from one floor to another. They ride the elevator to the ground floor and run across the street, in the middle of traffic, to the strip of park on the other side. Thea stands on the sidewalk, not knowing what to do, for we have told her never to cross the street by herself.

I had heard baboonlike shrieks in the stairwell both times we had gone, as well as the sound of the elevator door rattling open and closed and the clopping of kids' sandals in and out, but had chosen not to think about it. Then when Thea had come home, both times I had been on my way out and had not stopped to hear from her how it really was.

I am a white trash mom, it comes to me now with searing-clarity. I have also been, and am, the worst kind of non-Cuban, dumping all Cubans together into one messy group, as if it were impossible for one Cuban to be bothered by the squalor and chaos of another Cuban. I have been colonialist and radically chic, too, with my 'when in Havana' insistence, and worse, I have been *pushing that insistence on my daughter.* The kids don't *have* to have Cuban friends and hang out in Cuban public spaces if it scares them.

Then I realize it's to *Juana* I have been trying to prove how 'when in Havana' I can be.

III. 43

An American woman whose husband works at the Interests Section has three little boys who play Little League with Cuban boys at a baseball field off the Malecón. The field is ringed by houses with small porches that face the field. The other day, the American woman tells me, one of her little boys had to do something more than just pee. She was standing with him at the edge of the field, wondering what to do, when an elderly couple, sitting on their porch, seemed to understand their

211

problem and beckoned to them that they could use their bathroom.

The bathroom, as usual, was barely functioning, but the people were so kind to let them use it that the American woman wanted to give them something. She thought offering them money would be too crass, so she offered them some home-made chocolate-chip cookies that she had in her bag.

The elderly man took one, bit into it, and started to cry. 'I remember this taste,' he said.

III. 44

Nick says an X——ian translator was stopped twice by the police – once for not coming to a full stop on the white line drawn on the asphalt. It was a very grievous offense, the police-men said. He would have to pay sixty dollars. The translator managed to negotiate it down to three dollars. Nick didn't know what the second offense was, but the policeman got really excited because there was a Cuban in the car with no identifi-cation. He said they would all have to go to jail. The translator managed to get out of that one for eight dollars.

AT A COCKTAIL PARTY, we learn that *policemen* in Cienfuegos and Trinidad now stop tourists' cars to ask for beer and soap.

A SIGN PAINTED on the side of a building: Yo ♥ MI C.D.R.

I PASS AN ART DECO building in a part of town I don't usually visit. I park my car and enter the lobby. Classical Roman women in togas in aluminum bas-relief decorate the elevator doors.

III. 45

Birthday party for the artist Ángel Toirac, combined with a housewarming for their new apartment. They are moving into a part of what was his wife's family's apartment, which covered an entire floor in a building in downtown Havana and was broken up into smaller apartments following *el triunfo*. A communal kitchen was installed in the rear. Meira's uncle was consigned the apartment they are now in. Meira and Ángel have constructed a loft bedroom and their own kitchen. It has taken them a year to do it.

Meira and Ángel show us remnants of pre-*triunfo* niceties, like a special shoe tree that goes into a wall fixture so that you can shine your wing tips at a comfortable level. You can keep the shoe tree in the wing tip the whole time, presumably, then put it back in your closet, alongside your other wing tips, all with their special shoe trees inside them.

The apartment also contains ingenious gadgets improvised by Meira's uncle, who was the right-hand man to Che in Santa Clara. He was jailed, though, after *el triunfo*. After his release, he spent his time producing the inventions that Meira now shows us: one is a small wind-speed indicator, which enchanted Meira when she was a child; another is a simple machine for twisting knotted-together plastic bags into clotheslines. He produced many clotheslines and sold them. They sold quite well.

They still have one of the clotheslines he made. She holds it up. 'This is especially precious to us,' Meira says. 'He hung himself with one like this.'

III. 46

A U.S. anchorman, Mark, comes for dinner. He is well known in some cities in the United States, though neither Nick nor I have ever heard of him.

He wants to do a show about how the Helms-Burton Act is hurting the Cuban people. Americans don't think about Cuba, he says. He is looking for a way to get them to think about Cuba. One way to get Americans to think about Cuba is through kids. He wants to go into hospitals and show how kids are not getting medicines.

We say that is all very nice but that the most senseless thing about Helms-Burton is that it is only helping Fidel and the hard-liners.

He listens, and he says that while he understands that to be true, he has to get at the people angle first: showing kids in trouble will get the American people to pay attention. Then maybe, depending on how the show does, he can get more into how Helms-Burton keeps Fidel in power, but for now he doesn't want to antagonize the authorities.

Sometimes, talking to newly arrived visitors on the veranda before dinner, I think we are conducting a well-practiced Disney World ride. First the public is ushered by us into an orientation room (cocktails on the terrace, the first course at the dinner table), where they watch an OmniMax movie, *The Cavalcade of Cuban History from 1492 to the 1940s*. The doors open about halfway through dinner, the public filters through barred walkways onto moving cars, and we wend them through the revolution and its aftermath and the paradox of U.S. policy, which seeks the overthrow of Fidel and Cuba's rebirth as a democracy but only achieves the opposite. The car stops for a moment and turns, and the public faces a fixed stage with holograms moving across it. Here you see Ángel Castro, a Spanish immigrant, and Lina Ruz, his cook, who became his mistress and bore him Ramón, Fidel, Raúl, and other children. Here you see the young Fidel as a university student in Havana in 1948, with a car, an apartment, a sizable allowance, and time on his hands. Here you see the tininess of Cuban prerevolutionary high society, which disdained rich but gauche provincials like Fidel.

It is at this point that a voice coming from a point somewhere above the holograms tells the public that of course it is not believed that Fidel's *entire* motivation comes from the fact that he was not invited to the right parties.

The holograms continue. You see Fidel running for student body president but losing. You see Batista and the indignities and injustices inflicted on most Cubans. You see the assault on Batista's palace, the assault on the Moncada barracks, Fidel's imprisonment on the Isle of Pines, and his release one year later because of his father's connections. You see the parts the public knows much better: Fidel's exile in Mexico and his meeting with Che Guevara, the disembarkation from the *Granma*, the triumph of the revolution, the nationalizations, the Bay of Pigs, and the solidification of Fidel's position. You see the intransigence of the Miami Cubans. You see the collapse of the Soviet Union and the golden opportunity the United States missed in not dropping the embargo then. And continues to miss. The ride ends with a small, rubbery bump, and the public emerges (in time for after-dinner drinks in the living room), blinking, into banality.

A DANISH TOURIST is shot by the army. He was drunk and wandered into a military zone.

'YOUR FRIEND MARK is so *simpático*,' Roberto says. I am sure Mark gave him a big tip. I threw caution to the wind because Mark called me the day after he came for dinner and said he needed a car and a driver right away. I told Mark about Roberto over the telephone and then telephoned Roberto and told him how to get in touch with Mark.

Roberto tells me that when Mark first went to the car rental agency to rent the car that Roberto would then drive, he was told that there were no cars available, but there would be one available in the afternoon. When he went back in the afternoon, he was told that there were still none available.

'That's too bad,' Roberto says Mark said to the agent, 'because I spoke to your colleague in the morning, and he told me there would be a car for me in the afternoon, and I have a fifty-dollar bill here, waiting to be given to the person who finds me a car.'

'But you didn't tell us that there would be a *cash reward*,' Roberto says the agent said, handing Mark the keys to a brand-new Mitsubishi: '*Ay, qué simpático es Mark*.'

III. 47

I go with the kids to say good-bye to Nicoletta, our half-X—ian, half-Cuban friend, at her poolside bungalow at the Hotel Comodoro. Her contract is not being renewed by the Laundromat firm that sent her to Cuba, and she has to return to Europe.

Sexual tourists and glistening *mulatas y negras de pelo* lie with the inertness and predictability of seals on the Discovery Channel on chaises along the vast pool's undulating edge. A limb flips up from time to time to shoo a fly.

'The stories you could tell,' I say.

'Someday,' she sings softly, her hands fluttering over the lamps, picture frames, and hems of the curtains where microphones are supposed to be hidden. 'Someday,' she sings again.

I ask Nicoletta who is using the white stretch limo parked outside.

'It belongs to the prince of Malta,' Nicoletta says. 'He comes to Cuba a couple of times a year. He gets his own villa, and a few bodyguards are put in front of it for him. He has girls – two fixed ones, and then others who come and go.'

'But what does he do for . . . ?'

Nicoletta rubs her thumb and forefinger together.

Nicoletta walks among the sexual tourists and their *mulatas y negras de pelo*, tapping with polished fingernails on a can of cat food. Cats come running from all over the Comodoro, meowing, with their tails up, and rub against our legs. Nicoletta leads them back to the steps of her bungalow and starts opening cans of cat food and spooning it into bowls. The sexual tourists raise their heads, blinking, taking in the sight of two fully clothed middle-aged *blanquitas* and two children, speaking English and feeding cats.

I ask Nicoletta what she will do now. She says she will be attending astrology school, of course.

III. 48

Two women, more friends of friends, arrived here yesterday from the United States. They will not be staying with us, but they will be coming for lunch. They faxed us from the United States before they left, asking if they could bring us anything.

I faxed them back, asking them for three things. I faxed them to bring me the smallest Ziploc bags available in the supermarket (outside measurements 5½ inches by 3½ inches, officially called 'snack bags'), clear plastic pages (available from photography supply stores) to hold 3½-by-5-inch photos, and some tennis balls.

The women arrive at the house at 2 P.M. For two weeks I have been pleasantly anticipating the arrival of those Ziploc snack bags in particular. They are the perfect size for the children's school snacks. There are no prewrapped kid-portion snacks to speak of in Cuba. Everything they take to school is either home-made or bought in bulk in the United States or in Europe and brought in – kilos of nuts, industrial quantities of raisins. That's where the little bags come in. They hold just the right amount of raisins, nuts, cookies, and so forth for school. The children enjoy opening the Ziplocs; it makes them feel they are getting something closer to store-bought prewrapped snacks. Lately we have had to improvise with plastic wrap and rubber bands. The children have no patience for the rubber band packages: they tear at the wrapping, spill the contents, eat less, and come home in bad moods. We find flattened raisins and smeared chocolate in the bottoms of the lunch boxes. Ziploc snack bags will make everything better.

Sandwiches, we put in pint-sized Ziploc bags, but we have plenty of those. I have been thinking happily, too, about how, when the right-sized photo pages arrive, I will be able to continue organizing the boxes and boxes of loose family photos (going back to the births of our children) that I have vowed to myself I will organize, a little every day. It is something that it's possible to do only in Cuba, because in Cuba there is often nothing – absolutely nothing – going on, and there is time, time like people had a hundred years ago, when they quilted or tatted or carved, a little bit every day, and who knows how much longer we will be here.

The women extract what they have brought me from a carrying bag. They bring out four containers of tennis balls, a box of *pint-sized* Ziploc *sandwich* bags and a large box of Ziploc *quart-sized freezer* bags. They also bring out two packages of photo pages to hold *4-by-6-inch photos.*

I have plenty of 4-by-6-inch photo pages.

'Are the sizes all right?' they ask.

'Oh fine, these are great. Thank you,' I say, but inside I want to cry. And this is not the first time this has happened.

Not receiving something you need is bad, but receiving something you don't need is somehow *worse.* Why do people think I go through the trouble of writing specific sizes in my faxes to them? Doesn't it occur to people that I go to the trouble of writing specific sizes of things because I *actually need those sizes* and not other sizes? Is it not possible for people to imagine that I have spent *two whole weeks* thinking of all the progress I would be able to make once those things arrived?

I go into the powder room, wash my face, say '*Shit!*' to the mirror as loudly as I can without other people hearing me. I grip the edge of the sink. '*I am a privileged foreigner,*' I repeat to myself. '*I am a privileged foreigner and I will be out of here someday.*' I take a deep breath and move back, smiling a smile that only I know the meaning of, onto the veranda.

The next time friends of friends come, I tell myself, I will write them the *reasons* for needing one size of a particular thing and not another size, *all* the reasons for needing a particular size, in long, obsessive, run-on sentences, not caring what they think, sentences that end with the ultimate reason, that of the well-being of the entire family, so that they, especially people from the United States, with stuff up to their eyeballs, will understand the reality here.

It's amazing what people think people need here.

People need anything made of rubber here. People need anything made of plastic. People need Tupperware boxes and Ziploc bags and coated rubber bands for hair, Brooklyn Bridge cable kind of hair. People need Rubbermaid dish drainers – the metal kind, coated with rubber, and the rubber trays that go underneath them – so that the wooden counters on which dishes drain don't stay perpetually humid and rot. They need solid Rubbermaid garbage cans, with snap-on lids to keep rats away. People need things to stack, conserve, preserve, classify, label, repair. People need things to make the things they already have last, to repair them and organize them, for two-thirds of the population of Cuba was middle class and has devolved. If a Rubbermaid store opened in Cuba, people would be lined up around the block six lines deep. People need ties for plants. People need tomato stakes. People need gaskets. They need gaskets very badly. They need the thick gaskets that go around refrigerator doors and insulated gaskets for oven doors, and they need the rubber rings for espresso pots and canning jars. People need coated wire that bends. People need golf tees to pound into worn screw holes so that they can insert screws again, and the springs and tiny screws that go inside locks and door handles and window locks so that the rain doesn't come in more than it already does. People need sheets of expanded metal to repair the seats of broken outdoor furniture so they can sit and play dominoes and wait for things to change, and they need Rust-Oleum so that the outdoor furniture doesn't rust through again. People need Thompson's Water Seal. People need burner parts for gas stoves, and new burners for electric stoves, so that they don't have to cook over fires in their backyards and cut down more trees and make their asthma worse than it already is. People need asthma medicine. Cuba has the highest rate of asthma in the world, from the dust and the mold and the humidity, which they can't get rid of or escape from, for lack of parts.

III. 49

Tomorrow is Thea's ninth birthday. I dig in the trunk and find some presents, from the stash of kid presents I buy for future use every time I go abroad. I wrap them with used wrapping paper, blow up some balloons I bought in Mexico, put them in her room while she's sleeping, and then sleep myself until she and Jimmie start yelling at 7 A.M.

Plastic toys from China, the very cheapest kind, which fall apart after a few weeks, are available in only a few stores attached to tourist hotels here and cost five to ten times what they cost in Mexico or the United States.

III. 50

Very few vendors at the *agro* today. Miguel explains on the way home that it's because the smallest farmers can't make it any-more, with the new taxes they have to pay.

Miguel tells me that because of a continuing low hemoglobin level and asthma, his wife can't have the operation yet to take out the plate they put in her bone after she broke it. The government is giving her special ration cards to buy lamb, to keep her hemoglobin up. She is running a fever sometimes, because of the plate, but it is too risky to take it out.

I tell Miguel that a Canadian doctor I talked to in the United States who was in Cuba recently told me that Cuban medicine was good, but that it was about twenty years behind the times.

III. 51

I spend the next few days feeling bad that I said that to Miguel.

III. 52

I go with Carey and another visiting American woman, a friend of a friend whose handicapped husband is an advocate for the handicapped in Washington, D.C., to Pinar del Río to visit the Social Integration Laboratory of Vulnerable Groups – the first of its kind in Cuba. It is a cooperative project, sponsored by the Italian government, to rehabilitate and integrate groups that have been marginalized, either through handicaps, age, deformities, or the barrios (neighborhoods) in which they live.

Our Argentinean guide, Sergio, who works with the project, explains that several years ago Cuba approached Italy to buy rehabilitation equipment, but Italy, examining the health situation in Cuba, convinced the Ministry of Public Health to try something much more far-reaching.

'Cuba's approach since the *triunfo*,' Sergio quietly explains to us as we are walking to the hospital, 'has been to classify infirmities and to relegate them to specific institutions – a school for the retarded, a school for children with discipline problems, a school for deaf children, a school for blind children. There was a school for each infirmity in each province. This was very expensive, and when the *periodo especial* started, all special institutions were in crisis. Italy convinced Cuba to try, in an area of the country selected by the Cuban government, the general and specific ideas of a program that had been tested in northeastern Italy and had resulted in the successful closing of many institutions in Italy and large savings of public funds.

'The idea of the program,' Sergio continues, 'is to use Cuban institutions already at hand – of the *médico de familia*, the CDR, the Consejo Popular (Peoples' Council, or City Council) – and to introduce them to slightly new ideas and ways of operating.'

'You mean—'

'The idea is ultimately to demonstrate the effectiveness of the bottom-up, rather than the top-down, approach.'

We look at him.

'The Italian psychologists, physicians, and sociologists who have been involved in the program have had to tread so delicately,' Sergio explains softly.

We are at the hospital. Sergio introduces us to Lidia, the *pinareña* doctor who is the coordinator of the program, and

Rigoberto, who is the head of the Consejo Popular. Rigoberto is a *blanquito* in his early thirties, with the close-cropped hair and well-pressed madras shirt and khaki pants of a young cadre member.

Pipo, the spokesman for the handicapped, sits propped up by pillows in a wheelchair. He is severely handicapped, suffering from progressive muscular dystrophy, which causes his limbs to atrophy. He has already had one leg amputated and will soon be losing the other. We also meet his wife, a woman with cerebral palsy who sits next to him, holding his hand. They met at one of the first citywide meetings of the handicapped, and married recently. Pipo describes some of the programs.

'There were living, in Pinar del Río,' Pipo says, 'many handicapped people who had never seen the ocean, which is forty kilometers distant. Those who had never seen the ocean were taken to the beach. Buses were found. Food was prepared. Those who couldn't walk were carried onto the sand. *Compañero* (comrade) Rigoberto carried many handicapped *compañeros* himself.' Pipo's eyes grow liquid; his wife squeezes his hand.

'Seeing those people see the ocean was the most beautiful thing I have ever seen in my *whole life*,' Rigoberto declares strongly.

Rigoberto stands before us in the tiny community center of Comandante Pinares, in front of a giant 'Map of Challenges and Resources.' Comandante Pinares, a neighborhood built in 1982 to house those left homeless following Hurricane Andrew, was, until the introduction of the Social Integration Laboratory, the area of Pinar del Río that produced the greatest number of juvenile delinquents. Any streetlight in Comandante Pinares, Rigoberto tells us, would be broken by delinquents as soon as it was installed.

The map, a visual aid to community involvement, is a keystone of the laboratory's program. It is a map made by the residents of the Comandante Pinares neighborhood and surrounding neighborhoods. Above it, on one side of the map, is a list, compiled by the residents, of the community's needs and challenges; on the other side is a list of the resources the community has that can be used to address the problems.

In the audience are the *médico de familia* (local doctor) of Comandante Pinares, the head of the CDR (a black grandmother who, she tells us, lives in a house with twelve other people), a sanitation engineer, and a youth representative. This last is a tall, good-looking fifteen-year-old black girl who has had one arm amputated below the elbow.

Rigoberto is half-turned so as to read the map and speak to us at the same time. One of the challenges, Rigoberto reads, pointing to the map, is 'fecality in the air.' Fecality in the air, Rigoberto explains, is, after crime, the thing that bothers people most in Comandante Pinares.

All heads nod affirmatively.

The grandmother who is the head of the CDR explains to us that her greatest challenge was getting people to open up to her, to tell her what bothered them. 'I would go from house to house, and the people, they weren't used to someone coming to them, they were suspicious, they were used to decisions coming from on high, but I said to them, 'You can be part of the decision-making process, you can help us make our map.''

'And since people from here have gotten involved,' Rigoberto says, genuinely impressed, 'new streetlights have been put in and *not one* of them has been broken.'

Sergio softly explains to us on the way back to the car that low-level and midlevel administrators have been very receptive.

Carey mentions Dolly the cloned sheep at lunch with Sergio, Lidia, and our group. Lidia keeps eating her soup tranquilly. Lidia is an M.D. She also meets foreigners. Carey's Spanish is not perfect, either, and neither of us knows how to say *cloning*. Sergio translates. Lidia says she knows about genetic engineering.

Carey says she's not talking about genetic engineering; she's talking about the making of a genetically identical copy of a complex organism. She says it has been done, in Britain, and that there is now this duplicated sheep named Dolly. The news came out two weeks ago, in newspapers and magazines. Lidia drops her spoon. Her eyes open wide. She looks at us. Carey describes how the cloning was done. Lidia's eyes open wider. '*No me diga*,' Lidia says.

III. 53

Nick and I are greeting the first dinner guests when Piñeiro enters the room. When you invite Cuban officials to dinner, they often say they can come and then don't come, and you end up with an empty place. But sometimes you invite them, and they say they can't come, then show up anyway. Now here Piñeiro is, making thirteen at the table. It is very bad luck in X— to have thirteen at a table.

Nick stands in the pantry, cursing and dialing the telephone. He calls Fritz, his number one assistant, and orders him to come to make it fourteen. Lorena turns the flames down, and Manuel makes another round of *mojitos* as the table is unset, expanded, and reset by Danila and Concha, rubber soles squeaking excitedly on the marble.

Piñeiro, alias Barbaroja (Redbeard), the former head of intelligence, recently brushed aside (it is said, for favoring reforms), sports the classic orthodox look of neck hairs growing untrimmed upwards out of his collar to meet a tobacco-scented, untrimmed beard, and tight *guayabera* with stomach hairs poking through. Some say Piñeiro is responsible for hundreds of deaths; others say thousands; still, Piñeiro remains the favorite of the international set in Havana, because if you have to have an old revolutionary over, Piñeiro is the most schmooze-worthy. He listens well, of course – he has spent his life listening. His conversation, on good nights, is not the spouting of prejudices and platitudes. He speaks English well. He attended Columbia University, was kicked out, he says, for 'improper activities,' and is the ex-husband of Lorna, the blond woman from Connecticut who teaches dance at the childrens' school and is perpetually on the lookout for oatmeal to make cookies. Some even find Piñeiro charming, on good nights.

The true fascination of Piñeiro, of course, lies in the contemplation of the size and scope of the secrets contained in one unkempt head. He *knows* how Camilo Cienfuegos died, he *knows* how on purpose it was that Che was not resupplied in the Bolivian jungle, he *knows* up to what level Cuba's leadership was aware of drug trafficking out of Cuba in the eighties. *He* knows *all these things*, the foreigner thinks, *and here he is, in* my *living room, enjoying* my *scotch, sucking* my *food out of his dentures*. It is minuscule, Havana.

Some foreigners think, *Here he is,* and try to crack him – through charm, food, and drink – like a safe. He winks, drinks, smokes, guffaws, eats, insinuates, and drops phrases of American slang. They urge him to write his memoirs. He smiles crookedly, squeezes elbows. He is told that he can write his memoirs and put them in a box and seal the box for a hundred years. 'You think so?' he asks, cocking his head.

This is on good nights. Tonight, though, he asks the European ambassador sitting on my left if his country is against the common position recently taken by the European Union regarding investment in Cuba (which ties investment to improvements in human rights and is more in accordance with the position of the United States). The European ambassador states that the position recently taken is a *common* position. Piñeiro says that he knows that is what they *say,* but his European country was really against it, right? The European ambassador, his face reddening, repeats that the position the European Union took is a *common* position. Piñeiro then says that he hopes that the ambassador's particular European country is not sacrificing its dignity and its sovereignty on the issue. Piñeiro's voice is raised, and his speech is slurred. *Dignidad* and *soberanía* are favorite words in orthodox speeches. The European ambassador looks at Piñeiro incredulously and says that his country remains *very independent* of the United States in its decision-making process . . .

A Spanish woman sitting beside Piñeiro bumps him with her shoulder. 'Leave it, *hombre,*' she says to Piñeiro.

Piñeiro slaps his chest. 'We have balls!'

'Ay, balls again,' the Spanish woman says, sighing. 'Don't be this . . . thing that everyone expects you to be . . . like something out of *National Geographic.*'

Piñeiro looks at me, ignoring her. He leans forward. 'I have nothing against the American *people*. It's the politicians—'

'But the politicians are elected *by the American people*!' the Spanish woman says, cupping her hands around her mouth and speaking into his ear.

'Only thirty percent of the people!' Piñeiro leans back smiling against his seat.

III. 54

An empty tanker has sunk – Italian, registered in Panama, with six Cuban crew members lost; another tanker on the way to Cienfuegos has sunk (the word is there was 'an explosion on board'); there was a bomb in the nightclub Aché, attached to the Meliá Cohiba Hotel; and a munitions warehouse blew up in Pinar del Río, sending bullets flying.

The Cuban government has asked the press not to write about the bomb in the Meliá Cohiba Hotel.

Nobody except the army can have explosives here.

There is speculation that the United States' Transition document, which details the role the armed forces could play in Cuba's transition to democracy, is being considered.

WE ARE TOLD BY a friend who was there that Eusebio Leal, the city historian and head of the corporation restoring Old Havana, gave a speech in Old Havana in which he declares that there needs to be greater respect in Cuba for human freedoms.

Some officials, we are told, looked down at their shoes as he spoke. We are also told Leal swept out of the room without shaking anyone's hand when the speech was over.

'*PE PE HAY, PE PE HAY* . . .' ('PPG,' an anti-impotence drug, pronounced *pe pe hay*). Young men and boys follow us and others in their forties and older in the Plaza de la Catedral muttering the name of the drug, trying to sell it to us.

'No, *gracias*,' Nick says sunnily.

'*Pe Pe Hay, Pe Pe Hay* . . .' They will not stop.

I turn to the two following us. I put my hands on my hips. '*Mi marido no necesita PPG!*' ('My husband *does not* need PPG!').

'*Señora, felicidades! Estamos tan contentos para ustedes!*' ('Congratulations! We are so happy for you both!').

A SWEEP OF *JINETERAS* before the May Day parade: The agents go in plain cars, with license plates that say TUR for *turista*. They pretend they are customers, then take the girls to waiting buses.

THE BIGGEST MAY DAY parade ever.

Jineteras are back on the street hours after it's over. I don't know how it is possible with the sweep that happened just days before. When they are picked up, *jineteras* are usually trucked into fields to harvest sweet potatoes and other tubers and stay out of circulation for weeks. These must be other *jineteras*, waiting in the wings.

Also hours after the parade, while we are stopped at a streetlight, a man shoves his arm into the car. 'Give me money! Give me money!' he screams.

III. 55

Mrs. Fleites – the Bette Midler look-alike at the school, whose parents 'went to Brooklyn because of Batista and returned to Cuba because of Castro' – and her husband catch up to me on the street, just outside of the school. She says she has a favor to ask of me.

Mrs. Fleites says she wants to travel to the United States this summer, but she needs an invitation from a U.S. citizen. There is a person she knows, a U.S. citizen, who is going to go with her tomorrow to the Consultoria Juridica (the place that certifies invitations to travel abroad), but the person may not be able to make it. She is wondering if, in case the person doesn't show up, I would be able to go with her to draw up an invitation letter. The place is just down the street from the school. It is just a formality.

I look from Mrs. Fleites to her husband. They are both nearly hopping, from one leg to another.

MRS. FLEITES CATCHES UP to me outside the school. She says the person she thought was going to go with her to the Consultoria Juridica is going to be able to make it after all. I will not have to go with her.

I am relieved.

III. 56

Juana tells me how her brother Ernesto, who now lives in Texas, got out of Cuba and into the United States.

Ernesto was determined to get to the United States in style: he didn't want to get in a *balsa* or be a wetback. Ernesto is an engineer. He has blond hair and blue eyes. Ernesto was often sent by the Cuban government to Mexico. Ernesto contacted some relatives in Texas. The relatives studied the situation in some border towns. They found a town – Juana doesn't remember the name of it – where U.S. college students go over the border into Mexico for the weekend, to drink and visit prostitutes. The relatives drove over the border in their car on a Sunday afternoon. They took with them some *yanqui* clothes: chino pants, a Lacoste shirt, Nike sneakers. They met Ernesto. Ernesto dressed in the *yanqui* clothes. He sat in the backseat of their car, between some relatives. The only American word Ernesto knew was *yup*. They went back over the border on Sunday night, when all the college students were returning from their weekend. There were so many people going back to the United States that the border guards couldn't check every car; they only checked the cars with Mexican plates or the cars with people in them who looked like Mexicans.

A guard shined a light in the backseat. 'You all Americans here?'

'Yup,' Ernesto said, and in they went.

'This is racism in action,' I say to Juana.

III. 57

Nick and I go to a performance of Tania Bruguera, plus a show of the works of fifteen other artists at the Faculty of Arts and Letters. It is one of the shows that is not part of, but is taking place around, the Havana Biennial.

The artists who are in the show lie in a circle on the floor. Tania, dressed vaguely as a sheep, walks on the bodies, planting red flags on them as she walks. At each body, she also binds either their mouths, their eyes, their hands, or their feet with red cloth. She then steps out into the audience, planting red flags and binding mouths, eyes, hands, and feet.

Alexis Esquivel has a piece in the show called *The Machine for the Fabrication of Tradition*. It consists of a row of Plexiglas boxes filled to varying degrees with water. A fighting fish is in each box. Above each box, a tube leading from a suspended intravenous bag drips water. Soon the fullest box will overflow, carrying a fighting fish with it into the adjacent box, to fight with the other fighting fish until death.

In a room marked LADIES ROOM there is a small bronze statue of a *guajiro* astride a giant penis – his own, but three times the size of his body. The foreskin is pulled back, and out of the head of the penis sprout the antennae of a snail. Testicles trail out the back. It is a plan for a monumental sculpture to be mounted at the entrance to the art school. There is a blown-up photograph of the sculpture, glued onto a photo of the entrance to the art school, so that you can see how it will look.

III. 58

Dinner at a European banker's house. An American diplomat is there. This is convenient because we want to hear the other side behind the headlines in today's issue of *Granma*: U.S. CONDUCTS BIOLOGICAL WARFARE AGAINST CUBA. An article states that a parasite is attacking the potato crop in Matanzas just where an American crop duster had crossed the island several months ago, emitting a cloud of black smoke.

The diplomat says the crop duster was on its way to Colombia. A Cuban airliner was getting too close, so it let out some smoke. The diplomat says he remembers Carlos Lage (a vice-president) complaining to him about the parasite a few months ago. The diplomat says the funny thing is that when the crop duster incident occurred, they gave the Cubans the explanation about the airliner getting too close and the Cubans seemed to be happy with that. Now they send a letter to the United Nations and to all its members, without even bringing it up with the United States first. It's probably because they have had a very bad potato harvest and need to come up with some reason. No news lately about the sugar harvest, so it must be pretty bad, too.

III. 59

News of the United States' biological aggression against Cuba has disappeared utterly from the news.

NICK DECLARES AT DINNER that Cuba combines the *souplesse* of Africa with the surrealism of Spain.

A LOW-RANKING U.S. diplomat speculates that the reason for the appearance and rapid disappearance of the U.S. biological aggression story is that the Cubans are continuing to expand their chemical and biological weapons program, in spite of their having signed a treaty, and if the United States ever calls them on it, they want to be able to point to U.S. biological aggression against potatoes in Matanzas. Making a story appear and disappear is a kind of putting-it-in-the-file, he says, for future use.

ARTICLES APPEAR IN THE *Miami Herald* stating that Cuba may be developing anthrax, and that Cuba has the capability of wiping out three million people in southern Florida before being itself wiped out.

It is true that a few weeks ago Fidel gave a speech about Cuba's being a 'poisoned lamb in the mouth of the beast' in the event of U.S. aggression.

NICK ASKS A DOCTOR who is visiting us how long it usually takes before Parkinson's begins to affect thought processes.

TOMATOES ARE ENDING now at the *agropecuario*, not to reappear until October.

WE REVISIT LA CABAÑA, the higher of the two Spanish forts overlooking Havana harbor, where most of the exhibitions of the biennial are taking place. Installations in one sixteenth-century barracks room after another. The theme is memory, and since most of the artists are from Latin America, most of the installations are about violence. Lázaro Saavedra, a Cuban artist, has a piece near the end of the show, in front of the *paredón*, or wall where enemies of the revolution were shot. The wall is in a grassy, elevated square, reached by a ramp. A flame tree is in flower in one corner. Havana harbor is visible through a crack in the ramparts on one side. A cement wall was built in front of the sixteenth-century wall when the number of executions started accelerating, so as not to further damage the ancient wall. The new wall was made more porous than the fort wall to absorb ricochets. We can see the deep gouges the bullets made, in three lines – head, chest, legs. Nick wonders why they would shoot legs.

In front of the wall, Saavedra has put tombstones, thin slabs embedded in piles of stones. There are about thirty of them. Many of them have fallen over, and whether they were installed already fallen over, or fell over later, or were put in sloppily so that they would fall over, one by one, eventually, we don't know. We walk on a stone walkway to the wall, turn left, and enter a long, narrow, airless, vaulted room. On the way, we pass the title of the installation: *Buried by Forgetting*. There are more tombstones in the room. At the end of the room, painted on its wall, are three figures, mostly human but with some elements of birds in them (their mouths are more like beaks), hurtling headfirst from the sky and spewing stones from their open mouths – actual stones are glued onto the wall below them, leading to a pile of stones heaped on the floor, out of which human legs and arms protrude. The bird-humans are machine guns of vituperation. It is hard to stay in the room. It is hard to breathe in it. Turning to leave, we see a cross, placed over the entrance to the room. The cross is placed so that you see it only as you are leaving.

III. 60

Fidel gives a speech in which he declares that internal immigration from eastern provinces is a threat to national sovereignty. It is a threat to national sovereignty because it has led to a rise in delinquency in the capital, and a rise in delinquency can lead to instability, instability in which CIA infiltrators can do their work.

III. 61

The right-wing Spanish newspaper *ABC* writes that three hundred thousand *orientales* have been deported back to Oriente province or trucked to cane fields to cut sugarcane.

Three hundred thousand is nearly one-sixth of the population of Havana.

When, where, I ask Lety on the way to the Tocororo, were the *orientales* rounded up, where were the trucks and buses, driving them off? I ask her if it happened in the middle of the night.

Without answering my question, Lety launches into how *orientales* are the most proud, the most *machista* of macho Cubans: "No one is more beautiful, no one more intelligent than I,' that sort of thing.' Lety preens in the car seat. 'Their expectations are too high. It's the problem of *tu lo sabes* (you know who). *Es puro orientale . . . Y también es delincuente!'* ('He's a pure Oriental . . . And he is a delinquent, too!'), Lety yells, laughing at her own joke.

'But how were they deported?'

'*Yo no sé*' (I don't know).

LETY CAN NO LONGER rent out a house her parents left her, which she has been renting to foreigners. There are too many laws and taxes now. She says she knew it was too good to last.

III. 62

The Palestinian ambassador is annoyed. He says a letter has just been sent to all embassies, stating that ambassadors will no longer be allowed to use the protocol lounge at the airport. The Palestinian ambassador says this is because some diplomats were using it for smuggling items out in their hand luggage.

'What sorts of things were they smuggling?' Nick asks.

'Artwork, antiques, black-market cigars . . .'

'No.'

'Yes.'

The ambassador says diplomats are being blamed for a general problem. Now ambassadors will have to use the VIP lounge and be there with businessmen and their *jineteras*.

'I beg your pardon?' Nick says.

'*Ay, disculpe*,' the ambassador says, patting Nick's arm.

III. 63

Crowds of people on a street corner in Habana Vieja. Half a building has collapsed. It is the half with the stairwell in it. Men, women, and children stand in every window of the remaining half of the five-story building. Firemen have pulled an extension ladder out of a truck. They are working the levers, trying to get it to stay up.

'Don't move!' one fireman shouts to the people in the windows. 'Don't make any movements, or the rest of the building will fall, too!'

III. 64

Pretty heated discussion at the parents' meeting at school. The school is a sweet school, but it is not challenging, especially for children whose parents are native English speakers. Two educators have come from Virginia to counsel the teachers, and the meeting is ostensibly for the parents to meet them. There was not going to be any talk of accreditation at the meeting, but the parents raise the topic. They want the school to be up to some kind of standard, somewhere. A representative of the business community says the businesspeople are especially concerned. The businesspeople are concerned because if they cannot find successors – if successors are discouraged from coming because the school is not good enough – it means that they, the present businesspeople, will be stuck in Cuba *forever*!

One Norwegian father says that he doesn't understand why they don't just plunk the kids down and give them standardized exams from time to time so that everyone knows where their kids stand.

One educator says it isn't accreditation and standardized tests that are going to get them into MIT . . .

The businesspeople and some diplomats don't let her finish. There is a loud grumbling. 'We need exams, we need accreditation, we need standards!' an Indian father says, slapping his hand with a rolled-up magazine on each word.

I put my pearls in my pocket and walk down Quinta after the school meeting to a dinner party we have been invited to, where Nick will meet me. Young Cuban men start muttering things and blowing kisses at me from a bench on the median strip. True, it is dusk, I'm not fat, and they can't make out much about me, but when you get to be forty-five and are beginning to look like a turtle, you wish you felt safe enough to be able to turn and ask them, *Are you doing this because you think I am attractive, because you think I am ugly and need the attention, or just because . . . ?* Just so you'd know where you, or at least they, stand. It, too, is an accreditation process.

At the party, one ambassador's wife says that even if the accreditation process takes five years, they shouldn't worry, because in five years, things are going to be a lot different here anyway, and maybe some of the twenty or more English-language-based schools that were here before the revolution might find their way back.

'Five years?' I say.

III. 65

Nick and I are introduced at a lunch to Báez, an official Cuban journalist. He has just written a book called *Secrets of the Generals*. Báez says Fidel didn't read the book before it was published. It was commissioned and organized, though, by Raúl. Lowering his voice and looking around, Báez says that at first the generals didn't *want* to talk, and I am thinking it is not just Reny who makes me think of *Alice in Wonderland*.

RENY AND I SPEAK about blackouts. He says he never has *apagones* where he lives because he lives near a lot of important people and the Sección de Intereses. I say sotto voce to Reny that *los yanquis* have to pay for the embargo by having *apagones* like everyone else.

Reny looks around and, lowering his voice, speaks about repression at the biennial, about artists who were not allowed to show in some galleries. 'This is the *war* they are making,' he says.

Reny is wearing a long-sleeved linen *guayabera* with a blue-and-white polka-dot butterfly necktie and two-tone shoes. I tell him I really like his look tonight, and he says it's men's formal dress from before *el triunfo*.

I say the greater war at the moment seems to be against *cuentapropistas*, against people who work for themselves or rent out houses.

Reny spies a *duro* within earshot and steers me to the side of the room. Reny then says that it is too bad the government is doing that, because people were using the money to restore their houses, to make them presentable for *tourists*, to bring in more money for *everyone*. They don't want to renovate *just for their own selves*.

I know I should stop, but I think I will just say one more little thing, and I say that the government prefers to shoot itself in the foot.

III. 66

The Cuban Communist Party Congress, which convenes every five years, has just ended, making no concessions and calling for greater sacrifice on the part of the people.

A law was on the table that would have allowed for the creation of private small- and medium-sized enterprises, but it was not passed because it would give too much satisfaction to the United States.

'Oh, *come on!*'

'I am not kidding,' a low-level European diplomat says to me at a cocktail party. 'That is how a Cuban official explained it to me.'

'I *can't believe it.*'

'It's not like anyone ever said we were dealing with emotional maturity here,' the European diplomat says after a pause.

Someone asks, at the same cocktail party, if anyone remembers the song 'Limbo Rock.'

Others check for Cubans and, when they don't see any, start bending their knees and leaning back and singing, 'Every limbo boy and girl . . . and how *low* can you go?'

A MICROPHONE IS FOUND in the wall behind the bed of the French ambassador, one of the few *viva la revolución* diplomats.

It is said he was so v*iva la revolución* that they couldn't believe it.

THE PALESTINIAN AMBASSADOR says another letter has gone out, saying that ambassadors and their wives and children could still use the protocol lounge, but that lower diplomats and their family members had to use the VIP lounge from now on.

'*MIRA COMO A ELLOS LES PASA TAMBIÉN*' ('Look how it also happens to them'), Lety says when I tell her about the letters going out to the embassies. 'First, the government announces to us we can never have any eggs again, and we say, 'No eggs! How will we get along?' Then after that, the government says, 'OK, you can have eggs, but only four eggs a month,' and everyone says, 'How wonderful! We can have four eggs a month!''

234

People are getting fatter. I don't know how it's happening, but they are. There are not as many thin people, in washed-thin shirts and dresses and broken tennis shoes, struggling down streets with their last bits of strength; many amble now, with half-full shopping bags. Some bicycle home from the *agros* with three-pound lettuces tied on the backs. There are not as many people pleading for *fulas* or talking to themselves. There are not as many people waiting in line at the Coppelia for ice cream, which was for a while – when milk was not available to families with children over seven years old – the only place to find calcium. People can buy fresh cheese now from the Diplo, if they have dollars, or from friends and neighbors who bring it from the country. There is more gasoline and there are more cars and motorcycles. Our street is much noisier. People with access to dollars even have new clothes. There is more hair dye available, and superfluous hair bleach and makeup, and the styles of shoes people have on their feet are more varied.

Buildings are being done over, too, in Habana Vieja and on Quinta Avenida. In Habana Vieja they are being done over by Eusebio Leal, but on Quinta and in parts of Siboney and Cubanacán, they are being leased by foreign companies who are renovating them. There is a patisserie *française* on a side street in Siboney, offering croissants, éclairs, and cakes. It is air-conditioned and the windows and tables are clean and there is no guard at the door, and foreigners and Cubans with dollars go in it on Sunday mornings, when they are out walking their dogs, and sit side by side and are treated with equal importance, just like in most pastry shops in the world.

Cubans without dollars can't buy anything at the patisserie, but they can at least enter the patisserie and look and no one makes a fuss, and of all the shops in Havana, it is the shop in which one feels a little less Marie-Antoinette–like – and it's a patisserie *française*, of all places.

III. 68

I hear the story of the Swiss pastry chef, the *jinetera*, and her *marinovio*. A twenty-seven-year-old pastry chef, living in Switzerland, was in love for several years with a *jinetera* he met on his first vacation in Cuba. The *jinetera* was married to a Cuban, or was living with a Cuban and either was divorced or had done *divorcio a lo cubano*: that is, she had gotten involved with the Swiss chef as a way of bringing in extra income with the consent of the *marinovio*. The *marinovio* would make himself scarce when the Swiss was in town. The *jinetera* had two children, the first one with the *marinovio*, and the second one – it is not clear whether it was with the ex-*marinovio*, the Swiss, or someone else. The Swiss knew the *marinovio*, but the *jinetera* always said he was her cousin, the children were trained not to call him Papa, and the Swiss didn't suspect a thing. The *jinetera* and the Swiss started to make plans to go to Switzerland, and the *marinovio* (when the Swiss was absent) freaked out and smashed all the furniture in the *jinetera*'s apartment. The Swiss thought it was an extreme reaction for someone who was just a cousin, but the *jinetera* told him, 'My cousin is just concerned that I will be leaving my children behind.' The *jinetera* did not press any charges, and the Swiss bought her all new furniture.

Three days ago, the *marinovio* stabbed the Swiss in the chest. The Swiss went after him until the *marinovio* shot him, execution style, behind the ear. The *marinovio* then picked up the body and threw it off the terrace onto the street. The person who told me the story didn't know where the *jinetera* was at that point, but the *marinovio* let the oldest child go and took the youngest child and kept a gun to its head. The block was cordoned off; psychologists were called. The standoff lasted for many hours, but the *marinovio* finally surrendered.

III. 69

Nick is depressed. He always gets depressed, he says, in June, when the kids and I take off. He joins us when he can, but he usually has to spend six weeks alone. It's the heat, he says, and the fact that he's alone, and the shoddiness and the idea that things now will only get shoddier. Even if there *is* a change, at this point he doesn't see how things can ever be anything *but* shoddy, they are so far gone already: grim hotels, sad restaurants, *jineteras* and *jineteros* with it all out there, every single minute.

'And *paladares* and beaches and orchids and music . . .' I say stupidly, as if I have to be up when he is down, like carousel horses.

It's for the *children* that I leave, I tell myself. They need fresh air. They also need to see another kind of world from time to time. If it weren't for the children, I'd be right here with him, *sharing* the shoddiness, I tell Nick, I really would.

III. 70

Torrential rain, making lakes of intersections. Cars drive on the hump in the middle of the road but still make waves. We watch from the balcony overlooking the street. Waves wash up under the gates of the driveway. A dinner is canceled, because cars can't get to our house. The children are restless. The rain doesn't take away the heat; it only makes it steamy. 'For Daddy's next job, can we go to *Norway*?' they ask. Only four more days until summer vacation. The children draw grids on several pieces of paper and write an hour in each square, crossing the hours off as they pass.

III. 71

Miguel and I try to cross the river to go to the *agro* in Vedado, where I have heard there is still spinach, but both the Quinta and Socialism or Death tunnels are closed. We try to get to the bridge over the Almendares, but the traffic leading to it is so thick that we finally give up and go to the *agro* on Forty-second Street.

There is no spinach and no rice, and flies dot hunks of pork like raisins on a pudding. I *do* find watercress, though, a big bunch, unusual for this time of year, and so we are able to have salad for dinner.

I check with Nick as we eat our watercress, asking him if eating a vegetable he hasn't eaten for a while makes him as happy as it makes me, and Nick says it sends him absolutely over the moon.

The Fourth
School Year

IV. 1

Back from vacation with four hundred pounds of luggage, the usual haul. Twelve hours and three different airplanes, it takes us, to get from Newark to Havana.

Tums, we bring back for the help, Pepto-Bismol, Advil, Tagamet, foot powder, corn pads, false-teeth adhesive, hemorrhoidal suppositories, antibacterial soap, vitamins E and C, multivitamins, calcium pills, cod-liver oil pills, support stockings, underpants, bras, socks, raincoats, and sneakers. For ourselves, we bring tennis balls, books, a dish rack, ten pounds of kid's snack food, and sneakers, sandals, and dress shoes one and two sizes bigger so the kids won't run out, as well as every size of Ziploc bag and photo sleeve so we won't have to depend on visitors.

I am wondering if this is the last time I will have to make such a haul.

I hold out my hand to shake hands with the baby-faced guard who was there before we left, and before I know it, he kisses me on both cheeks.

THERE WERE FOUR BOMBS in one day while we were gone – three fifteen minutes apart at the Triton, Chateau Miramar, and Copacabana and one later in the day at the Bodeguita del Medio. An Italian was killed at the Copacabana while sitting in the bar with his father. He was hit in the jugular vein by a shard from a glass ashtray and bled to death. An El Salvadoran was caught, a mercenary trained in Georgia, the TV says, and paid by the Cuban-American National Foundation.

I FIND A SATIN BOW among my stash of present-wrapping supplies and carry it to the veranda along with a small aluminum suitcase I have brought from the United States. It's the kind of suitcase used for carrying camera equipment, lined with foam rubber. I tie the bow on the handle and put it on Nick's chair before he comes down for breakfast.

'Surprise!' I say as Nick unlocks the suitcase with a tiny key. Nick has already been back in Cuba for two weeks.

Inside are two dozen half-ripe beefsteak tomatoes.

A SMIRKING CUBAN NEWSCASTER reports that the Cuban government finds it incredible that security forces as efficient as those in the United States were not able to know about the attempts beforehand.

NO SUGAR OR FLOUR at the Diplo, Lorena reports.

THE POPE IS COMING. It is confirmed now. He will come in January.

IV. 2

Jaime, a gay Cuban man in his fifties, comes for dinner. Jaime tells us he was out for dinner with a friend at a *paladar* when they got the idea to go to the nightclub Perikiton because his friend had never been. The Perikiton, basically a large fenced-in open-air space, started as a place for gays, but now more than half the people who go there are straight. There were between three and four thousand people there the night Jaime and his friend went. The Spanish director Almodóvar was there, as well as the actress Bibi Andersson and the French fashion designer Jean-Paul Gaultier. Jaime and his friend were standing there, remarking how whenever they were in a place like that, they always felt that they had to be on their guard, because of what used to happen in the old days. They were just saying that, when suddenly there were screams and they felt themselves being shoved by a wave of people. Plainclothes policemen scattered throughout the crowd pulled out guns. They herded everyone outside – foreigners on one side, and Cubans on the other. They had waited for Almodóvar and Bibi Andersson to leave before they busted the club, but they didn't know about Gaultier. All the Cubans were photographed, then loaded into one set of buses, and all foreigners were loaded into another. Cubans had to pay fines of thirty pesos each, but the foreigners were set free. We ask Jaime what the charges were, but Jaime says he doesn't know. Jaime says that he and his friend, for some reason, were allowed to leave. '*Pasa, pasa,*' a guard said to them. They got in their car and started to drive away, when another guard stood in front of their car and said, 'Who do you think you are? Diplomats?' They had to get out of their car and be checked all over again.

I say that I thought it was no big deal anymore in Cuba when someone was gay.

Jaime says the roundup was designed to humiliate.

I say you can humiliate large numbers of people up to a certain point, but humiliating *four thousand* people on an island of eleven million seems kind of counterproductive.

Jaime says they don't see it that way.

IV. 3

Mrs. Fleites *se quedó* ('stayed,' which in Cuba means 'went for a visit to another country and stayed'), another teacher tells me. She will not be coming back. She is making a living for the time being giving private English lessons in Miami.

'But what about her husband?'

'It's *divorcio a lo cubano*. He will get to Miami someday, or maybe not.'

MRS. FLEITES IS GONE, the first-grade teacher is gone, too, and the school's Spanish teacher and Gonzalo and Raulito, a man who sold us fruit out of the back of his 1959 Nash Rambler. Now they live in Miami, in Venezuela, in Michigan, in Canada. Most slip away, but the fruit man announced, 'I'm going. Maybe I will stay.' One friend's brother left in a boat. He now has a job in a bakery, and a house and car. A film critic, too, has gone. He went to teach a course at a U.S. university and stayed. His wife and children are trying to join him and have been given refugee status so that they can now travel to the United States, but they still have not been allowed to leave Cuba. The film critic's wife lived all right for a year after her husband left, but now that she has been given refugee status, her son and daughter have been kicked out of school and she has lost her job. Still the family has not been given an exit permit.

A TEACHER AT THE school gives me a slip of paper. 'This is Mrs. Fleites's telephone number in Miami. She wants you to call her the next time you are there.'

I spend the next few minutes thinking about how much I will not call Mrs. Fleites.

IV. 4

I go to Lola's. A friend of a friend has gotten in touch with me over the summer. She is a Cuban American who left Cuba in the early sixties, along with her whole family. She married an American American ' and has one son. She meant never to return to Cuba, but now she is feeling more like visiting if only to show Cuba to her son. I tell Lola that she doesn't want to visit like a regular tourist. She wants a car, a driver. She wants to stay in people's houses.

Lola moves her abundant body to the edge of her chair. She asks me where the woman is from. I say her family is from Camagüey. They had a ranch there, but she grew up in Havana. Lola says she can find her and her husband and son a car, a driver, and places to stay in Havana, in Camagüey, and in places along the way to Camagüey if they are interested in stopping. Lola then says she also knows someone in the archives department and that if my friend needs any deeds or any other kind of documentation, her friend could get them for her.

I ask Lola if her friend could get into trouble for that.

Lola explains patiently to me that the deeds in the archives are the deeds of *private* properties that were taken over, just taken over by the government . . .

I ask Lola if she could get into trouble for that, and Lola explains patiently that people have to make a living.

IV. 5

A party in yet another spacious but dilapidated mansion in

Cubanacán. The host is yet another European man of about fifty-five with adolescent Cuban girlfriend, this time a six-footer in a backless polyester evening dress and sixties hairdo. Her long face is sullen, as if she doesn't know who to blame for being in that dress with that hair in that place. A Middle Eastern ambassador, about fifty, is also there with his adolescent girlfriend. Both the host and the ambassador look utterly unembarrassed. The Middle Eastern ambassador tells us he knew the Italian who was blown up in the blast.

There is a buffet of rice casserole colored bright green with food dye and pasta salad heavy on the mayo. The host says he hasn't been back to Europe in a long time. Nick whispers in my ear that this is obvious. The host, squeezing the waist of his slouching girlfriend, says he doesn't know why anyone would want to go. The host wears a white linen suit over a black T-shirt. He is in the import-export business. Medicines, he says.

Nick says he has to get his secretary to explain better to him, when an invitation comes, who exactly is inviting us.

LOLA TAKES US TO a pleasant modern house in Miramar, where we are greeted by a couple and led into an air-conditioned bedroom. The shutters are closed. The man carries a zippered case. He takes out a piece of green felt and lays it on the bed. He then takes out one piece of jewelry after another. He takes out necklaces, bracelets, earrings, and rings. Some have diamonds in them, some, sapphires, some, rubies, and some, emeralds. They are pieces from the end of the nineteenth century. He takes out a necklace with matching earrings and a massive, diamond-encrusted cross. He takes out a diamond necklace. 'They are from my family,' he says. 'We have to sell them because we want to renovate our house so we can rent it full-time.' It's getting trickier all the time to rent out houses, but people still do it. A miniature poodle tries to make love to my foot and has to be pried off. The diamond necklace is worth twenty thousand dollars. We select two smaller bracelets, art deco style with diamonds and sapphires. They are wrapped in smoothed-out pieces of Kleenex, which we are assured are clean, and put in the bottom of my purse.

I SEND A MESSAGE to the Cuban American through a friend of a friend who is traveling to the United States, detailing what Lola can do for her. The Cuban American gets back to me through the friend of a friend, saying she and her family have changed their minds about traveling to Cuba.

IV. 6

I ask Concha how her children, both of whom live in the United States now, are doing. She says they are doing very well. Daniel, who left first, has a job managing a tobacco warehouse in Tampa. 'The Americans in Tampa, they don't like Cubans, but for Daniel the owner makes an exception. Daniel says to me, 'It's not like in Cuba, Mommy: here you have to work.' He has bought a small *yate* (yacht), which he is fixing up.'

I ask Concha if there are a lot of Cubans in Tampa.

'Very few,' she says, 'but the ones who are there are Communists.'

'Communists?'

'They get there, then complain that they have to work.'

IV. 7

The El Salvadoran bomber who placed the bombs at the hotels and at the Bodeguita del Medio appears on television. There is a lot of hype about his television appearance beforehand. Officials move through a cocktail party we attend, telling all foreigners to watch the news at 8:30.

The bomber is a very young, very Native American– looking guy. He says he exploded all the bombs, including ones earlier at the Capri and the Nacional. He says his *s*'s precisely, the way Mexicans do. He demonstrates how he brought the explosives in, in the back of a television. He unscrews the back of a television and points out the hiding places inside it. The bomber also says to the journalist that he was part of a group of terrorist *narcotraficantes* financed by the Miami-based Cuban-American National Foundation, but neither he nor the Ministry of the Interior spokesman give other supporting details.

'GIVE US THE SUPPORTING details and we'll go after them,' Mike Kozak, the new chief officer at the U.S. Interests Section, says he says to them, but they won't do it. Mike says they believe that the U.S. government already knows everything there is to know about the CANF and its activities.

IV. 8

Roberto is tan to the point of looking weather-beaten and very thin after the summer, like a man dragging himself out of the desert. He has had no income for the three months that we have been away. I told him when he started that he had to be prepared for that, and I'm trying not to feel responsible, but still he is twenty-nine and has a degree in computer science. Roberto's blue eyes look even bluer and his hair is bleached almost white from the sun. When I remark on how tan he is, he says he is tan because he got divorced, moved back into his family's house, and spent the summer working on his parents' patio and garden because there was nothing else to do.

I say I am sorry about the divorce, and he shrugs and says, '*Eso no es nada.*'

We have no visitors, so I give Roberto our iron to fix. In addition to knowing computers inside and out, Roberto can also fix appliances. The iron is a Black & Decker that I brought to Cuba only six months ago from the United States. Roberto takes the iron apart and says the *resistencia* is broken. He says he will take it to a friend who he thinks will have some *resistencias*.

IV. 9

Roberto's friend has no *resistencias*. I tell Roberto to take the car and look for an iron so that our firm can apply for permission to buy an iron and then we can send someone from the firm to buy it, a process that can sometimes take weeks. Cubans are not allowed to buy high-energy-consuming appliances, such as irons, air conditioners, and microwave ovens, and non-Cubans can buy them only with permission and only from special stores. Estrella has very kindly loaned us her iron (acquired when Cubans were still able to buy irons), but we can't keep it forever.

ROBERTO SPENDS THE WHOLE day driving around Havana,

checking in every store where there might be an iron. *Nada.*

I call the secretary in Nick's firm who is in charge of material things since Ivan has gone. I don't like to deal with her because she is so deer-in-the-headlights about stuff. After a painful question-and-answer session, I finally get it out of her that the Korean firm GoldStar, the most recent company to supply irons to Cuba, used to sell directly to firms and embassies but now sells to Cubalse, who are in turn supposed to sell them to firms and embassies, but the irons disappear from the Cubalse warehouses before they are able to sell them, the result being that there are no irons to be found anywhere in Havana. She says I will have to ask someone in Mexico or Panama to *conseguir* one and ship it to us.

THERE MAY NOT BE visitors for quite a while, I tell Roberto, but I tell him I will pay him ten dollars per week to give computer lessons to Jimmie. Forty dollars per month, plus the twenty he has just made driving around Havana looking for an iron, should help to tide him over until visitors arrive.

IV. 10

A diplomat tells us that Piñeiro told him at a small lunch that the bombings were arranged by a secret military cell within the Cuban-American National Foundation and that the U.S. government knows about it and supports it. He says it is impossible to have enough security at Cuban airports and that the bombings will probably happen again.

We ask the diplomat if Piñeiro was less cootlike when you got him alone, the way people said he was, and the diplomat (who, though not a native English speaker, possesses an extensive English vocabulary) says without skipping a beat that during the lunch Piñeiro was, on a scale of cootlikeness, about a four, but he's seen him as high as nine and as low as two. It has to do with whether *reformistas* or *duros* are in ascendancy, the diplomat says, and how much Piñeiro has had to drink. Piñeiro even expressed the view that it is Fidel himself, who has the charisma, who must initiate change – now – to prevent a total collapse of society following his death.

Coot is a word I've dusted off recently. I have looked it up in the dictionary to be sure of all its meanings: 'coot (koot) *n* 1. a kind of waterbird, especially one with a horny white plate on its forehead. 2. (informal) a stubborn or foolish man: *an old coot.*' I have taught it to Nick. I have also taught Nick the words *geezer* and *codger* and have discussed with him how they differ from one another and from *coot.*

There are geezers and coots in both Havana and Miami, we agree, but codgers, who are fatter, are only in Miami.

This is a cootocracy, I say to Nick: bearded, fragile, isolated, in ill-fitting clothes, unchallenged, long fingernailed, muttering to itself, obsessing about the reality of forty years ago, because in the end, not enough human beings feel strongly enough on the planet.

Nick gets up from the table and turns off all the electric lights, and I realize that I am being a bore again, the way I am getting to be more and more these days.

The generator hums. There is an *apagón* in the neighborhood, making the circle of candlelight at the garden table where we eat our dinner even more of a cocoon, or like an illustration from some old-fashioned storybook, our little circle bathed in rings of yellow watercolor. A night-blooming jasmine is in flower nearby, its perfume wafting over us. Elephant's ears nodding next to the table deflect a drip from the air conditioner above us in a way that seems to agree with them, for they have grown huge since we planted them, and the ferns we planted underneath the elephant's ears seem to like the drip as well, for they are furry with health. A double hibiscus, whose blooms are in the process of closing for the night, arches over Nick's head.

We eat grilled shrimps with lime juice and garlic; rice and white beans cooked with garlic, onion, ham, and minced sweet pepper; avocado salad; and homemade bread. Insects sing. A green lizard on the wall, our nightly companion, distends a bloodred bladder under his chin. Dogs bark in the distance and our talk fades, as it often does now in the evenings, into how we won't miss the Cuban *day* after we are gone, but the Cuban night we will miss for the rest of our lives.

IV. 11

Still no flour at the Diplo, and our reserves are nearly finished. Everyone talks big, they can get us flour, but in the end not even Lorena can get us flour.

I HAVE A SMALL HEADACHE. Nick says I should go swimming at the Comodoro with him. He says it will make my head feel better.

The Comodoro has been improved. Algae has been scraped off the seawall, so you can walk on it now without slipping and you can climb down a ladder to the sea. The mast on the seawall sports new flags, fluttering in the breeze.

'Oh my God, Piñeiro in a bathing suit.'

Piñeiro sees us and bounces up from the lounge chair he has been lying on between two good-looking forty-year-old women.

Piñeiro's body is trim, relatively young looking, with a not unusual amount of cinnamon-colored chest hair. He is not *that* old, we realize: it is only the beard that makes him look like an aging werewolf.

'This looks like Cape Cod, don't you think?' he says to me gaily in English, gesturing to the flags, his beard coming at me at the same time. I brace myself: he kisses me on both cheeks. He has always shaken my hand before. The beard is surprisingly not bristly. He introduces us to the women in the lounge chairs.

'I was thinking more of Caribe,' I say. *I have been kissed by a murderer,* I think, though it doesn't come naturally, thinking that. I have to kind of make myself think it, just as I have had to make myself think it the times I have been kissed by other people in Havana who, if they haven't killed people themselves, have certainly arranged for their deaths.

COCKTAILS AT THE KOZAKS'. Naty Revuelta is there. We start chatting. I know that her daughter, Alina, has just published a book, *Rebel Daughter of the Revolution,* but I don't dare ask her about it. The Portuguese ambassador comes up to Naty. He tells Naty in a loud voice that he has just read an interview with her daughter in a French newspaper. Her daughter was very critical of Fidel.

'You don't say,' Naty says.

She and the Portuguese laugh. She and the Portuguese ambassador talk about Alina's emotional development. Naty doesn't know the Portuguese ambassador any better than she knows me, but there they are, talking about very intimate things, very openly. I realize that I've been here three years and still don't quite know when not to mention something and when to jump right in. Naty asks me if I have read the book. I lie and say I have. The Portuguese ambassador says, 'It seems that Alina is more developed emotionally now.' Naty says that Alina was a girl who was very developed intellectually but was not developed emotionally at all. The gap was . . . Naty makes a wide gesture with her hands.

Naty tells us that Alina is in Los Angeles now, promoting her book, but it is not known if it will be translated into English. Without prompting, Naty then goes from talking about Alina to talking about her relationship with Fidel. She and Fidel had, she says, '*una amistad amorosa*' ('an amorous friendship'). It is a practiced phrase, and I realize I am finally realizing something everyone else in Havana already knows: that Naty is *used* to talking about her relationship with Fidel at cocktail parties.

A VISITING CUBAN AMERICAN says to us that the driving force here and in Miami, too, is hurt feelings. More than people being killed even, what operates is hurt feelings.

DINNER PARTY. I AM placed next to a young member of the Foreign Relations Committee of the National Assembly. He is an associate of the man who told me, soon after my arrival, that 40 percent of Americans have sex with animals.

This man goes the other way and tells me that the big difference between Cuba and the United States is that the first settlers in the United States were people seeking religious freedom, whereas the first settlers in Cuba were criminals.

'What?' I tell him I knew that about Australia, but Cuba?

'It's true,' he says. Some of Cuba's first settlers were given the choice between prison in Spain and exile in Cuba.

I say criminals ended up in the United States as well. I quote Thomas Wolfe's line about the Georgia slattern. Then follows a little competition between us: *My country was settled by more dubious types. No, mine. No, mine* . . .

IV. 12

This is the first time I've been able to write in a week.

Felt bad the night after the dinner. It's October, diarrhea time, but better me than the children. Showered in the morning and managed to make it through my time for reading to the third grade at the school. Came home, collapsed on the bed. Switched from Kaopectate to Binaldan. Managed to get through a cocktail party. Got home, put on my nightgown, and was in bed by 8:30.

Diarrhea again in the morning, more Binaldan. I dropped the children at a friend's house, went home, tried to write, but kept being drawn back to bed for little lie-downs. Went back to bed after not eating the boiled chicken and rice Lorena made me for lunch. I was getting a fever. Maybe it was a stomach virus, not bacteria or parasites. Nick came home. José was about to leave for the day. 'Stop, José,' I said. I called Dr. Silvia. She was home and could come. José went in his car to pick her up. Managed to capture a *muestra* in a bottle. There was blood in it. Cramps were coming every few minutes. It was as if someone had shaken four Coca-Colas in my stomach. Dr. Silvia was almost sure it was not a virus. José took her and the sample to the laboratory. Time crept by – one hour, one and a half hours, two hours. Silvia finally called me from her home. I had amoebas, she said, and a high leukocyte count, evidence of infection. I probably had shigella also. She said I should take some medicine she was prescribing against amoebas. As for the shigella, they couldn't do a *coprocultivo* over the weekend, but if on Monday I had a fever and the diarrhea was still liquid, I was to collect another *muestra* so they could do a *coprocultivo* on that. Also, José's car had broken down. It broke down ten blocks from her house. She walked home. José was with his car, she said. A heavy rainstorm was going on outside. I asked Dr. Silvia if she could get some medicine. She said she could. I asked Dr. Silvia if she could get some medicine and walk back to José, and then José could take a taxi back to the house with the medicine. I lay back, listened to the soda fountain in my stomach, and waited. Nick was getting excited. He said I should go to the Institute for Tropical Diseases. He said amoebas could enter the liver. Two more hours passed with me in the bathroom the whole time. José showed up with medicine and oral rehydration salts. I scarfed the medicine, and after about a half an hour there was a definite quieting of the rumbling. Ate some breakfast in the morning, lying back after bites. Cramps and bathroom trips then subsided, until by midmorning I had almost none. It was miracle medicine. Dr. Silvia was a genius. I was exhausted.

Felt almost normal in my stomach the next day but had a migraine headache. Lay in the dark until the sparkle vision was over. Nick called, said he had made an appointment for me at the Institute for Tropical Diseases. I said I felt silly going since I felt so much better. Nick then had a strained sound in his voice, so I said I would go, but I wanted him to go with me so that he could hear with his own ears what they said to me and ask the doctors questions right then, so that he wouldn't say later, when he heard their diagnosis from me, that it was wrong and the doctors didn't know what they were talking about: it was one of our cultural differences.

LIKE MANY INSTITUTES in Cuba, the Pedro Kouri Institute for Tropical Diseases was nearly deserted, and the remaining staff wasn't even faking that they had anything to do. Desks visible through open doors had nothing on them; eyes in hallways fixed on us with total interest for the entire duration of our passage through them.

The Pedro Kouri Institute was established in the 1930s and enlarged in the 1970s for the wars of liberation in Angola and in other parts of Africa.

We sat down with the director and with another doctor. We were offered coffee. Nick was offered cigars. I described my symptoms to the director and the other doctor. I showed them the pills I was taking. We then went with the other doctor to an examining room, our steps echoing in the empty hall. The other doctor asked me how many pills I took before starting to feel better. I said two. He said it was impossible that I could feel so much better after just two pills. He said maybe I didn't have amoebas. He said he wanted to make two *coprocultivos* and led us down another empty hallway to the *recepción de muestras*, where a dozing attendant gave us two sterile plastic jars with labels. We were taken back to the director to thank him and say good-bye, then taken on a meandering walk through another empty corridor, the doctor opening the door of one empty office after another, mumbling something that sounded like an apology; we wondered if it meant we were supposed to pay.

The appropriate office was finally found; in it were a woman and an ornate, open, empty safe with 'National Cash Register Company' written along the top of it in flowing golden script. The woman smiled and wrote some numbers down on a pad marked 'Cubanacán,' the state tourism company. We were then led down another corridor to a place marked CAJA (Cashier). A nurse was called to pull a metal cash box out from the drawer of an empty desk. They were beginning their new operation, the doctor explained, as a place of *tourismo de salud*, where people could come and cure their tropical diseases in a relaxed atmosphere, with experienced doctors who had been in Angola. Some patients had already come, and they were hoping for more.

On the way out, we were led past a series of bulletin boards detailing the history of the institute. On the one marked 1930 there were the words 'Cornell University.' I wanted to look more, but Nick said we had to go. On the board marked *hoy* (Today) there was a picture of a *turista de salud* lying on a gurney, swathed in white cloth with his head raised, smiling, with a circle of doctors and nurses around him.

Cramps returned in the late afternoon, until by bedtime, I could not sleep. Wondered if it was the second generation of amoebas hatching, and found myself routing for Dr. Silvia. Spent the night waiting until 5:30 A.M., when I could collect a *muestra* that would still be fresh by 8:00 A.M., when José showed up and could drive it to the institute. Spent the night dreading not the collecting of the *muestra* so much as the having to leave the air-conditioned bedroom and walk down the fluorescent-lit sweltering back stairs, wearing my disgusting bathrobe over my disgusting nightgown, sweat rolling underneath it, saying to Manuel, who would be there kneading bread, 'Manuel, it's only me,' and putting an envelope the whole world knew the contents of in the refrigerator door next to the capers.

IV. 13

It's been a week now. I still have cramps and can run to the bathroom four or five times in an hour and then be fine for twelve. Blastocytes, the institute says I have, not amoebas, but the medicine Dr. Silvia gave me works for them, too, and so I have just kept on taking it.

I will be leaving for New York tomorrow. I was planning to stop in New York on the way back to Cuba after a trip to X — Nick and I will be making at the end of the month, but Nick now says that because of my illness, I should go to New York first and see a specialist there. I tell Nick I think it's overreacting, to change plans, leave the children so soon after the beginning of the school year when I felt so much better, but Nick, lying next to me, drawing an imaginary doodle on my stomach with his finger, says he wants to be *sure* I am well, and besides, he has been talking to Fidel's secretary and the only time Fidel can come for dinner is right after our trip to X—' so there is no time for me to go to New York after X—.

'Fidel is coming for dinner? Coming to this house?'

'Yep.'

'*Caramba.*'

I TRY SURRENDERING MYSELF to New York anticipation (a prickling in the palms of my hands, as if from the points of tiny Chrysler Buildings) but I cannot let myself go. A trip to New York *already*, and for *six whole days*. My rule has been that I have to be in Cuba a lot longer to earn a trip to New York – not that there *is* a rule, really (I have Juana), but the last time I came back, Jimmie said, 'I cried in computer class because I missed you, Mommy.' According to my rule, I have to be in Cuba for at least three months before I can go to New York and enjoy myself at all.

IT'S NOT BLASTOCYTES OR amoebas at all that I had, the New York specialist tells me after several kinds of examinations. He does not see the traces amoebas or blastocytes make. Moreover, the medicine they gave me is not the medicine that is given for blastocytes or for amoebas in the first place. I tell him the medicine worked for me. He says he cannot tell me what I had, only that it wasn't blastocytes or amoebas and that whatever it was has gone away.

IV. 14

There's a new class in business travel: funky first. That's the unofficial name of the class I am in, on the Cubana de Aviación flight, paid for by Nick's firm, from Europe to Havana, with a stopover in Santiago de Cuba. The only other travelers in funky first are two Cuban bureaucrats in polyester business suits and basket-weave loafers and one non-Cuban woman. The non-Cuban woman is the only other woman on the flight besides myself and the stewardesses. All the other first-class seats are empty, and all the other passengers, in *class tropical* and economy, are male.

The men, about eighty of them, are between the ages of twenty and fifty-five, not ugly, and you wonder what it means, that they have to go so far. The men appear to be utterly undisturbed at seeing almost no women on the flight; some men, in fact, look so serene that you feel as if their wives, mothers, or girlfriends ironed their clothes, then dressed them, packed their suitcases, and sent them off with kisses, saying, 'Now run along and play, dears!' and then sat themselves down, with sighs of relief, to glorious, solitary cups of coffee and cigarettes at their kitchen tables, their feet up.

No champagne, no tablecloths. Silverware in plastic bags. I try to prop my legs up with two triangular bolsters put together, but they keep sliding. None of this would be so bad if the ticket, one-way, did not cost sixteen hundred dollars. Chipped paint everywhere. The grime is so built-up in corners that you would need a trowel, then a wire brush with Ajax, to dig it out. The aisle carpet, where not worn through, sports shiny black stains. The seat bottoms of two seats in funky first are completely gone, and many of the armrests show only metal supports. I try to go to the one bathroom in first class, but the handle has fallen off the door.

'There's no handle on the bathroom door,' I say to the stewardess.

'*Ven pa'ca*,' she says in Cuban (meaning 'Go over there'), jerking her head to the back of the plane, where ten men are waiting in line in front of the only bathroom that seems to be working.

'There's a line back there. Can't you fix the door handle?'

'No.' The expression on her face is one of absolute contempt.

Later I see the crew putting the door handle on the door and using it to open the door every time they need to go, then taking it away again when they finish.

We view a newsreel of Fidel reaccepting the presidency of the country, the leadership of the armed forces, the chairmanship of the Communist Party, and Raúl reaccepting the vice presidency. This is followed by an announcement of the name of the film we will be viewing during our flight. The film is *Absolute Power*, starring Clint Eastwood.

We deplane for refueling in Santiago. It is one o'clock in the morning, European time; six o'clock in the evening, Cuban time. A salsa band blares in the single waiting room. I look around the edge of the room for deep angles or halls to wait in, but there is no escape. 'Do we *have* to listen to this music?' I ask a guard.

'*Ven pa'ca*,' he says, indicating a gift shop with the doors wide open.

I pay fifty cents to an attendant sitting at a table outside the bathroom for four squares of toilet paper, which she keeps in a stack in front of her. I roll them into balls, stuff them in my ears, and wait, as far away from the salsa band as I can, for the plane to reload.

IV. 15

I promised the children before I left that when I got back we would go, the three of us with a friend of theirs, Megan, to Varadero. Nick will be returning from X— in three days, and Fidel's office called while we were away and said Fidel will not be coming for dinner for another ten days, so there's time.

We have not been back to Varadero since the time soon after our arrival in Cuba three years ago. After we had admired the color of the sand (white) and the water (turquoise) and swum in the sea, Varadero got pretty boring. No shops to speak of. No restaurants that weren't empty (of food) or grim or dirty, except in tourist hotels blaring salsa. *Jineteras* galore. No shade. Nick had said he never wanted to go back. Even the children had said they were bored.

Varadero, though, has taken on an allure for the children since their friends have reported going there many times. We have also heard that it is less squalid. The police rounded up *seven thousand jineteras* in Varadero several months ago and put a barrier across the road, and visitors are now charged two dollars to get onto the peninsula and two dollars to get off. Tourism dropped 30 percent after the *jinetera* roundup. *Paladares* were also banned and there was a clampdown on people renting out rooms. Friends said there are still a few *jineteras*, though, but very discreet, just enough to make it not a total cemetery, and people still rent out rooms, but they have to be very careful. I will do anything twice.

Megan's mother calls just before we leave. Megan has a sore throat and a temperature. We set off on a grimmer trip.

We enter Varadero. Jimmie says he is hungry. We pass a corner open-air restaurant that looks like a regular restaurant: people are sitting at tables, there is a freshly painted sign at the entrance, there are freshly thatched palm-leaf umbrellas, and the chairs look new. There is a menu on a sandwich board. They have plates of food for one dollar – meat or fish, rice and beans, french fries. And sandwiches. There are about twenty-five items on the list. We have not been in a state-run restaurant since the trip we took to Trinidad soon after arriving in Cuba. Maybe they have improved.

The restaurant looked cool from the outside, with its palm-leaf umbrellas, but when we sit down we realize the palm-leaf umbrellas trap heat blasting from the kitchen. There is music playing, too, which I didn't hear at first. It is Barry Manilow. A gift shop tucked in one corner sells T-shirts with cartoon characters on them, the bottoms of the T-shirts shredded to look like fringe. Geezers and *chicas* for customers, I now make out, and jet-lagged, stalwart, but slightly angry *mittel*-European retirees. A sullen *mulata* shuffles to our table, the light changes, and swaths of grease and flies are visible on every table.

They have no pork. They have no chicken. The fish is two fish fillets stuffed with ham and cheese and fried.

'What *do* you have, then?'

'Ham-and-cheese sandwiches. French fries.'

We order those.

We see a sign across from the hotel: MONTE A CABALLO (Horseback riding). I speak with a man named Bigote (Mustache). He says he can take all of us on a ride that will last two hours. We will ride for a little while along the highway, then cut through to a place where there is white virgin sand. His voice lilts over the 'white virgin sand' part and his hand flutters like a hula girl's, but I still trust him. We arrange to ride tomorrow.

I take the children to a Chinese restaurant in the hotel for dinner. Even Chinese *paladares* in Cuba are terrible, but I'm still in the where-do-I-think-I-am mode.

The food is terrible, but there is beer, fried noodles out of a bag, soy sauce, and little bowls to pour the soy sauce in, and the children have fun dipping noodles in the soy sauce. I keep hoping 'less squalid' means 'better,' even though I know that's not what our friends meant.

Four young men sit down next to us. They hear us talking and ask me if I am Canadian or from the States. I say I am from the States. They say they are, too. They say I am the first person from the States they have seen on their trip. Two have dark eyes and dark hair, and two are blond. The two dark-haired boys, who are brothers, have Cuban parents who left in '61. They are visiting Cuba for the first time. Their parents have never been back.

They ask me where they *can* get a good meal. I tell them about *paladares*. They were only in Havana for one day, then headed out. They are on their way back to Havana now. They write the names of *paladares* I recommend on napkins. The Cuban Americans say Spanish words with strong American accents.

'We have no relatives left in Cuba,' one of the Cuban American brothers says to me. 'But we came with a list of friends of my parents from the old days and distant relatives. We drove up to this one place. The guy was up on his roof, nailing something. 'Do you remember Davide, the *hermanito* (little brother) of Omero?' '*Sí.*' 'We are his sons.' The guy almost fell off the roof. We stayed with the guy and his family. The family really put themselves out for us. They gave up their *beds* for us. We didn't want them to do that, but they insisted. They cooked pork. As we were leaving, we didn't want to exactly *pay* the people for the rooms, we thought they would be insulted, but we thought we should make a contribution. We gave them a hundred dollars. Only when we opened our suitcases at the next place did we discover they had taken our shoes, some shirts, some shaving stuff . . .'

'But maybe the stuff was taken by someone else between the time you left and the time you got to the next place,' I say. 'Maybe someone got into your car.'

'No way that could have happened. There was someone with the car the whole time. We know not to leave the car alone. After we packed, the bags were sitting in our rooms for like about an hour. That's when they took our stuff. They were nice to us, and then they took our stuff. I'm telling you' – he points at his chest and leans forward – 'it makes me ashamed to be Cuban!'

The other brother nods. 'Me, too.'

I feel a flash of uptightness and see in my mind's eye the wide stripes of the red, white, and blue Cuban flag: Cubans and foreigners who live in Cuba can say things like that, but not people who are just *visiting*, even if they *are* Cuban Americans. I find myself making up more rules: People who have left Cuba can say things like that, too, but they have to have left in the past five years, they have to have stood in line for hours on end, they have to have *conseguir*ed and *resolver*ed until they were ready to drop, they have to have experienced new shoes only in the imagination. Then they could say things like that, if they still felt they had to.

I tell the brothers they just had bad luck. Then I tell the brothers that it was a lot better that the people they stayed with were nice to them, then took their stuff, than it would have been if the people they stayed with were mean to them, then took their stuff.

HORSEBACK RIDING WITH BIGOTE. The children are gung ho before we actually get there, but after Jimmie is put on his horse, he starts to cry. 'It's so high up!' he says. Bigote says this is no problem: he will ride with him. Thea looks like she is about to ask for company, too, but I cut her off, for I can barely stay on a horse myself.

Most of the trip turns out to be on the road. Massive hotels in various stages of completion on the beach side of the road, cement-block sheds with images of Che and revolutionary slogans on the other side of the road, tour buses blowing soot in our faces. We pass a Club Méditerranée that has just opened. We turn in to a construction site and make our way to the beach. An official-looking car passes us. Bigote dismounts, has a conversation with the man inside the car. I am sure we are going to be turned away; it is evident that no one has paid Bigote to ride this far in a long time, but Bigote remounts and we go on. We come to a gate. There is a padlock on it. 'They didn't tell me . . . ,' he says. We ride along a wall to where there is a gap. A pile of sand is filling the gap. We dismount; Bigote leads the horses over the pile of sand one by one.

We remount, duck under some branches, and step onto the beach. For a moment in our sight, if we don't move our heads or use peripheral vision, it *is* paradise, magazine-type paradise: the sea is clear, then turquoise, then violet. The sand is just short of blinding white. Turn our heads a little to one side or the other, though, and there is one construction site after another.

Varadero is a series of beaches separated by small bluffs. On one bluff is a former vacation home of the du Ponts. There used to be no hotels or houses beyond it. It is now a restaurant, and on the beach beyond it is the Meliá Varadero. On the beach beyond the Meliá is the Club Méditerranée. We are on the beach beyond that, which is the last beach to be developed. Beyond it are rocks, trees, and mangroves. It is a *zona militar*. There is a small *cayo* (island) in the distance. It, also, is a *zona militar*.

'*Ojalá* (God willing), they will be able to save some of the natural parts,' I say to Bigote.

'*Ojalá*, they will,' agrees Bigote.

It is like riding stuffed animals across a bag of sugar, riding on sand, and for us it is yet another original sensual experience, taking its place alongside 'orange grove in full bloom' and 'evening breeze on upper arms.' These are the last few weeks people like us will be able to experience it here, this unintended nice thing, the last few weeks kids and horses will be able to ride through gaps in walls and find no one on the beach on the other side.

I GO WITH THE children to check out the new shopping mall in Varadero with the game center Megan's mother told us about.

The windows are clean. There's a small dollars-only food

store and a small dollars-only department store. We are the only ones in the department store. There are the fringed T-shirts and wooden items with images of Che burned into them for tourists; bike shorts, bras, cheap shoes, and stonewashed jeans for Cubans; and one sixty-dollar toilet seat displayed on a kind of plate holder for visitors to buy *for* a Cuban, for a visiting Cuban American to buy for his or her relative, or for a tourist to buy for his or her Cuban *marinovia* (-o) or *jinetera* (-o).

There is a room with electronic games in it; another room contains a bar and a six-lane bowling alley; an air-hockey table sits on the patio outside; and on a back lot are bumper cars.

Hotel workers' pay at Varadero is 230 pesos a month – about $10.00. On top of that, every month they receive a *jaba* – a plastic bag containing soap, shampoo, and toothpaste. They also receive a percentage of the service charge, which amounts to about $35.00, making their total monthly pay about $45.00 plus the *jaba*.

The cashier at the bar of the game center, where tokens are sold, is surrounded by Cubans pulling $5.00 and $10.00 bills out of thick wads of bills for bowling, at $3.00 a game, and for bumper cars, at $1.50 a turn.

The bowling alley is Brunswick, with automatic setup and ball return and brightly colored balls in a variety of weights. The noise of the bowling balls, of salsa at high volume, and of girls in *jine* wear and their boyfriends (mostly Cuban, with some Europeans), screaming and jumping up and down as they bowl, means you have to yell to be heard.

'*You can bowl barefoot or with special shoes!*' the bartender screams.

'*Just one game!*' I yell at the kids.

'*OK!*' they yell back.

We pay and find an empty lane. It's new, the bowling alley, but you can already see gaps between the boards of the lanes as well as warping in some boards. The wood has been finished with a lumpy varnish, leaving gaps and air bubbles, as if they got a kit but didn't follow the instructions or used the flooring that came with the kit for someplace else. Our balls keep veering to the left.

We buy more tokens and go out to the bumper cars and go seven or eight times – for a total of a hotel base salary. The bumper cars look pretty new also, but three are already out of commission, with the rods that are supposed to connect them to the electrified roof rusted and bent.

Roberto drives us through a barrio in back of the shopping complex – dozens of tiny concrete houses packed together, with patched tin roofs.

'Here's where they live, and there's where they suck it out of them,' I say.

'*Hay una pipa directa*' ('There's a direct pipeline'), Roberto says.

IV. 16

Caligula is playing at the same theater where we saw *Te Sigo, Esperando*. It is a Cubanized version of Sartre's play.

At the end, a woman in traveling clothes picks up a suitcase. '*Me voy*' ('I am going'), she says. The crowd responds mightily.

IV. 17

There is no flour at the Diplo. I do manage to buy 191 rolls of toilet paper, though. The ones we brought from our last country are finished and we are into the Kleenex, so I buy all the rolls on the shelf. They are twenty-five cents each, speckled, made in Cuba. There are no perforations, and the beginning of the roll is fixed to the rest with a swath of yellow glue. You have to toss the first foot or so away. We have enough toilet paper now to last until we leave. If we run out, we will move back to the Kleenex. We have had lots of diarrhea in Cuba, but not that many colds.

LORENA DRAGS A fifty-pound bag of flour in through the door. '*No fue fácil*' ('It wasn't easy'), she says, letting go of the bag, straightening her back, and wiping the sweat from her forehead with her hand. 'But it's good quality. I told them it had to be good quality for the *comandante in jefe* (commander in chief).'

IV. 18

Radio Martí has announced that the Cuban American

National Foundation will be sending a flotilla to just outside the twelve-mile limit, from which they will project a laser show, which will be seen in the sky above Havana. The laser show will begin at 9 P.M., after the *cañonazo* (traditional nightly canon salute from the fortress of La Cabaña). At nine P.M., all *habaneros* are requested by Radio Martí to start banging cooking pots to express their solidarity with the democracy movement, as they did in East Germany. There is even a rumor that they are going to beam the words LIBERTAD Y DEMOCRACIA in the sky.

We go to the *paladar* Prado 20, with its view over the harbor. We think that it will be the best viewing spot.

We stand on the terrace waiting for a table to be free, watching a laser test in the sky. A waitress serves us water, explaining to us that water is the only thing she can serve on the terrace. Prado 20 has just opened again after having been closed for several months. It was closed for serving drinks on the terrace, where they did not have a bar license.

We are called in to eat. I keep watching out the window.

The *cañonazo* sounds. We rush outside.

The light show begins. A green beam streaks up into the sky, but then it fades. It searches the sky, wobbles. It continues to shine in the sky, feeble and intermittent. There are no words, and after about twenty minutes it is over. No cooking pots bang.

'They may be the opposition, but they are Cubans just the same,' declares a man with a British accent sitting at a table next to ours.

IV. 19

Jimmie lies on the floor of his room before dressing for school. 'It's kind of boring here,' he says. 'It's always the same.'

IV. 20

The first security detail arrives around noon. Men in stonewashed jeans and imitation Lacoste shirts. We sit on the veranda. I serve them coffee. The head of security asks me to list the names of the help. He asks me to give him and his men a tour of the house. He asks me what bathroom the president will use. I say we have only one downstairs bathroom. He tells me the president will use that bathroom and that all other guests should use the guest bathroom upstairs. He asks me what kind of toilet paper the president will use. I show them one of the rolls I have just bought from the Diplo. He asks me if it is Cuban toilet paper. I say it is. He asks me if we don't have any better-quality toilet paper. I say we don't. The head of security asks me to take the roll, put it in a plastic bag, tape the bag shut, and leave it beside the toilet for the president. He asks me how the food will be served. I say it will be served buffet style, with identical dishes on both sides of the table so that the guests can serve themselves more quickly. He asks me to show him what side of the table the president will be served from, and after I walk with him to the dining room and show him, he tells me to serve Fidel only from that side. He then asks me where we will sit down to eat dinner. I escort him to the veranda, which is open on two sides. The tables have already been set up. Some of the tables have chairs with their backs facing the garden. The security man tells me to seat the president with his back facing the wall.

At two o'clock, the house checkers and the food taster come. The food taster spends the rest of the afternoon in the kitchen with Lorena. The checkers start combing the house delicately, looking under every piece of furniture with flashlights, tapping the furniture in some places. They get ladders and peek into chandeliers and rub the insides of lampshades with the flats of their hands. They pick up cushions and squeeze every part of them between their hands. They take out the telephone in the *despacho* and install a red one. They install a green one in the garden in the bushes near the entrance.

At five o'clock, Nick's secretary calls to tell me Fidel likes Chivas Regal. I go to the Diplo for the third time that day.

The security men check the dining table after it has been set, sliding on their backs under the tablecloth with flashlights. This is a signal for Jimmie and Thea to jump up giggling from the glass table on the adjoining veranda, where they have been eating their dinner, and, before anyone can stop them, dive under the dining table with the security men. '*Te cojí!*' ('Gotcha!'), Jimmie says, flopping onto one of the security men's stomachs with a ketchup-stained napkin still stuffed into his pajama collar.

One hour before the guests arrive, closed trucks park on the street by our fence. Machine guns are hoisted to the tops of the trucks. Soldiers in combat uniforms stand beside them.

The guests assemble. We wait without drinking anything. We wait nearly an hour. 'He likes for everyone to be here before he makes his appearance,' one Cuban whispers to me.

He arrives in a loud rush of black Ladas and one Mercedes. We greet him on the steps. He asks permission to use our hall mirror, stands in front of it, and with great concentration combs his hair with a small black comb, as thirty guests look on, beaming.

He appears top-heavy with what seem to be two layers of olive green polyester, even though it is at least ninety-five degrees out-side. Olive green pants over legs that look all the slenderer in contrast to the top-heaviness. The pants are gathered at the ankles, combat-style, but instead of combat boots he wears zip-up, Beatles-like boots with heels that seem to be just the slightest bit higher than the heels on normal men's shoes. The hands on the comb are thin, pale, hairless. The beard is long and sparse. You can see through it all the way to his skin. Old hippies, I think of, and the Fab Four and the gruff but whimsical top-heavy executives in old *New Yorker* cartoons.

Danila stands with a tray at the entrance to the living room. Fidel finishes combing his hair, walks up to Danila, puts his arm around her, and enters the living room with her, raising his other arm and calling a general, cheerful greeting to the room. Danila beams. Her *café con mucha leche* cheeks blush dusty rose. He releases her gracefully. She whirls off with her tray into the kitchen. Nick introduces him to the most important guests in the room. I ask Fidel what he would like to drink. He says he would like a sweet vermouth. I apologize and say we have no sweet vermouth. He says he would like some French wine, then. I say that unfortunately we have no French wine, just Chilean. Nick looks at me impatiently; Fidel, mock humbly (it's a look I have seen him use on TV). 'I will have some red wine,' he says supplicatingly, 'or some white wine.'

'Bring him some white wine,' Nick says abruptly to Danila, who has reappeared.

Nick tells Fidel almost immediately that I am a *norteamericana* (Nick has taken to telling everyone almost immediately that I am a *norteamericana* because he doesn't want to give them anything that they can discover). Fidel opens his eyes wide. 'But I have nothing against the American *people*,' he says, putting his hands on my shoulders and shaking them gently. He says he doesn't understand why the same Torricelli who exposed the abuses of the CIA in Guatemala is so much for Helms-Burton. His tone is one of hurt, puzzlement. It is just a shade different from mock humility.

I sit between Fidel and the featured guest, an X—ian manufacturer of pipelines, who I had thought would have some distinction because his company is so well known, but instead turns out to be a ferrety little man with a sizable gold bracelet. A translator sits on the other side of the featured guest. The man is so ferrety and so excited to be sitting with Fidel (I catch him once or twice grabbing his crotch) that he is able to get a lot of words in edgewise and ends up talking nearly as much as Fidel. He tells us that many Chinese have Ferraris now. He talks about how they have yachts now, and two hundred suits, and vacation homes. I expect Fidel to be taken aback at this but he listens, with his eyebrows arched. 'You don't say?' he says. The man talks about how they like to go hunting – Chinese hunting big game in Africa – and about how he likes to go hunting, too. He talks about how thrilling it is to shoot an elephant.

'But I didn't think it was legal to shoot elephants anymore,' I say feebly, but the ferrety man tells us it can be done on certain reserves in Tanzania. He tells us where to go, the name of the man to contact. He likes to hunt lions, too, with a bow and arrow. He likes to hunt ducks. He chuckles. He even – he wouldn't do this all the time, but just once – shot ducks with a machine gun. He got three hundred ducks at once. I expect Fidel to be appalled at this and I get ready to do lots of covering, distraction – I don't want Fidel to think that *all* X——ians are like this little guy – but Fidel simply says that he likes to go duck hunting, too. He says they have beautiful duck-hunting reserves in Cuba. The ferrety man tells Fidel what kinds of guns he likes to use. Fidel tells the ferrety man what kinds of guns he likes to use. He tells the ferrety man about their special features. The translator leans forward, sweating. He is having to work fast, with unusual words. Fidel makes like he's breaking open a gun, putting it together, sighting along it. And night hunting, the ferrety man says he likes to do. He was sold a special sight for his rifle – the kind used by the CIA – for night shooting. His voice drops an octave; he pulls on his crotch. It was sold to him by an Arab he met in Africa.

Fidel moves forward on his seat and, winking at me, says he would like to get his hands on one of those.

I am very aware of my back in a red dress, facing the garden with the bushes beyond and the neighboring building with its second floor clearing our dividing hedge, its dark windows looking at us, and I am aware of the soldiers with machine guns in the trucks on the streets outside. I glance at my watch. 'Ah, *señora*, you can't imagine how many attempts there have been on his life, and one just recently,' the surprisingly voluble young translator, with whom I had been chatting before Fidel's arrival, said to me within earshot of bodyguards as we were moving into the dining room.

Fidel sits in an armchair in the living room after dinner. There are not enough chairs to seat everyone, so Nick sits on a small ottoman beside him. The ferrety man is in another part of the living room speaking to other people. Fidel asked for a Sambuca, but we have no Sambuca, so he is sipping a cognac. Fidel is speaking about frozen shrimp. I don't know how long it is that Fidel has been speaking about frozen shrimp (I have been off talking with other people) but it seems that he has been speaking about frozen shrimp for a while, for the eyes of people around him are starting to dart around the room. Fidel has finished his cognac. Nick asks Fidel if he would like another cognac and takes advantage of a split second of silence to ask Fidel a question about the war in Angola. I think Fidel will be jarred by such a different subject's being introduced, but he launches immediately into the war in Angola without batting an eye. Fidel talks for twenty-five minutes about Angola, and then Nick, offering Fidel a third cognac, asks him about Eritrea. Fidel moves serenely on to Eritrea for twenty-five minutes more.

Eyes dart. Nick steals a glance at me, grinning with satisfaction. Nick loves footnotes in history, lesser-known military campaigns. Fidel keeps talking.

At midnight the head bodyguard approaches us. '*Commandante*, with your permission . . .'

'Is it time?' Fidel says.

The bodyguard nods.

'Hmm, time already. Amazing, how time flies' – he chuckles – 'when one is doing all the talking!' He glances at Nick, then at me, his eyes sparkling. We smile. The guests laugh appreciatively. Fidel then pushes himself forward on the armchair. The head bodyguard nears the chair, but Fidel waves him away. He grips the two arms of the armchair, moves his chest toward his knees, and on a second rock forward pushes himself up stiffly onto his feet. The head bodyguard and other bodyguards remain alert as Fidel steadies himself. Fidel holds his hand out to Nick. Nick takes the hand, his arm rigid to help Fidel steady himself more. It is a combination of steadying himself with Nick's help and shaking Nick's hand. Fidel thanks Nick for the pleasant evening and for the intelligent questions Nick asked. The ferrety man approaches. Fidel shakes his hand and grips his shoulder while the ferrety man beams.

Fully steady now, Fidel turns to me. '*Señora norteamericana, muchísimas gracias a usted igualmente* (to you, too).' The guests chuckle at the *norteamericana* part. Fidel puts his hands on my shoulders, leans forward, and kisses me on both cheeks. As with Piñeiro, I prepare myself for a bristly experience with distinct aroma to it. I marshal every nerve end in my nose and cheek, to remember and describe, but the beard is even softer than Piñeiro's – whispery soft, in fact, odorless, and withdrawn in an instant.

With Nick on one side of Fidel and a bodyguard on the other, the bodyguard's hand cupped a millimeter below Fidel's elbow, his eyes on Fidel's feet, Fidel makes his way down the entry stairs and into the black Mercedes while black Ladas rev their engines in front of the Mercedes and behind it. The Ladas fill with green uniforms and tight *guayaberas*. The car doors slam shut, the gates creak open, and the cars roar off, tires screeching, Nick's pant legs and my skirt flattened by exhaust, as are the pant legs of the ferrety man and the X——ian guests fanning out on the steps on either side of us – all male guests, whom we don't know well – their faces beatific.

IV. 21

Concha back at work after several days at home with bronchitis. She was sick, she said, because of the powerful cleanser she was using to try to get white film off the green marbled toilet seat in the guest bathroom – residue of a powder the security men sprinkled on the toilet seat when Fidel came to dinner. We told Concha not to bother with it, but she was determined to get it off.

IV. 22

Cuban Americans are arrested on the high seas on their way to Isla Margarita to kill Fidel Castro at the *iberoamericano* summit.

I ASK A CUBAN historian (not Leal) if he thinks the revolution and its continuance was and is the result of the romanticism of the Spaniard conflicting with the pragmatic coldness of the Anglo-Saxon.

The historian says romanticism was losing its platform, American pragmatism was rejected for being *too* pragmatic, and so surrealism, which is desiccated romanticism, took hold.

IV. 23

We are supplied with haute X—ian cuisine to serve at a reception we are giving for participants at an X—ian trade show – several kinds of preserved artichokes, mushroom salad, dried tomatoes, smoked pheasant, several kinds of truffle pâtés, cheeses, smoked trout, a variety of hams, wine, beer, and liqueurs. The bottles, cans, jars, and packages are wheeled into the house on dollies and unloaded into the *despensa*. Thea, Jimmie, the help, and I take turns going into the *despensa* to stare.

Nick says the Cuban government is beginning to figure out that elite tourism is the way to go.

I tell Nick you don't get elite tourists by feeding them pâté: that's like serving French tourists potatoes out of a can from Europe. Elite tourists would like good-quality *Cuban* food, since they are in Cuba – they would like *sopa de platano*, they would like *escabeche*, they would like grilled shrimps, *boliche cubano* (Cuban pot roast), *judias* or *frijoles negros*, chicken baked with honey and mint, stuffed peppers, banana pie, mango pudding – and besides, he's an energy consultant, he's not in the *tourist business*.

Nick, sighing and closing his eyes, says he *knows* this, but the X—ian National Chamber of Commerce *asked* him, 'elite tourist' doesn't mean *quality* tourism, of the standard of *Mme. Isadora B. Tattlin,* it doesn't mean people wanting to get out and experience a new country; it means hardworking, lower-middle-class people from some blighted place wanting to change their social status for a while in a place that's different, but not *too* different.

I tell Nick he doesn't have to get mad.

IV. 24

Lola tells us how a foreign man will pay a *jinetera* a hundred dollars a month or more as a retainer to have her on hand for his return. The only trouble is most valid *jineteras* get their hundred dollars or more a month from several sources, and sometimes two of a *jinetera*'s 'sponsors' show up in Cuba at the same time.

A BOMB IS FOUND at the airport and defused.

THE TRIAL OF THE CRAZY American Van der Veer, who handed out anti-Castro leaflets at intersections, begins tomorrow.

Van der Veer has said that he has asked Cuban authorities to execute him 159 times.

IV. 25

Miguel is not at work today because his wife is being operated on to have the plate in her leg removed, the one that was put there after she broke her leg. Her hemoglobin was up, she had no fever, and she had not had an asthma attack in a long time, so the new doctor Miguel and his wife found felt that it was finally the right time to operate. Miguel and his wife changed doctors because her hemoglobin was not going up. The new doctor told them that she could eat all the lamb in the world, but if she didn't eat tomatoes with the lamb, to fix the iron in her system, it just went out. She started eating tomatoes and lamb, and now she can have the operation.

IV. 26

The cocktail party we are supposed to give with the X—ian haute cuisine products has been canceled.

I do a jig. We will invite Cuban friends.

Nick says not to touch the food until we hear from the X—ian trade show organizers.

'You don't really think that they will come and *take the food away*,' I say, even though I don't know why I think we should be entitled to keep the food. Then I know: it's because we live *here* that I think we should be entitled to keep the food.

'Could be . . .'

Nick calls later in the day to tell me that a truck will be coming on Saturday to pick the food up.

IV. 27

Juana's brother Frederico, a Cuban doctor on loan to Angola, *se quedó* in Spain. He was on a stopover in Spain on his way back to Cuba from Angola and *se quedó*. He is the third sibling out of six to *quedarse en el exterior*.

IV. 28

We go in the afternoon with Ramón, our antique finder and sometime intermediary, to El Viejo Loco's. El Viejo Loco lives with a male companion in an almost windowless downstairs flat in Centro Habana, and once you're in it, you literally can't take a step, for on the floor, on chairs, in display cases, on beds, in the pantry, on every piece of available furniture except the toilet and hanging from hooks on the walls are porcelain lords and ladies, harlequins, flappers, Swiss peasant kids, Moors, a few caricatural blacks (but very expensive, as they are in demand), every kind of dog or bird you can name, lions, tigers, elephants, horses, Indians, geese, fish, clowns, cowboys, and all the tchotchkes no one thought of taking out of Cuba or bothered to try to sell until now. No child under fifteen has ever been permitted inside El Viejo Loco's, and if you find yourself at El Viejo Loco's for more than half an hour in any month except November through February, you want to run screaming out of it because it is so steamy and so obsessive.

El Viejo Loco, a very pale, expressionless sixtyish *blanco* with a sparse comb-over and a sizable paunch, dressed in shorts, flip-flops, and an undershirt, moves ahead, grunting, shifting objects to make room for us to pass. In addition to the figurines, there are vases, vases with every kind of bacchanal or pastoral scene on them, Chinese urns and busts of Homer, Pasteur, Beethoven, Marx, Lenin, Martí. There are boxes, lamps, bronzes, books, and paintings. There are decanters, punch bowls, Murano bowls and ashtrays, and glasses for champagne, port, liqueurs, and punch. There are candelabras and cut-glass hurricane lamps and a Tiffany table lamp that belonged to Batista, worth ten thousand dollars. We skirt wide past a snarling mastiff, straining against his chain, around a basket full of sweet potatoes, and enter a back room hung with ceiling lamps and wall sconces. There are twenty-five thousand things there that anyone would be hard-pressed to live with, but El Viejo Loco has a fast turnover of the more beautiful and more fashionable pieces – Murano glass and art nouveau and art deco items. He has Lalique glass, too, and Steuben. It's worth it, when it's not hot, to visit him. When it's hot, you might as well be in a sauna. El Viejo Loco wheezes as he pulls still more things out of locked cabinets and grunts rhythmically when he is at rest.

The only thing that is not for sale is an oil portrait of a little girl. It's his sister, he takes the trouble to tell us between wheezes, every time we go there, who died of typhus when she was five.

Nick and I select some Murano ashtrays, two Victorian lamps, and one art nouveau lamp. El Viejo Loco wants seven hundred dollars for everything. We argue and cajole, we go into the other room for consultations with each other and with Ramón, we pretend we're going to leave, but El Viejo Loco remains firm. Nick got mad at me last time for saying I was hot and leaving in the middle of a negotiation, so I tell him to handle it. Nick handles it by agreeing to pay seven hundred dollars. El Viejo Loco nods, grunting, his expression unchanged.

'You've got your price, so why aren't you in a better mood?' Nick asks.

'I *am* in a good mood,' El Viejo Loco answers.

Nick and I tell Ramón on the way home that the guy's name should be not El Viejo Loco but El Viejo Deprimido – the Old

Depressed Guy. We ask Ramón why he's depressed when he probably makes more money than twenty-five Cubans put together.

'Because he has no other life than his stuff. His kids are all in the United States.'

'But he's a homosexual, isn't he?'

'*O, eso,*' Ramón says, batting the subject off as if it were a fly. 'He's got money, he's got a house full of stuff, but it's not enough, even for someone as materialistic as him. And he's going to die, and who cares?'

'But he loved his sister,' Nick says.

And I love Nick. He makes me live in these weird places, but I really did the right thing, marrying him.

IV. 29

We go to visit one of the two members of the Arte Calle (Street Art) movement still remaining in Cuba. Arte Calle was a movement begun by students at the San Alejandro High School of Art at the end of the 1980s. They performed their most notable works when they were seventeen. One of their works was a large poster of Che, exhibited on the floor of a gallery. The words of a poem were at the top and the bottom of the poster: '*Dónde estás, caballero bayardo / Hecho historia o hecho tierra?*' ('Where are you, courageous gentleman / Have you made history or have you soil?' – i.e., nothing, blended with the soil).

At the 1988 opening, as the crowd became larger, people finally had no place to go and were obliged to walk on the face of El Che. A teacher became enraged and fought with some of the artists. Police were called. One policeman drew a gun. Several women took off their shirts in protest (which, we are told, was a form of female protest in the 1980s and before). The gallery was compelled to remove the piece. The director of the gallery was fired and now lives in Venezuela. All the other artists involved in the show (except the two in the apartment we are visiting) now live outside Cuba.

The upper half of the poster has been pinned up on the wall for us to see. The lower half is unrolled on the floor. We see a video of the 1988 opening. As we are watching the video, a couple emerges from a back room marked OFFICE. They mumble something to our host, who accompanies them down the stairs.

'That was a love couple,' our Elegguá confirms rapidly in a whisper to us while our host is downstairs. 'They have no privacy where they live. They have to go to other people's apartments.' Then, about our host: 'His family begged him to give up art after the exhibition. He has just started painting again.'

Our host (a thin and still very young *blanco*, with dark circles under his eyes, who hardly speaks) shows us a painting he is working on now. It is hanging on the wall next to the portrait of Che. It is a picture of a crying woman who, though crying, continues to put on makeup in front of a compact mirror, blue mascara lines running down her face.

IV. 30

There have been almost constant *apagones* lately and no explanations. Finally an explanation comes: it's to save gas for the visit of the pope.

IV. 31

Sunday. Rain almost the entire day. Take the children to the nearly normal pastry shop in Siboney as a way of going somewhere and run into Kcho, the artist who won UNESCO's young artist prize three years ago, for his piece representing a *balsero*'s raft as a crown of thorns. One of Kcho's teeth has been knocked out. It was knocked out in a brawl at a bar called the Fox and the Crow, and Kcho did have – it was agreed by all who knew him and heard about the brawl – the whitest, the squarest, the healthiest-looking teeth imaginable. It was what you noticed about him, after his eyes and his large *leche con una gota de café* head, and you didn't expect it, that someone who was capable of producing art of such urgency and profundity could have teeth out of a toothpaste ad.

Kcho's show of five hundred terra-cotta boats is now on display at the Museum of Contemporary Art in Los Angeles. The U.S. Interests Section in Havana denied him a visa to attend the opening, for having entered the United States illegally the time before. He was on his way back to Cuba from Korea a few months ago, after having won first prize at the Seoul Biennial. He had bought a plane ticket from Korea to Cuba through the United States, not realizing he needed a transit visa. He had gone through Korean immigration, and the Korean immigration officer, excited, had said, 'I know you! You are Kcho! You are famous!' and had not looked thoroughly at his passport. He was put in handcuffs when he got to the United States and kept in them until he was put on a plane home.

IV. 32

Sunday again, and absolutely nothing going on. It is as if more than oil is being saved for the visit of the pope. Nick goes for a walk by himself on the Malecón. He runs into an American diplomat he knows, who is in Havana on a visit. They start walking together. They are asked the time by two *jineteras*, and when they actually tell them the time, the *jines* start to giggle and pull on the men's clothes. They have to shout at them to get them to stop.

The diplomat, whom Nick invites for dinner, says things have gotten a lot better than they were in the early nineties. He used to go to the church of San Antonio de Padova in Miramar. The authorities tried to discourage Section diplomats from going to churches then. Once, they smeared the contents of a diaper on the door. Another time they got a woman to come in and start yelling and disrupting the service. He says they've stopped doing most of that kind of stuff.

The diplomat says the shooting down of the planes was not something planned. He says it was a gross miscalculation. Fidel gave an order to use 'whatever means necessary' to prevent territorial incursions, and the commanding officer was following what he thought were orders. The Cubans now say that Helms-Burton (which has been signed but not yet implemented) is a sure thing, but the diplomat says it is not a sure thing. He says they have an opening again now with the visit of the pope. He says the shooting down of the airplanes is well enough behind everyone now.

LETY TELLS ME IT'S going to become illegal now for a Cuban to buy a videocassette recorder or to bring one in from another country. Worse than that, merchant marines, from whom everybody bought their VCR's, will not be allowed to bring them into the country any longer, either. 'And this is strange,' she says, shrugging, 'because everyone knows that all we want to do is tape speeches of the *comandante*!'

IV. 33

'And socialism,' Fidel says at a dinner we are attending, speaking of his visit with the pope in Rome and of their discussion about Poland, 'coming to a country that was ninety percent Catholic, it must have been *terrible* for them . . .'

The foreign guests watch Fidel with clinicians' half-smiles on their faces as he says this; the expressions on the faces of the Cuban guests (low-ranking members of the *nomenklatura*), however, remain in the range they've kept all night, from admiring, through rapt, to in love.

Three years it has taken us to see Fidel in person, and suddenly we're seeing him all the time.

Alex, the same diplomat who, two years ago, told me Fidel's outfit reminded him of gays in the West Village circa 1978, who remains convinced that there is an unexpressed, subliminal homoerotic thing going on between Fidel and the men around him, has asked me to notice the next time I am with Fidel, the *height* of the Cubans Fidel has been surrounding himself with lately: they are all short.

It is true: except for one five-foot-tenish man in Fidel's entourage, all the other Cubans (I noticed in the living room while we were having cocktails) are under five foot six, and there is one man tonight who is under five feet tall.

This smallest Cuban guest, a kind of human dormouse, whose nose barely pokes above the table, and whose hair, unbrushed, sticks straight up from his head, does give one wide-mouthed yawn as Fidel speaks, but then goes back to looking totally in love.

Alex says short, lower-ranking members of the *nomenklatura* look totally in love when they're with Fidel, whereas medium-sized, higher-ranking members of the *nomenklatura* look less in love.

* * *

AN ENCOUNTER WITH FIDEL, I say to Alex, brings to mind Asian theater: Kabuki, No, Chinese opera, Bunraku, with their carefully contrived movements, stock facial expressions, masks. He speaks for twenty-five minutes, listens for three, speaks for twenty-five, listens for three. Thai dancing, too: reenactments of scenes from the *Rāmāyanda*, flights over water, the powerful monkey general (Hanumān) of the North. This goes on in daily life, too, as if daily life in Cuba were one long rehearsal for an encounter with Fidel, in the formulaic responses, in the limited movements of *conseguir*ing and *resolver*ing, in the dissolving and re-forming line of the permissible, which one must locate, agilely, on a daily basis. Encounters with Fidel are full-dress performances: porcelain masks, pointed golden headdresses, false fingernails, dog-faced devils, mice. The room becomes electrified, as if stage lights have gone on, when he enters, and norms of human interaction are dispensed with. The beard and uniform are his masks. He performs and we watch, responding within defined limits, with our own less-splendid masks and stock facial expressions.

There is also the element of religious adoration. He arrives in mysterious, roaring procession, is extracted from a black Mercedes, unfolds, performs his timeless rite. His time is up, he is carried, an animate reliquary, by phalanxes of devotees to another location, to perform again. He is the ark of the covenant, a moving holy Kaaba, the virgin goddess of Kathmandu.

IV. 34

Tennis at the Hotel Nacional. Jimmie lobs a ball over the fence. I go to look for it on the condom-strewn grassy slope leading from the court to the plaza below.

I step in something soft. I look back, hoping that it is mud (it has rained), but next to where I have stepped are some pages of *Granma*, heavily used, uncrumpling in the sun.

I race to the most pristine patch of wet grass that I can find. Luckily it is just one shoe, and a sturdy one. If it were both shoes, I tell myself, I would take them off and leave them for a sexual tourist to find.

* * *

WE DRIVE TO MATANZAS for the launching of a book, *French Memories*, about the French presence in Matanzas. When the French were driven out of Haiti, they went first to Charleston, South Carolina. From there they went to Matanzas. They became rich exporting sugar. The wealthiest Frenchmen built neoclassical houses that you can still see, in an area called Versailles. In addition to becoming wealthy, Matanzas became so culturally developed, its tastes so refined, that Matanzas was known as the Athens of Cuba.

The launching is in the building of the printing house La Vigia. La Vigia makes books by hand and never makes more than two hundred copies. La Vigia printing house is in an ancient and very pleasing building opposite the Teatro Sauto, with stone floors and a stunning clock face, made in London in 1870, capable of telling the hour, the day of the week, the date, and the phases of the moon.

A French writer visiting Cuba makes a speech in which he says that fantasy is more important than gasoline.

At the reception afterward, a vice-director of La Vigia says that the editions sell for ten pesos each – less than fifty cents. They have already been sold out. The money they have made for the whole edition is a little less than one hundred dollars.

'But if they are all sold out, why don't you make some more?' I ask.

'Because the books are hard to make. They require a lot of time.'

'But if they are popular, and people want to buy them— '

'They are hard to make,' the vice-director repeats.

'But here the law of the market doesn't operate!' I say, answering my own question.

'*Asi es*,' he says and the people around us say, nodding their heads in affirmation.

We walk to the Río San Juan. We see where the barges came up the river to be loaded by cranes with oak casks full of sugar. From there the barges would pass through one of the world's first pivoting railroad bridges to the bay of Matanzas, where the oak casks would be loaded onto larger boats bound mostly for Charleston, South Carolina, but also for farther north in the United States and for Europe.

We are driven for miles outside of Matanzas to a 1940s country house, now some kind of official guest house.

The dining room is very clean and the help are cheerful and willing to serve. We are served fruit first, which is typical of Cuban meals, but a Frenchman, recently arrived in Cuba, makes a face at me over the fruit when no one is looking.

I go into the bathroom. It is a spacious bathroom in a building all by itself. It may have been part of a pool house, for there are rusted supports for benches and partitions still in the walls and on the way to the bathroom I passed a pool-sized depression in the earth, filled with gravel and weeds.

Most of the tiles in the bathroom are missing. There is no toilet paper, no seat, one dripping cold-water faucet, and to one side of the toilet is a gaping hole the diameter of a soccer ball, edged with a white crust.

A fat fly bites deeply into my ankle; I smash it with my hand. Grateful for the small trickle of water, I rinse fly cadaver out of the contours of my wedding ring, wipe my hands on my dress, and retake my place at the VIP table.

IV. 35

Lunch with an acquaintance from X——. He speaks about his meeting with a Cuban vice-minister. He speaks about how agitated the vice-minister became when he brought up the question of human rights and religious freedom. 'And I suppose you're also going to ask me whether there is going to be *Christmas* this year or not?' the acquaintance says she said to him. 'Why is everyone always asking me whether there is going to be *Christmas*?'

IV. 36

This is the third Thanksgiving we have celebrated here. I am unable to find a turkey in the *agropecuario* this year as I did last year, though. I find one at the Diplomercado for twice the *agro* price.

Corn kernels cannot be eaten straight here – corn grows tough in the tropics, and the fresh kernels have to be ground into *maíz molido* in order to be eaten. I try making a chowder out of it to serve as a first course, with onion, crab meat, and sherry. I think the soup is going to be a failure because it tastes very floury at first, but then it starts to thicken, the fresh crab is added, and it becomes one of the best soups Lorena and I have ever made.

Lorena has been using dried cranberries in the oatmeal cookies because we have run out of raisins, and I have forgotten to tell her to save some, but there are a few left. We mash them in the blender with one orange, skin and all. The pieces swell in the orange juice and make a convincing sauce. Cuban *calabazas* make a fine pumpkin pie.

'The fish-and-corn soup,' I find myself telling our guests, all Cubans and X—ians who have never had Thanksgiving before, 'is a reference to the corn Squanto showed the Pilgrims how to grow. He placed a dead fish next to each planted kernel to act as fertilizer in the sandy soil of Cape Cod.'

I don't know whether it's having a third-grader and a fifth-grader at the table with us or being in Cuba that makes me invent this culinary tradition. I don't know, either, whether it's having kids and reading the Squanto story over and over again with them while being in a place that's not the United States at Thanksgiving time – it could be any place – that puts a lump in my throat now when I recount the Squanto story, embarrassing me totally and making me hope people don't notice.

I raise my glass of champagne after the pumpkin pie is served. '*Imperialismo no*, pumpkin pie *sí*!' I say loudly, the lump in my throat mercifully disappearing. This starts rounds of '*Socialismo o muerte!*' '*Imperialismo o muerte!*' '*Pumpkin pie o muerte!*' '*Pumpkin pie y socialismo!*' and '*Pumpkin pie o socialismo!*' delivered around the table with booming voices.

I am aware of Juana at the end of the table, sitting next to Jimmie, who is trying to keep his eyes open, and of her revolutionary father, who died in the eighties.

'I hope in the future people will not have to make such terrible choices,' I say.

'Why is it such a terrible choice?' an X—ian guest says. 'I would choose pumpkin pie any day.'

I am aware, too, of Juana's grandfather, the self-made man, who emigrated from Spain to Cuba as a young boy and moved back to Spain after his stores were nationalized. I am aware of

281

how he killed himself after he returned to Spain. This is the part of the story I didn't have until Juana filled it in for me, in a moment when we were alone together, about a week ago.

IV. 37

Miguel tells me on the way to the *agropecuario* that there is going to be a new law that sailors and merchant marines will no longer be able to bring electronic equipment into the country.

I tell him I already know this.

He says he has heard of doctors and academics who received grants and are studying abroad who are cutting their stays short so that they can return to Cuba with the VCRs they bought before the end of the month.

There is silence. Miguel lifts the palm of one hand, as if weighing something. 'People get so bored here,' Miguel says, 'but at least, until now, they have been able to watch nice movies.'

IV. 38

Nick and I explore an abandoned Catholic old people's home in Miramar. It covers an entire block. The guardian, an elderly *blanco* who lives with his family in the back of it, shows us around. It was closed two or three years after the *triunfo*, the guardian explains, when the Spanish monks, nuns, and priests who ran it were expelled. It was built in 1922 but already a section of it is in ruins, with a large hole in its roof and in the floor below, fringed with bent steel rods.

It's not the buildings built in the sixteenth, seventeenth, and eighteenth centuries that are in perilous shape – they are in Habana Vieja and are protected by UNESCO; it's the buildings built in the nineteenth century and afterward in Centro Habana and beyond that are in perilous shape. Most often they are the big institutional buildings because their sheer size makes them impossible to maintain. They are the most difficult to keep people from pillaging, because such long fences would have to be built. Bathroom and kitchen fixtures were the first to go, the guardian explains, and then copper roof gutters and copper pipes. People dug holes in the plaster to pull out pipes.

Doorknobs and window latches were then taken, and then in the seventies people started digging electrical wires out of the walls, for their copper and other metals. Bathroom and floor tiles were pulled off and taken, and roof tiles, too, as neither could be found anyplace in Cuba for a long time. He was hired as guardian and given the apartment in the back in the early eighties, but by that time it was already too late. People take bricks and cinder blocks now. He tries to keep them out – he has a German shepherd, too – but there is no fence, and the walls are full of holes.

IV. 39

Opening of the Festival del Nuevo Cine Latinoamericano. Alfredo Guevara's speech is back on the mild side. Che is mentioned, but the speech is not shrill. It is also brief. I find myself wondering if the black Lacoste-type shirt he wears tucked in and the blazer he wears draped over his shoulders is in emulation of Sartre.

The floor show this time is a lone musician onstage singing a song, the words of which are, 'The problem is not . . . ,' and he sings a list of a lot of problems or reasons for problems. At the end he finally sings, 'The problem is love.' The floor show, like the song, is over after a short while.

The movie, kept secret until now, is announced. It is a joint French-Spanish production, *The Cosmonaut's Wife*. It is a situation comedy, stretched out to nearly two hours, with labored humor. The star of it, Victoria Abril, is there. She makes a brief speech before the beginning of the movie. I take a little nap near the end of it.

IV. 40

A statement is released by a group of bishops in Rome in which Cuba is described as a 'totalitarian state.'

PIÑEIRO SAYS THE BISHOPS' statement is no big deal, just some rightist elements sounding off.

Nick has managed to get Piñeiro to come for lunch by himself.

Piñeiro has two *mojitos* before lunch, wine through lunch, and scotch after lunch. We eat garbanzo soup with cumin, grilled snapper, roast potatoes and carrots with rosemary, spinach sautéed with garlic and lemon, green salad, and Lorena's lemon meringue pie. Piñeiro eats hunched over his plate, making low noises of pleasure.

Piñeiro says something toward the end of the meal about Cuba's elections being free. I burst out laughing. Nick turns red in the face. 'What are you laughing at?' Nick asks me. It is me getting Piñeiro's tone of voice wrong, but I should know never to laugh when someone like him says something like that. I have had a *mojito*, too, but just one. It *seemed* like an ironic tone of voice he used when he spoke about Cuba's elections being free, as if he were scrunching his body apologetically and putting quotation marks around the word *free*. I should know by now that when he drinks, he is more *duro*. I do a save: I say I hope Cuba is preparing itself for when the embargo ends. The embargo's ending will be the greatest challenge to the revolution, in my opinion. Piñeiro nods. His eyes are heavy-lidded. He makes a contained burp, puffing out his cheeks.

Piñeiro weaves to his Lada and gets in the driver's seat. He shuts the door. The Lada clatters into first gear. Manuel opens the gate. Piñeiro hunches over the wheel, the way you have to over a Lada steering wheel when you don't have a lot of upper-body strength. We wave at him under the blazing three o'clock sun. I feel as if we are releasing a deadly weapon into the traffic. I tell Nick that Piñeiro is going to kill either himself or someone else.

'Maybe both,' Nick says.

PRIESTS AT A MASS use the word *derechos* (rights) for the first time.

A Spanish priest is expelled from Cuba for what is described in Cuban news media as 'counterrevolutionary' activities. It is not explained what the activities were, nor can anyone tell us.

NICK SAYS HE SAW the pope on television, celebrating mass. He was so weak he could not lift the chalice.

All reports still say the pope is really coming.

FIDEL HAS NOT BEEN seen in public for many weeks.

I ASK NICK HOW often, when people are in a historical moment, do they *feel* they are in a historical moment.

Nick says he thinks not very often.

FIDEL APPEARS IN PUBLIC for the first time in months, accepting his nomination as a representative of Santiago in Cuba's parliament. The speech lasts three hours. Those who watch it tell us later that Fidel looked blank a few times and that sometimes his mouth moved, but no words came out.

IV. 41

All shoes of the Cuban *nomenklatura* are curious. And Raúl Castro's shoes, visible below the pant legs of a snug-fitting olive green military uniform at a dinner party we attend, are no exception. They look custom-made. The heels of the shoes are slightly higher than normal men's heels and there is probably a lift inside them as well. This is to be expected, for Raúl is a good five to eight inches (depending on who is telling you) shorter than his brothers, Fidel and Ramón. It's the *last* on the shoes (I think that's what you call it – the slope of the shoe, from heel to toe) that makes them curious. The lasts of Raúl's shoes are more *swooping* than the lasts of modern men's shoes, even of shoes with lifts. They are more like the shoes of burghers in late Dutch Renaissance paintings, swooping down to square toes, or a more stolid version of the shoes men wore in France during the reign of the Sun King. They are shoes of *The Nightwatch* or *The Anatomy Lesson*. They are laced but would take buckles well.

It is curious how Raúl does look entirely different from his brothers, Ramón and Fidel, who greatly resemble each other. But the rumor that Raúl's father was the Castro family's Chinese cook and that he is gay – hence the nickname La China – seems to me a little extreme. Ramón and Fidel are both around six foot one. Raúl's height, according to different assessments, ranges from five foot five to five foot eight. Raúl's face is round, flat, and beardless, with slanted eyes and high cheekbones. His fine hair, which is light brown and still has very little gray in it, is straight. His voice is high and nasal.

Raúl says people say he doesn't talk as much as his brother

Fidel, but that it's not true: he talks just as much. The guests laugh politely. Then what follows is a play-by-play of the campaign in the Sierra Maestre, without anyone's asking for it, without any conversational lead-in, lasting throughout the entire dinner. He gestures, he bobs, he smiles, he grimaces, and you can tell from the degree of his absorption that he is not with us in the dining room at all, but back in the Sierra Maestre with his men.

The high-ranking members of the *nomenklatura* at the dinner table remain absolutely silent while Raúl talks, even more silent than they are when Fidel holds forth. The expressions on their faces are neither rapt nor adoring nor in love, but this is Raúl, and these are ministers, not vice-ministers nor the dormouse-like lower-ranking members of the *nomenklatura* with whom Fidel prefers to surround himself these days. The ministers drink sip after sip of wine as Raúl talks. Some ministers slide forward on their chairs, their tailbones giving way until their underarms are nearly level with the table. They play, straight-armed, with the stems of their wineglasses, draw with the tines of their forks on the tablecloth, steal glances around the room.

Then, just as abruptly as he started, Raúl stops talking. The ministers who have sunk push themselves back up in their chairs. There is a collective inhalation. Raúl rises. Chairs grind back. We move into the living room. People break up into smaller groups. Conversations start. Standing in one group, Raúl says that he hopes that Cuba can normalize relations some-day soon with the United States. It is a fact of geography that the United States is Cuba's closest neighbor, and you can't go on forever, having difficulties with your closest neighbor.

IV. 42

A Cuban tells us Fidel told him he invited the pope knowing that he was an anticommunist. Fidel then said, chuckling, that maybe he – Fidel – was an anticommunist, too.

IV. 43

The intercom rings. It is Manuel. 'You should come and have a look at Bloqueo. He doesn't look well.'

I sigh. Things have just gotten going at my desk.

Bloqueo's face is blown up to twice its normal size. One eye is shut and oozing. 'He hasn't been seen for two days, and he just showed up like this. He's been fighting.'

There's a new official veterinary clinic on Quinta. We have heard that, being so new, they haven't had a chance to go downhill yet. We bundle Bloqueo into the laundry basket, and off we go.

Claw marks, teeth marks on his face and legs, filled with pus. On one leg the skin has been ripped off, exposing bone. Miguel and I hold Bloqueo down as the doctor drains the wounds and paints then with purple disinfectant. The doctor gives him an injection of antibiotics.

We make an appointment for castration for Bloqueo and a complete ovariectomy for Embargo.

IV. 44

We move to the living room between the main course and dessert to hear the archbishop of Havana, Cardinal Jaime Ortega, speak on television about the visit of the pope. It is the first time since *el triunfo* that any religious person has been allowed to speak on television in Cuba.

The cardinal's speech is well constructed. First he speaks about poverty in the world and the scourge of neoliberalism, and he takes a potshot at abortion; then he gives a brief biography of the pope. He speaks of the pope as a young man, of his struggles against the Nazis, and of his struggles against the domination of his homeland by a large neighboring power, which imposed its system on his country. He concludes by speaking of the need to achieve the widest truth possible.

I think he has done a good job, but others in the room say he is tense and that he uses too many complicated ideas and words for the average Cuban.

IV. 45

I have rented rooms for Mark and other journalists in Cubans' homes, as they asked me to, but it's getting more and more illegal all the time to stay in people's houses, so I faxed them that I reserved rooms for them at the Hotel Lincoln. The Hotel Lincoln looks, from the outside, even more poorly managed than other hotels; the management probably has little idea who is going to be staying there, so (I reason) that if any one of the ministries that intercept my faxes should choose to check if Mark and his friends – among the three thousand other journalists who are coming to Havana to cover the pope's visit – are really in it, even it might have a hard time verifying this.

This morning, a decree goes out that all those renting to foreigners during the pope's visit will not have to pay taxes on the rooms they rent out, so now I can go ahead and fax, 'You're in a private house,' and give the address and telephone number. We rent a car for them today, too, even though they won't be coming for another week. There won't be any cars available by then. It sits waiting in Roberto's garage, costing one hundred dollars a day.

Within hours of the decree, the airport arrivals area is jammed with people holding up signs advertising rooms for rent.

INAUGURAL DINNER AT A newly refurbished tourist hotel, Arenal, in Santa María del Mar starts earlier than scheduled, in order to allow the guests to return home to listen to Fidel's speech on television about the pope's upcoming visit.

I ask the vice-minister of tourism, a brisk, open-seeming thirty-year-old, if his ministry is doing anything to discourage single-male tourism.

'We are raising prices,' the vice-minister says. 'We are developing more cultural activities.'

'Because the girls, you know, they go to Europe thinking to improve their lives. They are generally disappointed.'

'You don't appreciate what you have until you lose it,' the vice-minister says.

I ask him if hotel workers are given any more stimulus.

'It depends what you mean by *stimulus*.'

'I know many people on vacation don't care how much the people who are serving them are paid, but when I hear someone at a hotel where I am staying, or at a restaurant where I am eating, is making two hundred pesos a month, it cuts my appetite. I can't enjoy myself.'

'But in your country, you have to pay for your education, your hospitals, your housing—'

'But there is free education in X—, and medical care. There is free education and medical care in Italy, France, Sweden, Holland, and many other European countries.'

'There *is?*'

WE BEGIN LISTENING TO the speech in the bar of the hotel, move into the hotel director's suite, have another drink, listen to the speech on and off for an hour, drive back to Havana, turn on the television: Fidel is still speaking. I put Thea (who has been waiting up for us) to bed. We floss. I undo my face, pour water, put on hand lotion. Fidel is still speaking. At one o'clock we turn off the television, sleep, wake up at two-fifteen, say to each other, 'Let's see if he's still speaking.' We turn on the TV and there he still is.

IV. 46

We are invited by Eusebio Leal to the dedication of a park to the memory of Diana, Princess of Wales.

I thought, at first, when I read the word *Diana* in the invitation that they were speaking of a statue of Diana the huntress, rescued from some ruin and now used to adorn a park. But no, they mean the princess.

There is near universal shock on the faces of Cuban friends when I tell them what we are invited to. 'Now they are truly mad,' they say.

Nick can't go.

The monument to Diana is a ten-foot, entirely phallic column with, to the side of it and much smaller, a vaginal sun.

A Latin American journalist whispers breathily in my ear that the column must be the monument to Dodi Fayed.

A Cuban writer favored by the government comes up to me. The writer says it is good the pope is coming because it validates the Cuban process.

What process, I want to ask him, but don't.

He moves to the next group of foreigners.

Nick and an American journalist, Herb, who both speak Spanish a thousand times better than I, agree that Fidel's speech the other night on TV was brilliant. The speech, they agree, was Fidel's way of controlling the disgruntled *nomenklatura*; it was Fidel's way of showing that he was in control of the pope's visit, that it was he, Fidel, who was asking everyone to go to the Plaza de la Revolución, so that it would not appear that anyone's going to the Plaza de la Revolución was an independent act or an expression of anything other than support for the revolution.

I look at Nick. I didn't realize that Nick had actually *listened* to the speech, listened enough between the driving and the flossing and the dozing to be able to put it all together, but he had, and I realize, for the millionth time, how much more serious, thorough, and attentive Nick is than I am.

ON THE PATRIA O MUERTE sign next to the airport, they have taken down O MUERTE and left just PATRIA.

There is no slogan on the PabExpo traffic circle billboard, only the words THE CUBAN PEOPLE WELCOME HIS HOLINESS JOHN PAUL II.

AT LAST FIDEL SEEMS younger than someone.

The pope's speech is slurred. Fidel looks at him with surprise and concern. One wonders if the pope's dentures are slipping, or if he has had a stroke right there on the plane, and if this trip is some kind of abuse of the elderly, imposed by the pope on himself. His chin is on his chest, his hands and head are trembling, and his entire torso stays permanently bent over to one side. He manages to stay standing up, though, and when he says, with his trembling voice rising, that he hopes the world can open up to Cuba and that Cuba, 'with all its magnificent potential,' can open up to the world, his frailty is transformed into a giant, gleaming bulldozer pushing vanity off a high cliff into crashing violet waves.

THE POPE'S FIRST MASS, in Santa Clara. We watch it on TV. His theme is the family. I call the help to come in and listen to it with me. When the pope speaks about separation of families, Concha starts crying and runs out of the room.

ROBERTO STANDS IN THE doorway looking crestfallen. Mark comes up behind him. 'We have to go back to Washington,' Mark says. 'Clinton's been banging one of the White House interns and it's all over the news. Brokaw is leaving; Rather is leaving. I want to stay here, this is much, much more important, but we have to go.'

Mark was supposed to stay for six whole days, but now he will be leaving after three. That means $60 less for Roberto (or more, if you figure in the proportional tip that it is Mark's style to give) and $150 less for Roberto's aunt on his father's side, in whose house they are staying. Two hundred ten dollars is more than any Cuban makes in a year.

I want Roberto and his family to make money. I want everyone in our house to make money. I want all the *jineteras* except the underage ones to make money. I want all the *paladar* owners and the black-market cigar, lobster, fish, flour, sugar, potato, and cheese vendors to make money. I want all the people who work in the *agropecuario* to make money. I want all the artists to make money. I want all the people who rent rooms and houses to make money. I want all the people who rent out or show pirated videotapes to make money. I want the antique dealers to make money, as well as all the people who sell something precious out of their homes just every once in a while. I want the independent taxi drivers to make money. I want all the rent-a-clowns, magicians, and puppeteers for children's parties to make money, and the *piñata* makers and the independent tire repairmen. I want the man who powers his glass engraver by pedaling his bike and carves your name on your windshield – so that the windshield cannot be stolen right off the car – to make a lot of money. I want all the manicurists at their card tables on the street and the people who restitch tennis shoes and refill lighters with insecticide to make money. I want all the handmade greeting-card and party-favor people to make money. I want Alfonse the innovative vegetable farmer to make money. I want all the freelance masseurs and all the freelance Spanish, English, French, Italian, German, Russian, Portuguese, piano, swimming, dance, karate, tae kwon do, and yoga teachers to make money. I want the people who sell souvenirs in the Plaza de la Catedral and on the weekends in the parking lot on the Malecón to make money. I want the booksellers to make money, and the people redoing the houses of all the people who have made money to make money.

Every *cuenta propista* in Cuba will be making less money now because of Monica Lewinsky.

MASS IN SANTIAGO. The archbishop of Santiago speaks. He speaks of false messiahs and of those who confuse *patriotismo* with *partido* (the party).

PARTY AT THE HOUSE of the principal officer of the U.S. Interests Section, Mike Kozak, and his wife, Eileen, for the media. Five hundred people are expected, but many fewer show up. There are cardinals, also, and congressmen.

Most of the people we talk to acknowledge that the embargo suits Fidel to a T.

MASS IN HAVANA, at the Plaza de la Revolución.

Red Cross trucks are scattered throughout the square, and people in bibs with red crosses on them. A group tries to unfold a banner that reads DOWN WITH THE CASTRO BROTHERS! and are carried off, very quickly, by people in Red Cross bibs, to Red Cross trucks.

Three groups in the crowd appear to be organized. They pack themselves in tightly to keep the Red Cross people from getting at them. '*Libertad*,' they chant, all of them, in low voices, no voice louder than another, so that individuals cannot be picked out. They know that the Red Cross people know that arresting a group of them would cause the news cameras, which are now pointed at the dais on which the pope stands, to be pointed at the protesters.

One friend has bruises on his arms from being packed in so tightly.

IV. 48

Juana and I are alone in her family's Lada. Juana says she and Hernando have had problems and that he has moved out and is living with his mother.

I tell Juana I am so sorry.

Juana starts to cry.

I say to Juana that she is a treasure and if he doesn't realize that, that's his problem.

Juana continues to cry.

I ask her if it is the first time he has moved out.

Juana says there was another time, four years ago, but then he came back.

I ask her if it is definitive.

'For me it isn't.'

Hernando is an engineer. Working as a baby-sitter, Juana makes nearly eighteen times what he makes.

I say that the economic situation here must put a lot of stress on couples.

Juana says that all her female friends, attractive, competent women, are all divorced.

I say that I read in an article that in Russia, women were generally doing much better than men. Men felt sorry for themselves. They fell apart. Women, on the other hand, were like ducks. They kept floating.

'Courage,' I say to Juana through the open window after I get out of the car, and 'He should realize what he has,' which sounds lame as soon as I say it – like the verbal equivalent of using a twig to keep back a landslide, a landslide of broken families tumbling down whole mountain ranges.

IV. 49

The intercom rings.

'Roberto to see you.'

'Tell him to come to the upstairs hall.'

It's becoming a daily event, Roberto coming to see me to get cash – cash for Jimmie's computer lessons, cash for a computer part (I don't ask where he's getting it), cash for the purchase of a computer printer (I don't ask where he's getting it), cash for 'caviar' to upgrade the computer (once again, I don't ask), cash to reserve a rental car for an arriving friend of a friend, cash for touring friends, and sometimes friends of friends, around when they run out of cash in Cuba, who then reimburse my account in the States.

Apart from the journalist friends of friends, who came for the pope's visit, there have been fewer visitors this year. As the year goes on, it is becoming obvious that most friends, and friends of friends, who were curious enough to come to Cuba have already come, said, *Oh, it's like that*, and have not felt the need to come back again. I had the feeling, in September, that it would get to be this way. The visitors are now truly fewer and farther between.

Roberto has just returned from taking Jonathan, the last of the journalists, to the airport. Roberto tells me that Mark, who left first, asked Jonathan to give Roberto's aunt some extra money, for the trouble she took in making her house nice for all of them. Jonathan unfortunately ran out of cash and asked Roberto to ask me to give some extra cash to his aunt – $150 extra.

I go to my secret drawer, pull out $150, and give it to Roberto. Roberto thanks me and skips down the back stairs.

I can understand Jonathan not being able to telephone me from anywhere, but I can't understand Jonathan not even writing me a note about it on his way to the airport.

IV. 50

Nick and I slip into the swimming pool.

Nick tells me his replacement has been named. He's a nice guy, Nick says. We will be leaving in July.

It comes all of a sudden like that, as usual – the news. This time it comes even more quietly than usual, as we are slipping into the swimming pool on a weekday afternoon.

'Look at the orchids,' Nick says.

They are blooming now – purple ones and white ones, hung up on little boards on palm trees along the fence.

We walk back to our bedroom, wet feet tracking on the marble floors. We walk through the high-ceilinged downstairs rooms, through which the breezes are constantly blowing, for the doors are never shut and there are no glass windows, only eight-foot-high louvered panels, which bathe the rooms in cool half-light.

It's not our house, we know, but a ghost house.

We will have to go live in a house with glass windows now, which shut.

It's a center, a mandala, a stone in a pond, our house, with ripples spreading from it, describing memories: fish on a reef, our Elegguá, *sopa de platano*, stories every day. Beautiful stories, ugly stories, happy stories, sad stories, hopeful stories, hopeless stories – stories more than I can count, happening every day.

I cannot leave these stories here.

IV. 51

Concha cries; Lorena slaps the cutting board with the flat side of a cleaver.

'You get used to someone, you know their habits, and then they go,' Concha says, wiping a tear from the corner of her eye.

I put my arms around them. 'It's not our decision, you know . . .'

'*Y mis niños* . . .' ('And my children . . .'), Lorena says. A tear streaks down her *negra azul* face, causing me to cry now, too.

'I am from La Yuma,' I say. 'I'm just over there.'

The help, each one of them so distinct now, also in the ripples of the pond.

I think of them the way Cubans call one another, their physical attributes their handles, signifying affection: La Negra, La Mulata, El Chino, Los Narrow Faces, La Plucked Eyebrows, El Nose Hairs.

IV. 52

We *cannot* take Embargo and Bloqueo back with us to X—, I tell the children. It would not be fair to them. We will be living in an apartment. They would not be able to go outside. There would be no nice Cuban smells for them, nor lizards to catch. The people who will be living in this house after us say they will be happy to take the cats. They also told me they are happy I am going ahead with the surgeries the cats are going to have.

Jimmie and Thea look at me with tears pooling on their lower eyelids.

IV. 53

Friendly Gringo Delivery Service arrives, bringing mail and

articles about the visit of the pope, including an edition of the *New Yorker* dedicated entirely to Cuba. It's a thin magazine, though, and the articles just brush the surface. Maybe that's the way it always is when you live in a place that people write about.

The most detailed article is on architecture. Paul Goldberger calls Eusebio Leal's restoration of Old Havana 'Old Havanaland' and calls Eusebio Leal a 'very efficient capitalist.' Goldberger actually got himself and a photographer inside the Faxas house – the green-roofed one just before the tunnel under the Almendares River – 'through the roof of which,' Goldberger writes, 'you can drop breadboxes.' It is the one we pass at night in torrential rains, see rain pouring through the breadbox-sized holes in the roof, and see, inexplicably and eerily, electric lights on in what looks like the dining room, on the floor below. It is the house the fierce old lady lives in whom no one can meet and who will never move out or sell. It is the house the interior of which everyone tries to imagine.

The photos show the interior of the Faxas house as we imagined it: grandiose, warped, and surreal to the point of wooziness.

NATALIA BOLIVAR'S FAVORITE CAT has disappeared. She searches the neighborhood, she goes door-to-door, she goes to her local CDR. Finally it is discovered: some neighbors ate her cat.

Natalia goes to the apartment of the cat eaters. The wife opens the door. Natalia spits in her face. 'May your husband die in the same way my cat died!'

FIDEL TALKS FROM nine-thirty until well past midnight, sitting at a table with two journalists who never speak. One of the journalists is paralyzed from the waist down.

THE VETERINARY SURGEON calls me. 'There was only one ovary when we went in and it was infected. The doctor who operated on her the first time removed only one.'

'But they weren't supposed to remove *any* ovaries, just the womb . . .'

'Well, they removed one ovary while they were at it. It was a good thing we operated and found the infection.'

Miguel brings Embargo home with antibiotics for her

infection. We put her in the guest room, where Bloqueo is already confined, recovering from his castration. We have tied up the curtains, put a rubber sheet on the bed, and put down a pan filled with sand, which we collect every week from a spot in front of the former (i.e., before the *triunfo*) Havana Yacht Club.

THE HUSBAND OF THE couple who ate Natalia Bolivar's cat has a heart attack and is rushed to the hospital.

The wife goes to Natalia, crying. 'You must remove the curse you put on my husband! I beg you! For the love of God!'

Natalia remains firm. 'I will *not* remove the curse.'

TWO AMERICAN WOMEN traveling through Cuba come to see us. One is photographing architecture. She was told that in order to see Eusebio Leal she had to make an appointment a month in advance, so she gave up. She met him by chance, though, as she was walking around Old Havana with a Cuban architect. The Cuban architect introduced her to Eusebio Leal, and Eusebio Leal, for some reason, evidently mistook her for some kind of big shot, because he took time with her.

He talked mostly about his clothes. 'I'm a simple man!' he said. 'My mother still washes my clothes! Look at these old clothes!' He pulled on the front of his *guayabera*. 'I wear them because I go every day to the work sites!'

Leal seems more bothered, we agree, by the 'efficient capitalist' part of Goldberger's article than by the 'Havanaland' part.

IV. 54

We visit Papelería Cubana. It is a paper mill on the Almendares River, not far from Centro Habana. It has been in continuous operation since 1837.

We meet the vice-director, a stocky blue-eyed *blanco* who has spent many years in the Soviet Union. We sit around a conference table made of pale wood-patterned Formica curling at the edges underneath an intermittent fluorescent light.

The director explains that other, more modern factories built in the interior of the country are now standing idle. They used too much electricity and required too many spare parts.

Papelería Cubana uses American machines from 1914 and makes the simplest kinds of gray and brown paper – the thick gray paper for making cartons used to package prepared food in the *agropecuarios*, the thinner brown paper used for wrapping surgical instruments after they have been sterilized, and toilet paper.

I ask if the toilet paper is gray with speckles in it and if it is sold now at the Diplomercado. He says that it is.

This is an unexpected boon, for every time I am in that part of my sizable bathroom I find myself trying to imagine the factory that produced such toilet paper. It's because of the speckles, each one a different consistency (some are stiff, like wood chips, some flexible, some crinkly), composing endless constellations for my contemplation: giraffes, cars, a school desk, Independence Hall in Philadelphia, Munch's *The Scream*.

Nick says the word *stimulus*.

'My major concern,' the director says, 'is making sure that the workers and their families have enough to eat.'

I look at him. The director of Papelería Cubana is the first official person in any kind of managerial position whom I have met in Cuba (though Nick says he has met some) who has not, upon hearing the words *motivation* or *stimulus*, first lectured me about how in Cuba there is free education, health care, practically free housing, and so on, as if this were news.

The director describes the different ways he has devised to provide the workers with a supplement to their salaries of two hundred pesos per month (a little less than ten dollars). He describes how the workers profit from increased production.

We visit the factory. The paper-pressing machine, made of cast iron by the Beloit Iron Works of Beloit, Wisconsin, is a single machine, twenty-five-feet high by seventy-five-feet long. It's a cross between a pasta roller and a locomotive, and it is studded with *Modern Times*ian cogwheels, valves, gauges, and hissing pistons.

We start with the finished product, dry paper on rolls, and move backward. The machine, though colossal, is still dwarfed by the room in which it sits. Other machines, we are told, making other kinds of paper, were dismantled years ago and moved out. We end at the beginning: at the depository of used paper, and the vats in which the used paper is mashed and stirred with water and chemicals to make pulp. The factory uses only used paper. We see bales of Mexican telephone books. The director points to another bale, which he says is from Cuba. Nick pulls a crumpled volume out of it. It is a Marxism-Leninism textbook.

The director walks with us to our car. He studied in the Soviet Union, he says. He really believed in what he was studying.

Nick thanks him for the interesting tour.

It pains him, he says, to see waste . . .

Nick tells him he's doing a wonderful job with the situation he's got.

'But there's got to be *something* about socialism worth preserving . . .'

José stands with the car door open. Nick turns to the director and says that will become apparent with time.

IV. 55

Effusive fax from Mark. He asks for my account number so that he can reimburse me in the United States. He is reimbursing me for the deposit I paid on the car rental, plus the $100 extra he and Ted wanted to give to Roberto's aunt for all her trouble. He hoped I got the message about that.

Roberto asked for $150 to give to his aunt.

IV. 56

Juana comes to the house shaking. We go into the children's bathroom and lock the door.

'My mother has been denied an exit permit to go to Spain to visit my brother, Frederico, and her mother – my grandmother – who is in her nineties. They denied her because Frederico stayed in Spain and because he is a doctor. They get really furious when doctors leave. They denied her just to punish the family. They denied it out of meanness. My grandmother is going to die, and my mother is never going to be able to see her again.' Juana starts to cry.

We can hear the children calling us from the other side of the bathroom door. Juana takes some toilet paper and wipes her eyes.

'My mother was very cool about it,' she says, her voice still shaking. 'But I started to cry. The woman behind the counter, she was embarrassed, can you believe it? She had some genuine emotion, seeing us. I don't know how she can still have some genuine emotion, being in her job. "What can I do?" the woman said. "These are my instructions."'

Jimmie is kicking the bathroom door now. '*Juuuuuaaaannnaaaaaa!*'

'*Mira eso. No puedes darme un momento de paz!*' ('Look at that. You can't give me a moment's peace!'), she says, opening the door, picking Jimmie up and whirling him around the room in a looping waltz.

IV. 57

One of the women photographers who has gone off on a tour with Roberto receives a fax on my fax machine from a travel agent in New York, detailing how she can have a new airline ticket issued, to replace the one that was stolen.

I wonder if she wants me to know that she has been robbed. She has not called us; there is only this fax. Sometimes, visitors try to keep us from knowing that they have been robbed, especially if they've done something we have warned them not to do, like stray too far from Roberto.

Friends of friends don't like it much at first, my siccing Roberto on them. They say they can drive around Cuba by themselves, but after a day or two of potholes, roadblocks, scanty road signs, menacing, importuning, or begging people as they park, and smashed car windows and missing radios after they park, they say, 'OK, we need a *driver*, but we don't need a *baby-sitter*.' It takes another day or two of being harassed, propositioned, wheedled, ripped off, and robbed, and (worse) of eating in state restaurants because they don't know how to find a *paladar*, to admit to us they need a baby-sitter – that is, if it's not already time to take the plane home.

I wonder how far the American ladies strayed from Roberto. True, Roberto has seen a lot of movies, and plays his role a little too much to the hilt – insisting on walking right next to his charges, blond ducktail raised, eyes darting, torso puffed like Johnny Bravo's, arm out from his side as if over an imaginary shoulder holster. Friends of friends don't like being seen with someone like that. Friends, though, are amused by it. It's amazing how different friends can be from friends of friends.

We warn the friends and the friends of friends into getting Roberto. Then, once they get Roberto, we warn them that Roberto's favorite singer is Barry Manilow and they should not put themselves *entirely* in his hands, otherwise they will end up at a salsa concert on the rooftop of the Habana Libre with pensioners from Winnipeg and Aachen.

I wonder how many salsa bands the American women heard before they decided to break out on their own.

IV. 58

Danila, whose learning-disabled son is in the army, says that the army doesn't give soldiers long pants anymore. They wear shorts to save on fabric. She hopes the army will realize soon that it is more trouble having her son in the army than not.

THERE'S A RUMOR that the U.S. Interests Section will be able to hold a small ceremony in Colón Cemetery commemorating the one hundredth anniversary of the sinking of the *Maine*. They will not be allowed to display the flag, though.

IV. 59

The American woman photographer whose pocket was picked in Santiago says she is annoyed the travel agency sent the fax to my fax number, because she didn't want me to know. She was ashamed after our warnings. She felt stupid. All she did was spend *one day* in Santiago by herself, while her friend went off with Roberto to Baracoa. A little kid bumped into her. It was just a little kid. He didn't take her money, though – her major money – or her passport. They were in an inside pocket. He did take a little money, though, some immediate money that was in her pocket along with the ticket.

The American women then tell me that they think Roberto is a little funny about money. They paid him for his expenses, but there were twenty dollars in the end that he couldn't account for. He gave them some explanation, but . . . Maybe it was just their Spanish, but they thought I should know about it.

WE GO TO THE one hundredth anniversary commemoration of the sinking of the *Maine* in Colón Cemetery.

We meet at the chapel. The staff of the U.S. Interests Section and their families are there, along with the marines, us, and the two American women photographers, whom Mike Kozak says we can include, as long as they don't take any photographs.

It is the second time we have been asked anywhere (the first was during the pope's visit – to the party given at the Kozaks for the U.S. media), not because of Nick and his job, but because I am an American.

The marines are not wearing uniforms; they have only green tennis shirts on, with 'U.S. Marines' embroidered on them, in very small letters, over their hearts.

We walk to the place where the three hundred men who died were temporarily buried before their bodies were taken to the United States. Mike and his staff found the site of the plot in the densely crowded cemetery after researching old records. We walk to the middle of where the plot was. It is an empty spot, not much wider than a single coffin, filled with rubble and with a rusted fence on one side of it.

A fan of gladioli and roses sits on the ground in front of the empty spot. The marine gunnery sergeant holds the flag. It is a tinier, darker flag than the others, but Mike Kozak is pleased that they have been allowed to display the flag at all, for initially they were told that they couldn't.

Mike Kozak gives a speech. 'Diplomacy with Cuba has always been complicated. It was complicated one hundred years ago, and it is complicated now' is the only reference he makes to the relationship between the two countries. A Cuban priest, sent by the archdiocese, reads a prayer.

IV. 60

The director of an American center for the study of international policy calls me. He wants to come over to hear our opinions with an American group he is leading.

I tell him that Nick, who is much more knowledgeable than I am, is in X—, but they can come if they want to hear the opinions of a not very well informed X——ian American housewife.

I say the embargo suits the Bearded One very well. They nod in agreement.

They always nod in agreement – every single American who comes to Cuba – when you say that the embargo suits the Bearded One very well. Sometimes it's after an hour of being in Cuba and sometimes it's after five hours, but it's always on the first day.

A SECTION OF THE abandoned old people's home in Miramar that Nick and I visited has collapsed, killing three people. The people who were killed were on the ground floor removing bricks.

ROBERTO ASKS IF WE can keep a lookout for a job for him, for after we go.

IV. 61

The Centro del Nuevo Cine Latinoamericano was established in the outer reaches of Siboney, on a lush former estate of the Loynaz family. The *centro* is one of our favorite places in Havana. There are offices, a bookstore, a bar with a large patio, and a movie theater, all unobtrusively set in dense greenery. It opens to the public at 2:30 P.M. every day.

We approach the box office, past a stand of bamboo. There is a Cantinflas festival currently showing a Cantinflas film every day at 3:00 P.M. Nick and I buy tickets and enter the movie theater.

The movie theater is one of the nicest we have ever been in, anywhere. It is well air-conditioned and has comfortable seats. Glass sidewalls in the movie theater allow us to take our seats in natural light and gaze at well-tended greenery until the film begins. It is 2:55 and we are the only people in the audience. At 2:57, a Mexican diplomat comes in, nods at us, and takes a seat. At 2:59, the red velvet curtains are closed over the glass walls on either side of the movie theater. The film begins. One ticket costs two pesos (about ten cents); still, very few people in Havana have cars to get here, and buses to this sparsely populated section of Havana are few and far between. It's also 3:00 in the afternoon on a weekday. Nick can be here because he is the boss and can take off when he wants to; I can be here because we have Juana. Still, the *centro* does not change the schedule of its showings. A ticket seller waits in the ticket booth. Two bartenders stand in the bar. A bookseller stands in the bookstore. Gardeners rake and clip. The air-conditioning hums, cooling thousands of cubic feet of empty space around us and the Mexican diplomat.

We will miss the *centro* very much.

There is a film for children every Saturday morning at 10:00 A.M. Practically no one comes to the Saturday morning films, either, we are told, except the few mothers and children who live in scattered houses nearby and can get there that early.

IV. 62

We visit Cuba's greatest living lyric poet, Dulce María Loynaz, in her house in Vedado. It is an airless mansion of beige stone. Vedado is like the Garden District in New Orleans, but Dulce María Loynaz's house is more like a pared-down version of the Frick Collection in New York than like anything you would find in Louisiana.

Dulce María Loynaz is in her late nineties. She has not had to sell her things, like the Carrera sisters have, nor does she cover them with plastic, like Bibi Sebaya. She has let them age in glass display cases: opera glasses, plume pens, souvenir ceramic thimbles, signed matchbooks, kid gloves, ivory cigarette holders, photographs of her being given things by bald men wearing sashes and by little girls with big bows in their hair. Though widely acclaimed in the 1930s, 1940s, and 1950s, she has written little and made few public statements since *el triunfo de la revolución.*

Dulce María Loynaz sits in a smock of lilac-colored raw silk with a bow at her throat. On her feet are lilac-and-white-striped raw silk pumps. They are about size 4½, width AAAA. They are the kind of shoes you see in display cases of women's costumes, not of the nineteenth century, but of the *eighteenth* century, when women's shoes looked more like slightly opened pea pods. We are served tea in hand-painted cups, through which the afternoon sunlight shines.

Dulce María Loynaz quotes *The Song of Hiawatha* for us in English.

IV. 63

Back from an early spring trip to Europe for our last push before returning to X—.

I wonder if I am going to have a heart attack. I get pains in my chest when I think about all I have to do now. I try to think about one thing at a time but can't get the one thing to stay in my mind, just by itself: other things start coming in, crowding the original thing. After a while the things I have to do start buzzing and moving in beelike patterns of their own. That's when the pains start.

This is the time, always, when our acquisitions haunt us. The trick is going to be to get everything out – not only the stuff we bought in Cuba, but also the stuff we came with. We have already been told by every foreigner who has ever left Cuba about how people in uniforms go all over your house, how they watch all the boxes being packed, and how you have to prove to them that everything you are taking with you is either something you brought to Cuba with you or has an export license.

I HAVE BROUGHT BACK photos of the school Jimmie and Thea will be attending in X—. I have also brought back photos of some of the children who will be in Jimmie's and Thea's classes.

'*Qué pálidos son. Están enfermos?*' ('How pale they are. Are they sick?'), Jimmie and Thea ask.

FIDEL MADE A seven-hour speech in our absence, criticizing the Cuban Film Institute and the film *Guantanamera.*

Guantanamera has already been out for more than a year, but Fidel hadn't seen it until Raúl saw it, when he was in Rome, and told his brother Fidel to see it.

Alfredo Guevara resigned in protest after the speech but resumed his post after a few days.

THE BILLBOARD ON THE PabExpo circle now reads YOUNG PEOPLE OF CUBA: WORTHY OF THEIR PARENTS.

IV. 64

I take four foreign women who are new to Cuba to meet Alfonse, the vegetable gardener. I am trying to drum up some business for him, especially now that we are going.

We go slowly through the garden. I tell them how Alfonse started with a rubble-strewn empty lot. Alfonse points proudly to the raised beds he and his helpers have built, and to the site he has prepared for the well driller.

One woman says under her breath, 'But it's such a wreck!' and later, 'I'm scared.'

I am hoping it's because she is new, but at the end of the visit, with a bag full of vegetables, she mutters, 'I hope I don't get sick.'

I don't know why I bother with some people.

IV. 65

The thighs of a female member of the *nomenklatura* are as wide as two midsize Canon photocopiers, and her rather short skirt is tight, so that a large, empty triangle is formed, up which a member of a European undersecretary's delegation and I, who are sitting across from her, can see all the way to her crotch. She is wearing electric-blue nylon pantalets trimmed with black lace.

IV. 66

Piñeiro has died. He confused the brake with the accelerator, had a car wreck that didn't injure him very badly, was taken to the hospital, told the doctors he was fine, went home, and died.

We go to a viewing of the body at a *funeraria* on Calzada, right in back of the U.S. Interests Section, just a few blocks from the Malecón. Lots of people are milling outside. We are led to the fourth floor. We step into a large, low-ceilinged film noir set, dense with cigarette smoke, dimly and nervously lit by feeble fluorescents, packed with thin old men in imitation leather jackets. Some look shocked; others look furtive; and still others, guilty, as if they are worried that what they learned in Catholic school may have some basis in truth and that there may really *be* a final judgment coming for them, too. Some sit on grimy red Naugahyde banquettes placed at intervals around the room. Some of the old men are so thin that they look like cartoon characters after they have been steamrollered, then peeled off

306

the pavement. Piñeiro, I realize, with his in-shape pectorals, cinnamon-colored chest hair, and willingness to talk to foreigners and to drink large quantities of wine, whiskey, *mojitos*, and cognac, was a giant among them.

I look at the crowd and try not to think about how, at this moment, all it would take would be for the U.S. Marines to pull up to the *funeraria* with amphibious landing vehicles. They could get practically all of them with one sweep. The marines would broadcast on television and on the radio in Miami and on loudspeakers blaring over Little Havana that they were coming. But the time the marines would announce would be an hour and a half before the time the boats would actually come, giving plainclothes marines waiting on the docks time to disarm the aging Cuban Americans who came to the docks carrying clubs, knives, guns, and bombs to meet the boats. The plainclothes marines, masquerading as unarmed 'monitors,' would wait until the dock was full and the false time they had announced for the arrival of the boats had come and gone. Then, on a signal, a roadblock would go up behind the aging Cuban American warriors, and they would be told to surrender their arms. Those who resisted would be overpowered. The marines would then transfer all *nomenklatura* members and Cuban American warriors to a high-security retirement home with a hospice, an infirmary, three hundred domino tables, and a cinema with nightly showings of Glenn Ford, Cantinflas, Rita Montaner, María Felix, and Kim Novak movies, and all the marines and all the people under fifty-five, from both sides of the Straits of Florida, would walk away from the retirement home brushing their hands, a job well done.

I know it does absolutely no one any good to think like this, but I've been here three years.

'I'M GOING TO miss him,' Mike Kozak says about Piñeiro, shaking his head sadly.

IV. 67

Nick and I go to the Jardin Botanico (Botanical Garden) in the afternoon. It's what I would do if I had to live here – be a botanist, even though I have no inclination. It's what I would do if I had no choice but to stay. We see salami trees from Africa, their seeds in pods truly as big as salamis. We see a palm tree, its bark covered in long black spikes like a porcupine's, and another tree, the seeds of which are as big as zucchinis and swell and burst and rain down furry pelts like hamster skins. We see trees bursting with fuchsia-colored blossoms and dark brown blossoms, other seedpods round and yellow like lemons but with flip tops.

IV. 68

I have started asking Reny about his past when I see him at cocktail parties. He is not used to people asking him about his past – where he studied, what he did during the revolution, if he ever visited the United States before *el triunfo*, how many members of his family went to the United States or to any other country, if he still communicates with any of them – and watching him be evasive and weird. It's not fair, for the man can't escape, but he's at the party and so am I.

IV. 69

Embargo and Bloqueo are losing their fur in patches. The veterinarian scrapes the skin and looks at it under a microscope. They have mites.

Danila's father-in-law's present *mujer*, who is a nurse, is enlisted to come every morning to give Embargo and Bloqueo courses of subcutaneous injections that make their blood toxic to the mites. The cats are kept trapped in the bathroom every morning until Danila's father-in-law's present *mujer* arrives. They are held on the kitchen table as they bat their tails and moan.

IV. 70

The packing representative of Cubalse comes this morning to see what size container everything can go in.

My PERCEPTION OF TIME contracts and expands unreliably. Sometimes I feel like a runner, crouched down, waiting for the starting gun. Other times I feel like Butterfly McQueen, sashaying her way past the picket fence as the Yankees close in on Atlanta. Everyone has been telling me how awful it is when the people in uniforms go all over the house and you have to justify to them every single thing you are taking out of Cuba.

I feel that I should be doing something to get ready for the people in uniform besides throwing things away and giving things away, but I don't know what it is.

THE DIPLO IS BRUTAL these days. Long lines at the diplomatic checkouts spill over into the regular checkout lines, where we stand. Cases of cooking oil and Cristal beer stacked on hand trucks appear in the cramped aisles of the Diplo. They are piled, minutes later, into Vietnamese, North Korean, and African diplomats' shopping carts, which then block the lines at the checkout.

One Vietnamese diplomat has a blackboard hung outside her house in Miramar, posting what she has available, for 15 percent less than the Diplo price. As a diplomat she gets a 33 percent discount at the Diplo, so she ends up making 18 percent.

THE *MIAMI HERALD* HAS come out against the embargo. It also states in an editorial that the lack of direct charter flights, suspended after the Hermanos al Rescate planes were shot down, simply makes the trip to Cuba, now through Nassau and Cancún, a calvary for the passenger and nothing else. It inconveniences thousands for the sake of a few fanatics.

NICK CALLS FROM the office. Direct humanitarian flights are being resumed to the United States.

CARLOS VARELA, A CUBAN singer based in Cuba, has just sung in Miami and nobody made a fuss.

Maybe things are getting back on track.

IV. 71

Nick's replacement is arriving from X— today, with his wife, to check out the house.

Nick says the wife is the one who should be scared of me, not me of her. Still I'm scared of middle-aged X——ian ladies, with their serious makeup, streaked blond hair, straight skirts, stockings, and high heels all day long.

RUN INTO THE U.S. consul at the Diplo. I tell him that we have a Cuban nanny whom we would like to take with us to the United States this summer. I say she will be spending the summer with us in the United States, then going with us to X— and spending a few weeks with us there to help us get set up there.

He says the important thing is that she won't stay in the United States.

I say she doesn't have a reason to because she already has another job lined up with another family after she returns from X—. I say that she makes now and will continue to make about fifteen times the average Cuban salary and that she lives in a nice house in Miramar and has a car.

The consul is a big man with a round, impassive face.

I say that she has a grandmother living in Spain and a brother who has just emigrated there and that if she were to go anywhere, it would be to Spain.

The consul says to send in her visa application with a note addressed to him.

I thank him. I thank him for taking the time to talk to me. I thank him for thinking about her visa application. I tell him that she is a person who will really benefit from traveling. I tell him that she has a superior mind . . .

'Well, if she has a superior mind, then she will want to stay in the United States. There is nothing for her here.'

I backtrack quickly and tell him that we have a very open relationship and I have often asked her if she would like to leave Cuba. I say she has told me that she has hope for the future and says that Fidel can't live forever and that Cuba is one of the most beautiful places on earth, physically.

'It is that,' he says.

I ask him how long it will take to get the visa. He says she can get it in one day.

JUANA AND I GO to the Consultoria Juridico. The Consultoria Juridico is the place where I have to go to have Juana's letter of

310

invitation composed. Juana cannot even apply for her exit permit until she has a letter of invitation from a resident of the country she is visiting, who promises to act as her sponsor and to pay her medical and travel expenses.

The Consultoria Juridico is in a mansion in Miramar with chandeliers and clean, well-lit rooms. The whole operation takes just a few minutes. I tell Juana that I expected the Consultoria Juridico to be in some dingy place across town where we would have to line up for hours and sweat, but Juana says it's in an easy-to-get-to, nice-looking place because foreigners go there; it's the other offices Juana has to go to that are dingy and across town and make you sweat.

I pay $140 for a girl at a computer to compose a letter for me on official paper and put a stamp on it. Juana says she is embarrassed that I am paying it, but I tell her that it is normal for me to pay it, for I am inviting her. Juana says it is not normal, it is not normal to have to do this, and I say that it is not normal but it is normal that I pay.

Now Juana has to apply to the Ministry of Education for a paper confirming that the Ministry of Education has no objection to her leaving. It's because it educated her, she explains, and they want to make sure she's not taking her education off to benefit other countries. That process takes about a month and costs $40. If the Ministry of Education has no objection to her leaving, she can then apply for an exit permit, which takes another few weeks and costs another $150. I say I will pay that, too, and Juana, balking at the Mitsubishi door, says I will not. I say it is normal that I pay because she is coming to America to help me, and Juana says, '*Por favor, con este normal,*' and says that if she doesn't pay she will feel bad for the rest of her life. I say we will see.

In the meantime, Juana must get her visas to visit the United States and X—. They will together cost another $30 and will take a few days, but she says she wants to have them in plenty of time.

Roberto asks if we have heard of any jobs for him yet.

We tell him we have been asking all the diplomats and businessmen we know. We have asked Nick's replacement, too. So far we have found nothing.

IV. 72

I insist on driving to Santiago and back with Nick, stopping at towns on the way, some of which I have seen but Nick hasn't, and some of which neither of us has seen. I tell Nick he can't leave Cuba without having seen Camagüey, Santiago, or Baracoa and that we can't leave without having seen Remedios, Sancti Spíritus, and Bayamo. We go in the Land Cruiser, with Roberto driving. We take plenty of clean underwear in case we can't find showers. We take raisins, crackers, nuts, canned tuna, canned beans, and canned fruit and two dozen bottles of water in case we can't find places to eat.

The children started moaning, 'Do we *have* to go?' three weeks before the trip. I said yes the first week, wavered the second week, and by the third week said they could stay in Havana with Juana.

They are ecstatic.

OUR FIRST STOP IS Remedios, a swept-bare colonial town. It is devoid of cars and even more devoid of stores, of any kind of commerce, than other Cuban towns we have seen. It is more devoid of commerce than Dimas, Baracoa, or Mantua. We park our conspicuous car in front of the church we have read about in our guidebook, but our arrival elicits only mild interest from passersby. No one offers to watch our car, to be our guide, or to sell us *una moneda con el Che* (a current three-peso coin with an image of Che on it, which in Havana they try to sell you for five dollars). People are the way we have heard they were before the *periodo especial* – reserved and unmaterialistic.

We enter the church through a side door and come immediately upon a baroque, three-hundred-year-old gilded wooden altarpiece. It fills the entire back wall of the sanctuary of the otherwise bare church. It is naive, overpowering.

Nick, who was raised a Catholic but is not devout, kneels on the altar rail and crosses himself.

Nick asks the priest who has let us in if they will be allowed to have their Good Friday procession this year outside the church. It has been rumored that since Christmas was allowed, they will allow Good Friday processions again outside of churches, for the first time since 1960. Since 1960 they have had to mark the stations of the cross inside the churches.

The priest says that as usual the Good Friday procession will not be allowed outside the church.

THE AMERICAN WOMEN photographers who recently traveled around Cuba with Roberto said they managed to sleep in a private house in Remedios, on beds with Cabbage Patch Kids sheets, but Nick prefers a hotel, so we drive fifty more miles to where there is one, in Morón.

Morón means idiot in Spanish, too. The room is spacious and clean. There is CNN. 'I can't believe it,' Nick says. The bathroom, too, is modern and clean.

Eating a bland but edible dinner of chicken, rice, and beans in the dining room around nine-thirty, we look out through the windows to see two lone *jineteras* under a single streetlamp at the entrance to the hotel, one in over-the-knee boots with stacked soles. As we are ending the meal, we see them, with resigned gestures, clomp off in the direction of town. There are only five guests in the hotel.

We retire to our amazingly comfortable room, which costs thirty-four dollars with breakfast. We go to sleep but are awakened harshly at one in the morning by the noise and thump of a discotheque, which seems to be directly underneath our room. Nick puts on pants and goes downstairs. The night manager follows Nick back to our room, stands in the middle of the room, and says, 'It's true, you can't sleep with this.' I put on my bathrobe and we are moved as far away from the discotheque as possible, into a cramped, unrenovated room.

'This is more like it,' Nick says.

Before we leave in the morning, we are given a basket of fruit, a bottle of wine, a baseball cap, a T-shirt, a pen, a 50 percent discount, and a personal apology from the manager.

EVEN USING A LOT of pull, our Elegguá hasn't been able to get reservations for us in Santiago at the Hotel Casa Granda, on the main square, only at the ugly modern hotel outside of town. Nick takes one look at the modern hotel, and we head to the Casa Granda.

The desk clerk says there are no rooms available. We go outside to Roberto. 'No rooms,' we say.

Roberto goes in. Five minutes later, he comes out. 'You

can go back in now and take your pick.'

The same desk clerk greets us. We are shown three rooms – one a suite, one overlooking the square, and one in the back. We choose the one overlooking the square.

A PLAQUE IS BEING put back under the statue of the soldier with the Grace Kelly profile on top of San Juan Hill. The plaque sits on the ground next to the young people who are doing the restoring, two young women and a young man, who are carefully brushing the spot on the rock where the plaque will go and trying different sizes of screws. TO THE MEN OF THE NEW YORK REGIMENT, the plaque reads. There is another plaque on the ground next to another rock. It reads TO THE MEN OF THE MASSACHUSETTS REGIMENT. We take a photo of them working.

The young man and one of the young women look annoyed, but the other young women smiles. 'It's for the tourists – they want to know,' she explains.

'Siboney,' I see on the map. It is on the coast, with a little umbrella symbol next to it, indicating a beach. 'Siboney' is the name of one of the most beautiful songs by Ernesto Lecuona, the Cuban composer. It takes us more than an hour to drive there. The drive, over green hills under a rising moon, is beautiful. We pass the hut where Fidel planned the attack on the Moncada barracks.

When we finally get to the former resort village, there are so many men, women, and children watching our every move that we don't know whether to place Roberto near the parked car or with our towels on the beach. Finally we decide to leave everything in the car with Roberto, including our sandals and our towels, and walk barefoot over the gravel to the water.

A man swims after us holding up a coconut for sale.

WE STOP AT A deserted beach on the way from Santiago to Baracoa, just before Guantánamo. We plan to spend half an hour there but end up spending three hours. It is the kind of beach we have been looking for ever since we came to Cuba. It is utterly deserted and in a glorious setting – this we have found before. But this is the first time we have been on a deserted beach and not had to worry about our stuff. This is because it's *so* deserted. It's deserted because it's in a desert, a desert microclimate found between Santiago and Guantánamo. People cannot live here, and few have cars or reason enough to come here in the heat. Agave and cactus on steep hills frame small beaches, one after another. All we see in three hours is one spearfisherman.

THRONGS OF PEOPLE on the street in Guantánamo. We think there is some kind of festival, but there are no banners. Roberto says it's just people looking for a ride. We look around. There are no cars. A truck passes and slows (it's the law that a truck with any kind of space in it has to pick people up), and people throw themselves on it, packing themselves in until they are hanging off the sides.

EL SOCIALISMO, a sign in Guantánamo reads, ADEMÁS DE SER JUSTICIA, ES EFICIENCIA Y CALIDAD (Socialism, in addition to being justice, is efficiency and quality).

WE ARE AT THE Spanish fort turned into a hotel in Baracoa, where I stayed with my brother and Marianne. Looking out through the sealed plate glass window, between the curtain and the air conditioner sealed with brown stuff, which has remained (I check it with a fingernail) gooey after two years, Nick says he didn't think Baracoa would be such a dump.

I say I never said it *wasn't a dump*; I just said it had other things in it besides things that made it a dump.

I send Roberto to find the architect Nelson Figueroa. He arrives, with a trimmer beard, looking dazed. I ask him if he remembers me from when I was there two years ago, with my brother and Marianne, the Canadian photographer. He says, 'Of course . . . ,' but it is obvious that he doesn't. He looks stricken when I introduce him to Nick. I don't know whether it is because Nick is so tall (Nick is not really tall, just six foot one, but Nelson Figueroa is four foot ten) or because he is so serious-looking, but Nelson Figueroa is completely different from the way he was before. Then I figure it's the way he is around any woman with any tall, serious man attached to her.

Nelson Figueroa takes us on a walking tour of Baracoa. Baracoa is even more depressed than before. One or two buildings in the town seem to be operating as *paladares*, but to me the people look even more bedraggled than before.

Nick and I mention a kind of travel magazine that came out a few months ago, published by Benetton. It's a special issue devoted exclusively to Baracoa, in which Baracoa's poverty and degradation are presented as colorful tourist attractions to be exploited. There is an article on a coffin maker who makes five dollars a months. It is presented as a good thing, such a salary, as something that keeps him pure and unspoiled. There is an article titled 'I Like Sex,' showing the good-looking young men and women of the town. In it, they are quoted as saying that sex is their source of entertainment. Several young men and women are quoted as saying they especially like having sex with foreigners.

I am closer to Nelson Figueroa's level, and I can tell from his pleased expression when he opens his mouth at the mention of the Benetton magazine that he is about to say that it is a good thing, the magazine, that it has really put Baracoa on the map, and so on, but before he is able to say anything, Nick says the magazine is depressing and disgusting, and so Nelson Figueroa says, 'Yes, it is disgusting.'

In chorus, Nick and I say that it's encouraging the dregs of Europe and every other place to come here. It will also cause the spread of AIDS.

Nelson Figueroa, looking more stricken, nods vigorously. '*Exactamente*,' he says, pointing into the air in front of us for emphasis.

Nelson Figueroa mentions a Dutch woman who is living in his house. We ask what she is doing in Baracoa. Nelson says she is doing research. We ask Nelson what she is doing research on. Nelson says he doesn't know. We ask Nelson if she is his girlfriend. Nelson makes a face and says she is not.

WE ITCH IN THE night and find raised welts all over our bodies in the morning from *agua mala*, which we must have gotten the day before, when we lolled for three hours in the water.

Roberto goes to pick up Nelson Figueroa. Roberto finds him passed out in bed, having completely forgotten that we were supposed to meet. He arrives extremely hungover, his hair wet.

Nick wants to visit a chocolate factory. We have heard there is one in Baracoa. We pull up to it unannounced. An American family we know visited the factory a few years ago. They drove right up and went in with their four children. It is Saturday. Nick explains to a guard stepping out of a guard box that he is a director of Energy Consulting International (he gives the guard his card) and he was wondering if we could visit the chocolate factory. Nelson hangs back, after having said several times on the way to the factory that it would probably be impossible to visit it.

The guard calls a higher-up. The guard tells us that the higher-up says it is impossible to visit the factory without the permission of the director, who has to get it from the Committee of the 26th of July, who has to get it from the party.

Nelson Figueroa leads us to a fake farm geared to group tourism. *Bohíos* (thatched *guajiro* huts) with shined, intact cement floors. A *mulata* in *rumbera* costume smoking a cigar. Neat signs in front of plants: CACAO, PINEAPPLE, MANGO, GUAVA.

Nick keeps wandering off, leaving Nelson in midsentence.

'We want to go to a *river*,' I tell Nelson Figueroa. Last time I came here with Sam and Marianne, we heard about the rivers, but it was raining and chilly. Nelson Figueroa takes us to another fake primitive group-tourism establishment to look for a boat to take us up the Toa River. 'It's just for a minute, ' he explains quickly.

A man is roasting a whole pig under a tent for a group of Swedish tourists who will be arriving. The boat is not there. Nelson stands there.

'I am *from America*, too,' I finally say.

'Go farther, go farther,' Nick says to Roberto, as we drive on a rough road up a bank of the Toa River, every time it looks like Roberto is about to stop. 'Go farther,' Nelson, who has finally understood, says, too.

We put on our bathing suits, take off our shoes, and climb down an embankment into the Toa River. There is a small rapids. Nick gets in, feet first, hands behind his head, then Nelson Figueroa, then me. We float, letting the current take us.

Sometimes the river is deep and slow, sometimes shallow and rushing, but never rushing enough to cause us the slightest bruise or bang. The water is crystal clear. High above us on either side rise the riverbanks, covered in dense jungle. There are in the river no alligators, no snakes, and not one aggressive reptile, insect, or mammal. There are not many people, either, only an occasional hut with a woman outside it, washing clothes. The women smile at us and wave. Every hundred yards or so, there is a rock or a rise on which we can rest, feel the water rushing around us, soothing our *agua mala* welts, and contemplate Nelson Figueroa's hairy elfin body. The Toa is one of four rivers in Baracoa, the others being Doaba, the Miel, and the Yumurí. These rivers have never been exploited and cut through forests that have remained as they were when Columbus arrived here; it was on approaching a beach near Baracoa that Columbus said, 'Never have human eyes beheld anything so beautiful.' There is no boat in the river and no one else in the river floating as we are. We float without sandals, without keys, without keep-dry bags, like otters, always to another bend in the river, to see what is beyond, and it is such a nice clear run that we float down it, too. After two and a half hours, we know we must be tired, though we do not feel tired. We stop not because we want to but because Nick and I are middle-aged and it's weird not to feel tired after floating for so long. We figure it's something the river has done to us, this not feeling tired, and that maybe it does this, make you feel not tired, until you drop like a stone.

We have forgotten a towel and share our supplies of canned tuna, crackers, olives, nuts, and raisins with Nelson, standing on the sand. Nelson looks a little more relaxed now, but still stricken.

At the end of lunch we give Nelson an extra can of tuna from our picnic basket to take home, as well as a can of olives and a can of something we took out of the minibar of the hotel, thinking it was a beer, which turned out to be a nonalcoholic malt drink. When we have nothing else, we give money, but usually we give things. We think it is less embarrassing that way, when the recipient is a professional, but Nelson's fraught silence as we root in the picnic basket – a silence we understand only seconds after we have given him the tuna, the olives, and the malt drink – communicates telepathically: *It doesn't matter if I am an architect. Give me money.* Still we hold our ground – I don't know why.

ROBERTO FINDS A MUCH better and cheaper *paladar* for us than the one we were in the night before with Nelson. I take Nick afterward to the bar of the Hotel La Rusa. La Rusa is for dollars now. Cubans no longer go there. Three lone tourists sit on the back veranda, staring out to sea.

On the way back to the hotel, Roberto begins a long, flowery speech about how much he respects us. We are, he says, like, like . . . we are younger, of course, than his parents are, and he hopes we don't mind him saying, but we are like parents to him. Yes, like parents. His hand sweeps down in front of the steering wheel with a flourish on the word *parents*. He cares about us. He really does. If we were other people, he wouldn't feel the need to say anything . . .

We tell him that it is very nice of him to say this, but what is he trying to say? Roberto says he knows that we have advantages, privileges, but that we try to do what we can to help people. We help people, and we try to see only what is good in people. That is why it pains him when some Cubans try to exploit the situation . . .

We ask him if he is trying to say something about Nelson Figueroa.

Roberto says Nelson Figueroa is very talked-about in the town as a big drunk. He has the habit of taking his clothes off in public and getting up on tables when he is drunk. Roberto says Nelson said to him the night before, when Roberto was driving him home, that they should use our car to cruise bars and pick up women.

'But where are the bars that you can cruise to? People don't even have *boniatos* (sweet potatoes) here; where are they going to get beers?'

'*Señora*, he wanted to use *your car* . . .' Roberto says Nelson asked him if he thought we would give him some money for going around with us. And the Dutch woman? Roberto says Nelson told him she is some old woman in her fifties who is in Baracoa, hanging out, and Nelson is sleeping with her in exchange for being maintained. Roberto says Nelson told him, '*Me cuesta mucho trabajo*' ('It's really a lot of work').

I HAVE TOLD NICK to steel himself, but the Gran Hotel Camagüey, we discover, is now managed by a Spanish chain. The bronze girl still holds her globe lamp at the bottom of the stairs, but the rooms on floors that are open to guests now have hot and cold running water.

Nick and I lie in twin beds while I tell him about how

319

Marianne and I lay there, waiting for running water, our armpits smoking.

The top-floor breakfast room, lifted directly from a William Holden movie, has not changed, however, and it still takes more than an hour to get fried eggs.

IV. 73

The bank and Bienes Culturales come today. The bank is represented by the same two men who came and listed all the jewelry and silver we brought with us when we moved in. They come with the list they made that day. They also bring with them a man from Customs, who introduces himself as Nestor. Nestor is a smiling *blanquito* with curly black hair and large dark eyes. They sit at the dining room table, checking the list of silver and jewelry we brought into the country against the silver and jewelry we are bringing out, and adding the new pieces of silver we have bought here, which we have already gotten stickers for, after paying 10 percent of their declared value, from the government export-licensing entity in the state antique store in the Hotel Kohly.

All antiques, silver, and jewelry, no matter where you buy them (and strangely, they don't seem to be much concerned about *where* you buy something), must be taken to the Kohly for export licenses. All paintings must be taken to the export office of Bienes Culturales for export licenses, and all books more than fifty years old must be taken to the Biblioteca Nacional. With the export licenses come little stickers, which are placed on each item. The silver items and jewelry are checked again, before the movers come, by representatives of the bank and one Customs representative, the other items are checked by Bienes Culturales, and then everything is checked again by Customs when the movers are actually in the house and the packing is going on.

We can't find a piece of silver that we brought into the country and is on the bank's list. We think it must still be in the attic. Miguel, Danila, and I climb to the attic and kick papers and shift mattresses and rip open boxes. Miguel and Danila keep looking, and I start back downstairs. I meet the two bank people and Nestor coming up the stairs as I go down. I have not told them they could come upstairs; they are just heading on up. Standing in front of them on the stairs, I tell them that the piece of silver we are looking for will be down shortly, ask them what they would like to drink, and escort them back down the stairs to the dining room.

To gain time as Concha is serving drinks, I ask her if she is sure she has brought out of the pantry all the silver belonging to us that we will be taking out of the country. I go back into the pantry with her and rattle trays. I pull out some ladles and a soup tureen and take them into the dining room. 'We forgot these!' I say, sounding alarmed.

'It's silver plate. It doesn't count,' the older bank person says. Just then Miguel and Danila come into the dining room carrying the lost silver piece.

Bienes Culturales, which comes an hour and a half after the arrival of the bank, is Maida, a modified boarding-school-house-mother type in a plaid polyester skirt with a frayed hem. With her is Betina, the bouncy woman who was present three years earlier as our things were being unpacked – on the lookout for Cuban national treasures coming from Southeast Asia – and had handed us her card. Recognizing the name Maida and noticing the whiff of gentility about her, I ask Maida if she knows Nicoletta.

'We were at the conservatory together,' Maida says.

Maida is one of the childhood friends of Nicoletta's who stayed on, whom Nicoletta looked up when she came back to Cuba. They hadn't seen each other for forty years.

'She has a pitiful job,' Nicoletta said, describing Maida to me, 'going into foreigners' houses, checking what they are taking out of the country. "But how can you *do* that," I said to her, "checking the things that Cubans are forced to sell in order to survive. Going into foreigners' houses, checking every little thing, saying yes, no, yes, no. A Chartrand (nineteenth-century Cuban landscape painter) or a Pelaez (twentieth-century Cuban painter) painting, I can understand, but every little thing. You were such a talented girl at the conservatory. You can't possibly *believe* in what you are doing, now that you have seen how it has turned out . . ." '

I take Maida and Betina to the section of the upstairs hall where I have put the clocks, vases, ashtrays, door knockers, paintings, daguerreotype, furniture, china, opera glasses, mantilla combs, fans, glassware, pharmaceutical jars, and books more than fifty years old bought in Cuba that we are taking out of the country – the valuable objects with their stickers from the Hotel Kohly, the books with stickers from the Biblioteca Nacional.

Maida tells me we have to have export licenses for the ashtrays and less-valuable items as well. The less-valuable items are grouped in lots of five, on which we must pay an export tax of ten dollars per lot. Maida measures and describes every one of our forty biomorphic Murano ashtrays, measuring the distances between swoop points or bulges, and calling the measurements to Betina, who writes them down.

I point out the piano in the playroom.

'*Problema*,' Maida says about the piano.

It is one-thirty. Concha comes upstairs. 'The bank people are still downstairs,' she whispers.

'But I thought they finished . . .'

'I thought so, too. But they are just hanging around in the dining room.'

I seat the bank people, Nestor, and the Bienes Culturales women on the porch and give them *empanada de atun* (tuna cooked with peppers and onions in a piecrust), beer, salad, and ice cream; the table is set with doilies and cloth napkins. Concha waits on them, looking peeved.

Nestor shakes my hand, grinning, as he leaves. 'Be sure to ask for Nestor when you move.'

Maida says we can export everything except the piano, the pharmaceutical jars, the daguerreotype, and two door knockers in the form of ladies' hands.

I knew the piano and the pharmaceutical jars would be a problem and I suspected the daguerreotype would be, but I had no idea about the door knockers. Still, I act surprised about everything. 'A Chartrand or a Pelaez painting, I can understand . . .'

Maida looks at me, startled. Then slowly, with her eyes half shut, she explains in a quiet voice that it is forbidden to export pianos or anything that reflects *cubanidad*.

'*Cubanidad?*'

'Anything that is symbolic of Cuban history.'

Maida says she will ask her superior.

Nick says he will write to Bienes Culturales.

I get a chorus of reproofs afterward from Lorena, Concha, Manuel, Miguel, Estrella, and Danila that *I should have served them in the kitchen, with paper napkins.*

IV. 74

Smiling Nestor comes the day the actual packing begins with another Customs guy, an unsmiling six-foot-eight-inch *negro azul y trompudo* whose muscles strain the seams of his uniform and whose pants stop a good eight inches above his ankles. We didn't know Nestor would be coming with someone else. I explain to them and the packers that they can do downstairs first, then move upstairs.

I am not so worried about the two painted fifties side tables we have downstairs that we forgot to get an export license for as I am about another small table I forgot. It is caoba – Cuban mahogany. Some say they don't let you take out caoba furniture at all, but others say that if the piece is minor enough, you can take it out. Still, every piece of caoba furniture has to be considered by Bienes Culturales, and I am afraid that if we ask about it at this late date, they will just say no and we will have no time to appeal. I detach the tabletop from the base to make the top look like a tray and the base like nothing and put the screw in my pocket. I put them and the painted tables in the 'stuff we've always had' section.

Nestor stamps every juncture of strapping tape with a small stamp from Customs as the boxes are finished. Nestor is very talkative and asks questions about words and expressions in English and X—ian as he stamps. The *negro azul y trompudo* watches in stooped silence. I wonder if it is a good cop/bad cop routine or if Nestor's joviality is meant to give me a false sense of ease, and the seriousness of the *negro azul y trompudo* is meant to give me I don't know what. My heart races and there is a sweaty feeling in my palms as the packers move closer to the caoba table. There are lulls between stamping sessions, though, and after a while Nestor's attention and the attention of the *negro azul y trompudo* fall on the old copies of *El Nuevo Herald* (the Spanish-language version of the *Miami Herald*),

Herald-Tribune, the *Economist, Hola* (a Spanish gossip magazine), and other magazines and newspapers that are being used for packing. Nestor and the *negro azul y trompudo* sit on the floor, carefully smoothing rumpled newspapers and magazines, so absorbed in their reading that the packers, when they finish a parcel, have to yell, 'Stamp!'

They seem casual, but the caoba table, when they get to it, will trip an alarm that will cause them to go scuttering through the house, picking up on details that we didn't think were criminal, but turn out to be criminal.

THE *NEGRO AZUL Y TROMPUDO* is replaced today by a slender young *blanquito*, who is also silent and spends most of his time reading *Hola* and drinking Tropicolas.

ON THE THIRD DAY, the small table and base are packed in a box with such insouciance that I slip the fat screw I have been holding in my pocket since the first day into the box right in front of everybody.

Nestor has yet another partner today, who like the others is silent and spends most of his time smoothing out crumpled magazines and newspapers and reading them while sitting cross-legged on the floor.

Nestor and the packers move upstairs. His partner lingers downstairs. All of the books we owned before coming to Cuba, as well as those we bought in Cuba that are less than fifty years old, are still on their shelves in the upstairs hall.

'You are aware that all books have to be checked by the *biblioteca*?' Nestor asks, walking right up to and removing a sixty-year-old book from the shelf that was somehow not taken to the *biblioteca*. Nestor slips it into a box of books that are being packed. The box is sealed. Nestor stamps it, winking at me.

Nestor moves to a table on which I have put small objects to be packed. There are many seashells, some of which are from Cuba, but most of which we have collected from other places in the world. 'Do you know that it is illegal to remove seashells from the country?' Nestor says.

'But they are *ours*!' I say, truly surprised. I catch myself: 'I mean, they are shells Nick found in Africa.'

Ours. It is all ours. Still, Nick and I have taken to saying, 'This is ours,' about what we brought with us into the country, and 'This is from Cuba,' not 'This is ours,' about the things we bought or found here, *even to each other*.

'Listen,' he says, 'my *compañero* downstairs is from another division. Pack the seashells first.' Nestor motions to the packers to start packing the seashells now.

The *compañero* comes upstairs before the shells are completely packed. He gives the shells a desultory look and goes back to reading the weekly magazine supplement to *El País*.

SATURDAY. THE PACKERS load the final container this morning. It is also the day of Jimmie's birthday party.

I pleaded with Jimmie to have the party on Sunday ('It will be calm then – Mommy won't be so tired'), but Jimmie said *kids never had birthday parties on Sunday it was his last birthday party ever in Cuba in his life and he should have it when he wanted to have it why did we have to leave he was mad about leaving it was nice in Cuba you got to wear shorts all the time it wasn't fair he had to go to a scary big school now* con *pale, pale, mean* blancos *and there were no mangoes and no swimming pools and no tarantulas in the grass and no tostones*.

It is also the day Thea wakes with a temperature of 104 degrees. She is not able to hold anything down. I call the pediatrician at 7:30 A.M. I rummage through the remains of the medicine cabinet for fever-lowering suppositories. All we have are expired suppositories from when the children weighed less. Dr. Silvia is brought to the house by Miguel. Thea is put in a tub and sprayed with cold water – this as I am running out of the bathroom every few minutes to watch the loading of the container.

Dr. Silvia comes back in the afternoon in the middle of Jimmie's party. Thea's temperature is down, but Dr. Silvia thinks Thea should go to the hospital for tests. I am trying to keep kids from running around the pool and say I think she should be tested, too, but I ask Dr. Silvia why we can't go to Cira García (the foreigner's hospital) for once. I don't mind paying thirty-five dollars, I really don't, and I can't spare the people right now to drive a sample here, take her there, but Dr. Silvia, looking hurt, says she just can't do it, have me pay all that money when they, the doctors, get nothing. Dr. Silvia puts her hand on my arm and says she knows I am stressed and she will take Thea with her, she will pretend Thea is her niece. She is a doctor; she will get good service.

Dr. Silvia props Thea up. '*Tea, no dices una palabra, claro?*' ('Thea, don't say a word [i.e., let people hear your accent], OK?').

IV. 75

A week after Jimmie's birthday party. It is very hot and all the children's friends are otherwise engaged. Most toys were sent away in the container or given away. We have held on to one TV, but as happens every year, we have forgotten to pay the television satellite subscription – the satellite people in Cuba whom foreigners use (Cubans are not allowed to have satellite TV, or even extra-tall antennae) never send a bill – so there is no Nickelodeon. The children spend most of the day watching bits of stations until they are cut off. Out of desperation, I persuade Nick to go with the children in the late afternoon to see the film *Fanny and Alexander*. I remember its being about children.

We convince the Cine Chaplin to let the children in. In movie houses in Havana, no children under the age of sixteen are allowed in, regardless of the content of the movie. We guess it's because movies are so cheap and there is air-conditioning, so that parents, if they could, would park their kids at movies as a form of baby-sitting.

It's about kids, the movie, but it's also about child abuse, incest, et cetera, et cetera. People in the audience look at us. About fifteen minutes into the movie, Thea starts moaning. 'My stomach hurts,' she says. I think she's faking it because she has been fine all week. She just doesn't want to be at a movie in Swedish with Spanish subtitles. The hospital found nothing wrong with her when she went with Dr. Silvia last Saturday, her fever subsided, and by Sunday afternoon she was fine.

Half an hour goes by. More moaning. 'My stomach *really hurts.*'

I tell Nick we have to go. It's the ham sandwich she ate for lunch, which no one else wanted to eat, *conseguido*ed not from our regular source. We go up the aisle and into the lobby. Thea starts to vomit on the floor, just inside the glass door leading to the street. I take a sweatshirt I have brought along for the air-conditioning and hold it under her, thinking she will just vomit a little bit into it and I will be able to get her outside to the curb, where it won't splash so much. She ate very little except for the ham sandwich. Instead it's breakfast, too, she can't move, and Nick is yelling at me, 'Why are you trying to preserve it?' I bundle up the first sweatshirt, take out another, and Nick starts yelling at me that I am suffocating her. Finally we get her to the car and I ask Nick if we can give the lobby person some money to clean up the floor because I feel bad – first we persuaded them to let us in, and now one of the children has vomited on the lobby floor – but Nick gets even madder at me and gives me five dollars to give to them, which is way too much, but he doesn't have anything smaller.

We get home and I take her upstairs and clean off her face. Nick comes in and tells me he thinks she should drink some chamomile tea. Thea tells me she doesn't feel like drinking anything. 'She says she doesn't feel like drinking anything.' I say to Nick over my shoulder. Nick repeats what he said about the chamomile tea, louder. 'Fine,' I say.

IV. 76

Lorena calls to say she'll be late for work because her son had a problem in jail. When she appears, she explains that another prisoner attacked her son with a knife and cut off three of his fingers.

She says she is sorry to be telling me this.

I ask her why she is sorry.

'Because it is unpleasant for a *señora* to hear about a boy who did some wrong things in his life getting his fingers cut off. The blood . . . ,' Lorena says, not finishing, not looking at me but into the unlocked closet where we keep small amounts of basic foods, one hand trailing over a shelf.

'But he's *your son.*'

Lorena hugs me, crying. I steer her to the table on the kitchen veranda. She sits down. I sit next to her, holding her hand and crying, too.

WE SIT WITH Arquitecto Vasquez in his former gallery, which has been turned back into his living room. The tables in the small *paladar* area in back have been tilted on their sides and are pushed against the wall.

'It was a neighbor on my own floor,' he says. 'I tried to be so nice to him, too. We had some openings, but in general my visitors were discreet. It wasn't really the people coming and going and the sounds, though. It was the fact that I did it and that it was a little successful. You'd be surprised how many people don't like that.'

EMBARGO IS FOUND DEAD under the car in the morning by José. The night before, José says he had seen her fighting with Bloqueo and had seen her take refuge under the car. José found her in the same position in the morning.

Now the help tell me they noticed that her belly had been swollen for a few days. They thought she was pregnant. I want to yell at them, *How can anyone be pregnant who had her uterus and one ovary cut out in one operation and her remaining ovary cut out in another operation?*

We bury Embargo in the garden, between a lime tree and a palm. The children gather flowers. We scatter them on top of her grave. Manuel and Lorena come. The children and I sing Episcopalian hymns. I deliver a homily in English: ' . . . like Evita, like Marilyn, cut down in her prime . . .' Manuel and Lorena catch the names Evita and Marilyn and bow their heads respectfully.

I tell the children Bloqueo will need a lot of comfort now. Bloqueo lies under the kitchen table eating fish skin, unconcerned.

WE CANNOT TAKE Bloqueo to X—— even though he is by himself now, I tell the children. It is bad enough for a cat not to be able to go outside; it is worse for a cat to have to stay inside all the time *and be alone.*

'But we can get an X——ian cat to keep him company and teach him how to be happy indoors,' Thea says.

This is an idea and a good one. But I tell them Bloqueo is just too used to Cuba now. It would be cruel. We will find pets in X—.

'But we love *Bloqueo.*'

FRITZ READS ON THE Internet that Fidel, now in Switzerland for a meeting, is seeing a heart specialist.

ROBERTO ASKS IF WE have heard of any job for him. His voice is strained. He bites the side of his thumb.

We tell him we have asked everyone we know. We have made follow-up calls, too. We tell him we'll keep trying.

WE CALL ON THE Carrera sisters to tell them we will be leaving soon.

The tiny *mulata* is struggling with the front door. 'You have to lift it up on your side!' she calls to Nick. Nick puts his fingers under some trim on the lower half of the door and eases the door over the jamb.

Saida pulls us gently to her and kisses us on both cheeks. Nick turns to shut the door. 'You can leave the door open because I am expecting some people for bridge. Reny is already here. I think you know him already – isn't that so? Reny, where are you?'

Reny comes up shyly behind Saida. He kisses me on both cheeks and shakes Nick's hand. Reny is wearing chinos and a plaid shirt rolled up over his elbows. He looks relaxed – much more relaxed than at a party.

'Saida is a shark, an absolute shark at bridge,' Reny says.

Saida pushes on Reny's arm playfully. '*Que te vayas, hombre!*' ('Get out of here, man!'), she says, laughing.

A table on the veranda off the dining room is set with teacups and small plates. Lilian, Saida tells us, is not so well today. She is asleep upstairs. On the table there is a stack of sandwiches and a bowl of mariquitas (green bananas fried like potato chips).

Saida tells us to stay. She says that she and Reny and the others who will be coming have played together for so long that they can have conversations with others while they are playing, but we tell her we will be going. We will return another day.

'Wait a minute,' Saida says.

There is another small piece of furniture left over from before *el triunfo* – a semicircular Louis XVI legless console, which is mounted on the wall. She pulls open its only drawer and takes out a blown-glass bird – it is the size of a sparrow, light pink in color, with a blue beak. She puts it in my hands. I start to protest, but she folds my hands around it.

I TRIED TO KEEP stuff in reserve for the last few weeks that we are here, but some of it is already gone. No more kids' toothpaste, no more vitamins, no more face cream for me, the kids' shoes are falling apart, Thea's and my bathing suits are stretched out and billowing in the pool, Thea is bursting out of her shorts. No more electric toothbrush refills. No peanut butter. No kids' books: that's the worst. Thea goes through a book a day. I tell Thea to check more books out of the school library, but she forgets. Socks a mess. Beach towels that we will be leaving here, to be cut up for rags. One tape player that eats tapes. No television in our room to floss by, just the small one downstairs.

I should be grateful: I have time. Time to write letters. Time to read a thick book. I read *The Mambo Kings Play Songs of Love.*

I'm sick of Cuba, but what do I read? A book about Cuba.

IV. 77

We drive to Guanabacoa to see Nick's friend Aurora. Aurora sells books in the parking lot on the Malecón and told us when she last saw us that she knew of some Chinese furniture – *precioso* – some *manteles* (tablecloths), and a nice, old-fashioned wooden *maniquí* (dress mold) near her in Guanabacoa.

I don't know why Nick thinks we need a dress mold; he just says we do.

Thanks to a thriving book business, Aurora has *permuta* ed her old apartment for a grand, ground-floor railroad-type flat built in the middle of the nineteenth century, and in the three years that we have known her, she has been *conseguir* ing lumber, cement, tiles, and kitchen and bathroom fixtures and renovating as her finances will allow.

Aurora's flat is a flat without corridors, one room opening onto another in a line all the way back to the kitchen through swinging doors made of carved wood and etched colored glass, like saloon doors, cut off to let the breezes blow. Most of the etched glass in the doors is still intact, Aurora has pointed out to us on other visits, as are the spring mechanisms of their hinges, so the doors still swing.

We have seen Aurora's house in many stages. We have seen it

with no bathroom and the ceiling falling down. She and her daughter and her *marinovio* were already living in it then. It has been a struggle, the renovation – a fight, a sufferance, a maneuver, a manipulation, a feint, full of minitriumphs, defeats, and close calls, which she revels in sharing with visitors. She makes faces, she reenacts, she takes sides, doing both parts. She grabs your arm, throws her head back, and laughs in thorough appreciation of your comments.

We enter the first room, the old parlor, which is still a construction site. A pile of sand is in a corner of the room, with fresh dog turds in it. She's not got just the Doberman now, she explains; she also has a cocker spaniel puppy. We go through swinging doors to the next room (the old dining room), where Aurora's six-year-old niece sits on the floor, fitting doll clothes into a miniature closet. 'I'm making everything neat,' she says. Beside her, a lit candle flickers in front of a small Santeria altar. We enter the first bedroom. Aurora's *marinovio* is asleep in his undershirt on a chenille bedspread, one arm over his eyes, ripe beads of sweat sitting undisturbed on top of his *leche con una gota de café* armpit hairs. We hesitate for a moment, but Aurora says, '*Adelante! No se preoccupen*' ('Come ahead. Don't worry about it').

My thoughts turn back to the turds on the sand in the parlor. Maybe it's the heat or the *chaclera* I had in a *paladar* the night before (ordered because I didn't know the word: fatty ham, it turned out to be, fried with potatoes and onions), but I am feeling as though it would take very little more to make me vomit. I am feeling as though it would take very little to make me vomit a lot these days. I feel dust and (I am certain of it) powdered turds accumulating on my skin (which starts to sweat the minute I leave our house) like crumbs on a breaded cutlet.

In the next bedroom, Aurora's sister lies on a bed, wrapped in another chenille bedspread, attended by Aurora's mother and four other relatives, who sit watching an American Western on videotape. She has just had an operation this morning on her feminine parts, Aurora explains, and is here to recuperate.

Maybe it's the lack of ventilation (there are cutoff swinging doors in each room leading to a skinny, open-air courtyard, but it is filled with rubble), but even though Nick and I and the kids have already left Cuba more than a dozen times, sometimes

331

even for long weekends, still I have been worrying, more and more these days, that getting on a plane and getting the hell out of Cuba for good somehow won't really happen. I worry that we will lose our passports, forget X——ian, forget *English* even, and some all-powerful, hairy being will declare us Cuban and unable to leave.

Aurora gets in the car and directs Nick, who is driving, to the house of Usnavy (a Cuban first name, invented at the time of the Spanish-American War, from *U.S. Navy*), her friend who can guide us to *her* friend who has the Chinese furniture – *'precioso'* – and to another friend who can take us to the *manteles* and the *maniquí*.

We drive past a building with a guard holding a machine gun in front of it.

'What's in there?'

'*Blumes*' ('Underpants').

'*Cómo?!*'

'It's an underpants factory. They've had a lot of problems with people breaking in and stealing underpants.'

We are silent for a moment. 'Not having underpants can really put you in a bad mood,' I say.

'*Muy mal humor,*' Aurora agrees. Then to Nick, 'You see how your *señora* is? She understands us.'

We drive along a ridge under ancient ficus trees to a 'suburb' of Guanabacoa: low, flat-roofed houses with carports, looking like Miami. At the door is a living, *mulata* version of the late, great actor Divine, in curlers, pancake makeup, and etched eyebrows. She greets Aurora triumphantly. 'I did it!' Usnavy yells.

Aurora yells, hugs her.

Usnavy has managed to get a *certificado médico* so that she can retire a year earlier. '*Fueron los nervios*' ('It was my nerves'). In teaching, women can retire at fifty, and men at fifty-five. She has been teaching for thirty-seven years, she says. She was fed up.

I don't know if I am understanding everything correctly, but I don't dare ask if it means that, if Usnavy is forty-nine, she has been teaching since she was twelve.

Usnavy says it hasn't been possible to abduct the *maniquí* from the factory where it has been sitting unused for years, because King Kong was in Guanabacoa today, inspecting state enterprises.

Lazo, aka King Kong, is the Communist Party head in Santiago. He is one of the few *negros* of any shade in the Communist Party leadership. He is very big, very black, with a low forehead, so everyone – black, white, *mulato*, Communist, non-Communist – calls him King Kong.

We enter Usnavy's living room. Danish modern furniture covered in new-looking spring green Naugahyde. We drink more *cafecitos* and chat with Usnavy about her retirement. Usnavy gets up to guide us to her friend with the Chinese furniture.

As we are walking down the sidewalk to the car, Aurora pats Usnavy, who is ahead of us, on the behind. 'Will you look at that *culito* (little ass),' Aurora says, looking back at us, grinning, framing Usnavy's behind with her hands as if it were a work of art.

Usnavy's behind is the width of a Volkswagen, high, and utterly unselfconscious, clad in pink, green, and yellow floral stretch bike pants, which she has either made or miraculously managed to find big enough. 'I had problems today on the *guagua* (bus) with this *culito*,' Usnavy says, laughing. 'You should have heard the comments! Ooof!'

Usnavy and Aurora laugh, we laugh, and maybe it's the night air coming on, but suddenly I don't feel like a breaded cutlet anymore, but light and fresh, as if I have just taken a shower. And I feel as if we will leave – but leave or not leave (we are laughing harder now), what does it matter? For we are, all of us on this planet, just visiting anyway.

IV. 78

Another weekend gotten through. The heat and boredom of the weekend as we approach it is slightly terrifying, but it goes well enough: a Polar Bar; a visit from a friend of a friend of a friend, a lone man whose evasive answers to our simple questions lead us to conclude that he is a sexual tourist; two children's birthday parties to go to; and a concert by the Camerata Romeu at the convent of San Francisco.

Nick comes to get me during intermission. He wants me to speak to an American who has approached him. The American is an older man with a cane. He is a member of an association of amateur chamber-music groups. He is against the embargo. He says it fiercely to me, as if I am *for* the embargo. He gives me his card. He is a retired judge from Los Angeles. I ask him what group he has come with. He shrugs, as if that is something unimportant. He says his association has chapters all over the world, but not in Cuba. He says he would like the Camerata Romeu to come to the United States. I agree they would be a big hit in the United States. I tell him who to get in touch with at the Interests Section to arrange for their visit. He says, 'Interests Section, bah . . .' I say that's who you have to go through to get Cuban artists to the United States, and that they are really quite helpful these days. I introduce him to the manager of the Camerata Romeu. He asks if her group has ever been to the United States. She says they have been many times and have just come back from a trip to Los Angeles.

The judge steps back as if he has been slapped at the words *Los Angeles* and looks confounded. 'I don't understand why I didn't know about it – I just don't understand why I didn't know about it,' he says as he walks off with his cane.

We are introduced by Reny to a black diva in a white dress with a cascade of hair, gold fingernails, and gold shoes. She is a soprano, born and raised in Cuba, who now lives in Europe. She is the first diva I have ever stood close to. She has a tall black girl with her. It is her niece. The niece is a regular Cuban girl, Centro Habana, deer-in-the-headlights style. I ask the diva if she misses Cuba, and the diva says she lives in Munich now, but lived in Paris for fourteen years.

On the way home, with Fritz in the back seat, Nick says he *can't understand* why I didn't invite the diva for dinner, she was so captivating, and I say that I thought she was so compelling that I wanted to walk right into her, my eyes staring, like someone out of *Village of the Damned*, but we are leaving soon, I don't trust my instincts anymore, and every time I spread myself thin, he (Nick) accuses me of being like my mother or like some other ADD-ridden member of my family, spreading myself all over the place.

Fritz, from the backseat, says, 'Invite her and invite me.'

That night in bed it comes to me: she is *the* diva, of the French film *Diva*. She is the black goddess-singer the French boy is obsessed with. Our diva lived in Paris for fourteen years.

* * *

'MY WIFE FELL DOWN and broke her leg again yesterday,' Miguel says. 'They will have to operate on her.'

She has fallen and broken her leg in the place where the screw of the plate had gone through, where there was a little hole that, they find out now, never healed.

FRITZ HAS LOOKED IT up on the Internet. Our diva is not the diva of *Diva*, but we don't care.

IV. 79

Juana's letter of invitation and application for an exit permit were passed to the Ministry of Education, which had no objection to her leaving. The papers were then passed on to the Emigration Department. Now Juana tells me she has just received 'the white ticket' – a white postcard sent to those who have passed the Ministry of Education and Emigration Department hurdles – informing her that she can now go to pick up her exit permit. Her visas for the United States and for X— are already ready.

The tickets are the final hurdle. We cannot buy a one-way ticket for Juana to Miami, even though she will not be returning to Cuba through Miami, but through X— and Madrid. No Cuban can buy a one-way ticket from Havana to Miami without also buying a nonrefundable return ticket from Miami to Havana, no matter how the Cuban plans to get back to Cuba. In addition, there are no direct charter flights available the day we want to leave Havana: we will have to fly through Cancún. We cannot buy the Cancún-Miami portion of our tickets in Havana, nor can we buy Juana's U.S.-X—— ticket in Havana; they have to be bought in the United States and mailed to us via DHL courier service. Only when we have all the tickets that we have to get in the United States, as well as Juana's X— Madrid-Havana ticket, bought in Havana, Juana's nonrefundable return charter flight ticket from Miami to Havana, which she won't use, and a Mexican transit visa for Juana, required of all Cubans traveling through Mexico, are we allowed to buy Juana's ticket to Cancún.

IV. 80

Dinner with the diva, Fritz, Fritz's girlfriend, Belkis, and the Danish cultural attaché, Rolf. It seems to be a good combination, but I don't know how much we can talk about Cuba with the diva there. She is a German citizen, but her family still lives here, and Manuel, who has to make his report, is hovering near us with a tray. It's also tiresome to always talk about how weird Cuba is, but it's what happens in living rooms in Havana whenever two or three foreigners are gathered together.

Rolf says the Cuban Revolution is good material for an opera.

Pushing myself forward on the sofa, I say that I think of Cuban history, beginning with the war of independence, as a compendium of operatic and dramatic styles.

Rolf and Fritz say yes, they can see that.

I say I can see it beginning as an American musical, incorporating great Cuban music: Don Barreto, Lecuona, Bola de Nieve, Beny Moré, Celia Cruz, the Trio Matamoros, and other earlier and later styles. There would be the explosion of the *Maine*; there would be Cuba's victory snatched by blithe, oblivious, singing, dancing American soldiers (martial American tunes contrasting with Cuban melodies). There would be a Spanish-pride number, a Cuban-pride number. It would continue in the American-musical mode, through a part showing U.S. economic domination of Cuba. Hershey's and United Fruit Company would be represented. More blithe, singing, dancing Americans. There would be a gambling number, a prostitution number. There would be a Batista number and a gangster number . . .

I steal a sideways glance at Nick to see if I am going on too long (he's heard it before from me, but less developed) or being a boor, but Nick looks OK about it, the others are being mildly polite about it, I've been waiting for the right people and time to try my idea out, and now that I am in it, I might as well get to the end. Then there would be the rise of Fidel and the revolution. The work would turn to something akin to classical opera: there would be a small opera buffa number on the Castro family home life in Birán and on Fidel's never winning a student election; there would be Moncada, Fidel's exile and return, and the assault on Batista's palace. Students tortured, dying. There would be Fidel's sweep across Cuba and his early speeches: 'History Will Absolve Me' and 'I Am Not a Communist, I Am a Humanist.' It would switch back to American-musical mode for the appearance of Herbert Matthews and Fidel's visits to Princeton and Harlem and later contain a reference to *Hair* during a Venceremos Brigades number. The diva laughs. The others chuckle. I feel less embarrassed about going on: it would continue in operatic mode through the disappearance of Camilo Cienfuegos, the executions at the *paredón*, the mass exodus of middle-class Cubans, Che's disquiet in the USSR (Russian opera then), his speech in Algeria, the nationalizations, and Che's death (with another eruption of an American-musical number during the Bay of Pigs). It would move to insertions of Kabuki, No, or Thai dancing (something like the insertion of the *Uncle Tom's Cabin* play in the musical *The King and I*) within the operatic mode with the sclerotization of the revolution, its dependence on the Soviet Union, and its internationalist campaigns, becoming thoroughly Kabuki, No, or Thai following the death of Celia Sánchez, Fidel's last true confidante. The end, beginning with the Ochoa trial, is Greek tragedy, with Fidel and Raúl in platform shoes and a cacophony of musical styles as the revolution sells out and the island is overrun by foreign corporations and mass tourism.

The thesis of the musical would be that Fidel is one of the greatest actors the world has ever known, only Fidel doesn't walk into a play: Fidel transforms history into a play, directed by and starring him. The public would enter with Fidel talking and go out with Fidel talking, and there would be a ten-cassette pack of Fidel talking that you wouldn't have to pay for – it would just be given to you, for you to take home. There would be many, many scene changes, or maybe there could be an *Orlando furioso* type of staging, with the public loose in a big tent and islands of characters on rolling platforms pulled through the crowd. There would be José Martí, de Céspedes, Maceo, Hearst, Spey, Cervera, Teddy Roosevelt, McKinley, Ángel Castro, Lina Ruz, Raúl's alleged father (the Chinese cook), Meyer Lansky, Lana Turner, George Raft, Fidel, Raúl, Herbert Matthews, Che, Camilo Cienfuegos, Huber Matos, Nikita Khrushchev, Kennedy, Piñeiro, Celia Sánchez, the Venceremos Brigades, Black Panther fugitives, a bodega, Lincoln Díaz-Balart, Jorge Mas

Canosa, Ochoa, a neurologist in a white coat with a pointer and a chart of the brain, explaining the physiological origins of manic-depressive and obsessive-compulsive disorders, malignant narcissism and logorrhea, or maybe a different neurologist for each disorder, on platforms with slick swiveling casters, singly or in groups, entering, inveighing, exiting, being pulled by vigorous young people on a vast, smooth floor through dodging crowds. It would last seven or eight hours. You could go out and get something to eat – Cuban food served on stands outside – you could go home, even, if you liked, and come back the next day for what you missed. The ticket would be valid for three days.

IV. 81

Juana's transit visa is ready at the Mexican Embassy. All we need now are our tickets to arrive via DHL to get Juana's ticket out of here.

IT'S NOT THAT IT'S so terrifying to be without a baby-sitter anymore. I can leave the children alone in a hotel room for a few minutes now, if I have to go to a pharmacy or buy a snack for them, with a DO NOT DISTURB sign on the door. I can make it from Florida to New York on my own with them (we're supposed to drive, visiting friends along the way). It's that I'm nervous about it working out with Juana's visas and tickets because I really *want* Juana to see the United States with us. I'm nervous because of all the days and weeks I've spent thinking and fantasizing about seeing Juana see the United States: about seeing her see the stuff-a-thon shopping centers and fat people and eight-lane highways and jumbo-sized Styrofoam cups in cup holders coming out from dashboards and her saying '*Mira eso!*' or '*Qué curioso!*' about everything. I am fantasizing about explaining the fat people to her. I am fantasizing about watching Juana bite into a Cape Cod potato chip for the first time, and a tender ear of corn in season, and a pecan, and a blueberry, and hear obscure blues on the radio, and about going off the main highways with her and seeing her see mile after mile of just fields or forests, and seeing her see ranch houses and trailers, but wooden houses, too, with sagging gingerbread

338

porches, dozing at the bottoms of hollows, the picture of non-aggression, or maybe not. I'm nervous that the time I have spent and the time I am still spending fantasizing about her seeing the United States might be for nothing.

It's not just European men striving to get *negras de pelo* out of Cuba, I realize; it's all kinds of foreigners wanting to show all kinds of Cubans how the rest of the world *is*. It's also so that they can know how Cuba is for us.

I'm beginning to have fantasies about seeing Lorena see the United States, too.

WE HAVE DINNER WITH an X——ian who is restructuring a hotel in Habana Vieja. Nick talks about how tired we are. The X—ian talks about how tired he is. He says the Cubans who are working with him are insisting on putting the hotel bathroom's sinks, tubs, and toilets on the same waste pipe. He asks us to imagine what it will be like when the pipes back up.

Nick says that for every business that gives up, another one will come in and try, because it's Cuba.

STILL NO DHL ENVELOPE, but Nick's secretary tells me that she called DHL, and the envelope is in Havana and will be arriving later today. It has taken nine days to get the envelope via DHL from the States, but that is about average because it has to come through Mexico.

JUANA'S CANCÚN-MIAMI and U.S.-X— tickets are delivered by DHL.

Juana comes over to drop off her passport, which we need to buy the rest of the tickets.

I tell Juana that I am worried about what it says on her exit permit, that she can only be out of the country for thirty days.

Juana says that she can be out of the country for eleven months (if she is out for more than eleven months, her house will be requisitioned), but that for every month beyond the first month that she is out of the country, she has to pay a certain sum of money to the Cuban Consulate in whatever country she is in. If she does not pay, she cannot return to Cuba. She has to pay $150 per month to the Cuban Consulate in the United

States for every month she is in the United States, but it's less in X— and Spain.

I tell Juana I knew that a Cuban had to pay to *get out* of Cuba, but I didn't know, until now, that a Cuban had to pay to *stay out* of Cuba as well. I tell Juana that we will pay the monthly payments for her to stay out of Cuba, because it is for *us* that she is traveling. Juana tells me that she forbids me to pay it – she absolutely forbids me. She says she will not come with us if I pay it.

NICK'S SECRETARY GOES TO buy Juana's X— -Madrid-Havana return ticket and, once that is done, to get Juana's and our Mexicana ticket from Havana to Cancún and Juana's charter return ticket from Miami to Havana, which she will not use but is still required to have in order to be able to purchase her ticket from Havana to Cancún.

I wait by the phone all morning.

Nick's secretary returns, mission accomplished.

When you expect the worst, sometimes things work out all right.

Nick says he is beginning to believe we are leaving.

I will tell Juana this afternoon what I have not been wanting to tell her before we had the tickets: that in order for her to get a visa for the United States I had to promise to the consul at the U.S. Interests Section – I really did – that once we are in the United States I will not pay her the $350 per month I am paying her now, but a regular salary for someone doing a job like hers in the United States, which is $900.

IV. 82

I go to Miguel's house to see his wife, who is in bed with her leg up, following the second breaking of her femur and third surgery.

I follow Miguel's car to a neighborhood that is a ten-minute drive from our house. It is a tree-lined street, with rows of two-story houses with barred, gated carports. On the gate is a sign indicating that their home is the site of the local Committee for the Defense of the Revolution.

'You are the head of the local CDR?' I ask Miguel.

'It helps us get along,' Miguel says.

Miguel, his wife, and their two children live on the top floor. Miguel's brother Ysidro and his wife and two children live on the ground floor. Miguel and Ysidro's mother and father live in an apartment in back. Miguel's car is locked in the carport alongside his brother's motorcycle.

'We have to lock them in now because of all the robberies,' Miguel explains.

Ysidro's apartment is light and spacious. Salsa pours out of Ysidro's Sony stereo system. I tour Ysidro's apartment, making appreciative comments: it really is a nice apartment. Ysidro, his wife, their children, Miguel, his children, and Estrella follow me as I go.

'You have a very nice setup here. Congratulations.'

'We help one another,' Ysidro says.

'That is very important. Not all families can do that.'

I am near the door to Estrella's apartment. 'You don't mind my looking, do you?'

'*Señora, por favor,*' Estrella says, holding the door open for me.

'I am curious. I have known you all these years.'

Estrella and her husband's apartment is smaller but also pleasant, with furniture that looks new.

I walk upstairs to Miguel's apartment. 'These are the stairs she fell on last time,' Miguel explains. Miguel's apartment is smaller than Ysidro's apartment, but it is full of light and pleasant. Miguel shows me the electric range they were able to repair with the burners I brought them from the United States.

Miguel's wife lies on a white sheet in a room containing a bed and an armoire. She is wearing cutoffs and an embroidered blouse I brought her from Mexico. A straw purse, which I gave her on another occasion, is pinned on the wall. The blouse and the straw purse are the only decorations in the room. There is a stainless-steel brace on her thigh, through which the scar is visible. It is a neat scar and there are no bruises. From the brace, anchors go through the flesh of her thigh to the bone to keep it in place. 'They are trying this new method now, with this brace on the outside of the leg,' Miguel explains. 'They don't know how long she will have to stay like this.'

Miguel's wife answers my questions in quiet monosyllables, hardly raising her voice above a murmur.

'She is embarrassed that she cannot get up from the bed, that

she cannot offer you anything,' Estrella whispered to me before
we left our house to come here.

'It is good you have a light, pleasant room to stay in,' I say to
Miguel's wife, taking a *cafecito* off a tray brought by Estrella from
her apartment.

'We are very lucky,' she murmurs.

'You *are* lucky,' I say.

IV. 83

The official dining area of the Palacio de la Revolución is
beautiful in a 1960s-seat-of-power-in-the-tropics kind of way, with
large islands of space on the ground floor that are not floored
with marble, but filled with minijungles of native plants. Nick
and I and the president of Energy Consulting International sit
at a large table among the minijungles with Fidel Castro and
twenty other people – some foreigners, but mostly high-ranking
members of the *nomenklatura*.

The president of Energy Consulting International says to
Fidel that he doesn't agree with his belief that globalization is a
bad thing.

There is a shifting as the high-ranking members of the
nomenklatura who have sunk in their seats prepare to push themselves back up. They wait to see if Fidel will keep talking, but
Fidel stays silent. The members who have sunk push themselves
up halfway.

The president of Energy Consulting International says that
globalization will undoubtedly cause trauma and dislocation to
many populations in the beginning, but that in the end it is a
good thing because it will reduce tensions between nations and
it will create jobs.

'How will it create jobs?' Fidel asks.

'It will create jobs in the service sector.'

'How so?'

'Well, for example . . . even now, because of the computer,
many North American banks no longer keep their records in
the United States. They keep them in Bangladesh. They can
keep them in Bangladesh and use Bangladeshi workers, because
in Bangladesh, they speak English.'

There is a murmur. The members of the *nomenklatura* who

had sunk down in their seats are now all the way up. I have never heard that American banks are doing this. I do not know this because I don't read current magazines and newspapers. Judging from the rapid adjustments to the expressions on the faces of the members of the *nomenklatura* around the table, it looks like *they* don't know this, either, but are trying to look like they do.

Fidel pushes out his lower lip, then leans forward and silently checks the faces of the members of the *nomenklatura* on one side of him and on the other, his eyebrows raised.

There is silence. 'We should all learn English!' Fidel declares merrily, slapping the edge of the table. 'Here we were, learning Russian all those years, and while we were learning Russian, the Russians were learning English!'

IV. 84

We don't know what to say to Roberto. It has never happened to us before, to not be able to find a job for someone. We did try. There were the little suspicions about him, but they were never substantiated, and we are sure that if the salary were good enough – say, $150 a month – the little skims here and there (which may or may not have happened) would really not happen anymore.

'Good luck,' we say.

There are tears in his eyes.

IV. 85

We watch them through the back window of the car in which José is driving us to the airport until we cannot see them anymore – Manuel, Miguel, Concha, Danila, Estrella, Lorena, and Bloqueo, who is squirming in Lorena's arms, for Lorena is holding one of Bloqueo's paws and waving it at us.

Will Manuel and his *mujer*'s house be requisitioned for the *nomenklatura*? Will Miguel's wife's leg get better? Will Concha's son motor to Cuba in his *yate*? Will Danila's learning-disabled son be discharged from the army? Will Estrella and her husband live long lives in their apartment? Will Lorena's son get out of jail? Will Bloqueo be petted and loved by those who come after us and die a fat cat at sixteen?

I want people coming out of Cuba to keep telling me about them always, for I am going to miss them until the end of my days.

IV. 86

Juana, the children, and I are in the Cancún airport. Nick is on his way to X—— to get our apartment ready for us there. We go to the newsstand. I buy comic books in English and in Spanish for the children, and the *Herald-Tribune*, *Time*, the *Economist*, and *Vogue* for me. Juana buys *El País* and *El Nuevo Herald*.

We go to the gift shop. It's just a plain old Mexican gift shop, but everything looks wonderful, like it always does when you've just left Cuba. Juana and I talk about how we want to buy everything in the store. I tell her the impulse subsides after a few days. The important thing is to get over the first wave of wanting to buy. I tell her we have to buy a little something, though, to appease the wave. I buy hand cream for myself, some sandals for the children, and a key chain in the form of a Mexican sombrero for Juana. Juana buys a key chain in the form of a beach ball and gives it to me.

We go to the coffee shop. We order tacos even though we are not hungry and eat them all. We drink iced tea.

We walk to the gate for the airplane to Miami. The children sit in chairs, absorbed in their comic books. Juana is reading *El País*. I wait for the 'I'm not in Cuba!' feeling to come – a kind of singing and running in my mind over a mountaintop, like Julie Andrews in *The Sound of Music*, only it should be *more* this time, with alpine winds and fluffy clouds and hoards of liberated children on either side of me, because we're not going back and because Juana is with us – but it does not come. It has always come before, in Nassau, Miami, Cancún, and even European airports, as soon as I got off the plane from Cuba. I wait for it and wait for it; it has always come so easily before. This time it's like being on a swing with my legs pumping, but the swing won't go.

It will come, the 'I'm not in Cuba!' feeling, but maybe not until we get to the States, or to X—, in the fall. It will come, but not like Julie Andrews.

We board the plane to Miami.

Epilogue

Things have changed and not changed since we were in Cuba.

The salary of professionals such as doctors and architects and of Cubans in other peso-paying jobs continues to be a small fraction of what is made by Cubans in contact with tourists and with dollars. Against rising crime, policemen's salaries have been increased four times. This has led to increased recruitment in the police force and a still more visible police presence on the streets.

Until September 11, 2001, the economy was growing in all sectors but sugar. The number of tourists was expcted to rise in 2001 to 1,750,000 to the point that the Cuban Union of Artists and Writers worried that the ratio of tourists to natives in some cities and towns would turn integral elements of *cubanidad*, such as Santeria rites, into nothing more than sanitized shows geared to tourists. The events of September 11 drastically reduced tourism in Cuba; a subsequent devastating hurricane delivered a further blow. Some recent evidence of recovery, however, has been noted.

Terrorists and natural disasters do not affect the increasing worldwide popularity of Cuban art, literature and music, which continues to be Cuba's most effective and positive means for gaining international recognition. Increasingly large numbers of foreign architects and architectural historians pay homage to Cuba's astounding architectural heritage, bringing it world attention.

Independent tourism in the hinterlands continues to be a daunting experience, though Havana sprouts new (or newly refurbished), well-run hotels. Many *paladares* in Havana have closed due to punishing taxes, but those which remain are ever fancier.

The U.S. embargo, though softened, continues. The U.S. has approved Cuban purchase of medicines and food from the U.S., but Cuba is still denied access to the loans necessary to buy them. Recent puchases of food from the United States – the first since the imposition of the embargo nearly forty years ago – have been paid for in cash. Though there has been a clampdown by the United States on its citizens making unauthorized trips to Cuba, there has been, at the same time, a broader definition of authorized trips and greater facilitation of travel to Cuba. The hurdles set before Cubans wishing to travel outside of their country remain very high.

One of the most interesting developments since the first edition of this book was published has been the increasing visibility of the Varela Project. Conceived and developed by Oswaldo Payá, a member of Cuba's dissident Christian Liberatio Movement, the Varela Projct (named after Felix Varela, a 19th century Cuban priest who supported Cuban independence and died in exile) takes advantage of a provision within the Cuban constitution, which allows for revisions to its constitution to be debated within the Cuban National Assembly if the National Assembly is presented with a petition bearing at least ten thousand signatures. On May 10, 2002, a petition, calling for freedom of expression, freedom of assembly, for the right of Cubans to own their own businesses, and for the right to free and fair elections, was presented to the National Assembly with more than eleven thousand signatures. The Varela Project's petition was given a further boost, two days later, by the visit of former U.S. president Jimmy Carter. The former president referred to the Project in a speech broadcast live and uncensored on Cuban television and radio, making large segments of the Cuban population aware of the Project and its petition for the first time.

The leadership's reaction to the Varela Project's petition was to present, in June, a counter-petition, accompanies by mass rallies, calling for a constitutional amendment that Cuba's economic political and social systems cannot be changed. The petition received eight million two hundred thousand signatures – literally the entire electorate of Cuba. Following the massive signature drive of the counter-petition, Oswaldo Payá stated, 'No Cuban should feel paralyzed or hopeless for having signed [the counter-petition] against his will'.

Cuban history, like the history of most states, is a timeline riddled with brackets: brackets within brackets and brackets which overlap. Simply stated, the brackets mark times in which unexpected things happen. What makes Cuban history different even from the history of other Latin American countries is the extent to which magic realism is allowed to become part of its timeline, both within and outside its brackets of unexpectedness.

Without a doubt, the most distinct bracket of time since we have left Cuba has been the Elián González period. On November 25, 1999, a five-year-old Cuban boy was discovered by fishermen, lashed to the inner tube of a tire in the Straits of Florida, where he had been drifting for two days after a boat carrying his mother and thirteen others overturned in a storm. Elián González's mother, who took her son on the Miami-bound boat without the knowledge of Elián's father, from whom she was divorced, was lost at sea. Elián was taken to a Miami hospital, then released into the care of his great-uncle, a Cuban exile and Miami resident, who then sued Elián's father for custody of the child, in order to keep Elián in the United States. What ensued was ostensibly a legal battle between Elián's father and the Miami relatives, but came to be seen as a public relations battle between the Cuban-American National Foundation and Fidel Castro, ultimately involving the Attorney General of the United States. It conclued five months later with the removal of Elián by armed federal agents from the Miami relatives' home, following the Miami relatives' repeated refusals to release Elián after losing their final appeal in family court.

The case might have been concluded quickly had it not been for the seemingly miraculous circumstances of the boy's survival. Elián came to be equated with La Virgen de la Ciridad del Cobre herself, with Moses, with Elegguá, the opener of roads (who is often portrayed as a child) and with the child-saviour of Ifa (one of the five branches of Santeria) oracles who, it was predicted, would arrive by sea. As if there were not enough, Elián manages to be sincretic not only in an Afro-Cuban sense, but also in an Afro-Cuban-*yanqui* sense, hitherto unheard of.

Since Cuba has repossessed Elián, the leadership of the Cuban-American National Foundation has been replaced by a more moderate, younger generation. On September 12, 2001,

347

Rual Castro presided over a rally of 'solidarity with the American people over the tragedy they are living through'. Manipulations aside, the fact is that Elián is growing up with his one remaining parent in his native land. His future there becomes harder to imagine every day. Still, one cannot have lived in Cuba without being affected by magic realism oneself, without believing it a distinct possibility that Elián, growing, will experience more miracles. And maybe they won't even have to be miracles.

Isadora Tattlin
November 2002

Glossary

agua mala: 'bad water,' microorganisms in the sea that cause raised welts on the skin of sea bathers

agro, agropecuario: fruit, vegetable, lamb, and pork market

apagón: blackout

babalao: Santeria priest

balsa: raft

balsero: rafter

barrio: neighborhood

blumes: underpants

bodega: neighborhood food store where Cubans shop, using ration cards

bohio: hut

boniato: sweet potato

El Caballo: the Horse, another name for Fidel Castro

caoba: Cuban mahogany

cáscara de toronja: grapefruit rind that has been boiled, then pressed under a weight, in syrup

CDR: Committee for the Defense of the Revolution

chica, chico: girl, boy

chicharrones: pork cracklings

La China: the Chinese Woman, another name for Raúl Castro

chino: 'Chink,' 'Chinaman'

Cohiba: the best brand of cigars

compañero: comrade

conseguir: to achieve, obtain, get

coprocultivo: bacterial culture grown from a stool sample

Cubalse: state-run monopoly for construction, the distribution of construction and household materials, and the providing of employees to foreign entities, among other activities

cucurucho: sweet made of coconut, sugar, and almonds

cuentapropista: self-employed worker

Diplo, Diplomercado: Diplomarket, the largest and most well supplied dollars-only supermarket in Havana

dulce de coco: coconut sweet

duro: hard-line

un duro: a hard-liner

El: Him, another name for Fidel Castro

Elegguá: a Santeria saint who is 'an opener of roads'

ensalada de espan: spam salad

escabeche: fillets of *serrucho,* a type of fish, breaded and fried with onions, then pressed under a weight, in vinegar, for a week

fula: dollar

gallego: Galician, from the province of Galicia in Spain

guajira, guajiro: farmer or country person

hijos de puta: sons of a whore

jamon biki: a salami-shaped ham made of many parts of the pig

jine: short for *jinetera;* also, of or pertaining to a *jinetera,* as in *jinewear*

jinetera, jinetero: semiprofessional female or male prostitute

judias: literally 'Jews;' white beans

loca, loco: crazy

majá: small boa constrictor native to Cuba

malanga: an edible tuber

maricón: 'faggot'

mariquitas: green bananas sliced thin, then fried like potato chips; also, 'little faggots'

mojito: cocktail consisting of light rum, dark rum, lime juice, sugar, and crushed mint

mojo: garlic sauce

mulata, mulato: mulatta, mulatto

muestra: stool sample

un negro: a black person, a negro, a 'nigger'

un negrito: a little black person, a little negro, a little 'nigger'

El Niño: the Child or the Kid, another name for Fidel Castro

nomenklatura: the Communist leadership

oriental, orientales: oriental, orientals, meaning Cubans originating from anywhere east of Camagüey; also known as *palestinos*

panatela de Boston crema: Boston cream pie

panqué: pancake

paredón: a wall against which people were executed

periodo especial: special period, short for 'special period in time of peace,' the time in Cuban history following the withdrawal of aid from the Soviet Union, in which Cubans were asked to endure shortages and inconveniences for the sake of the survival of the socialist revolution while the government adjusted to new realities

perros calientes: hot dogs

permutar: to exchange houses or apartments

picua: a fish that is often toxic

la pincha; pinchar: work; to work

plátano: banana

plátanos verdes: green (nonsweet) bananas

P.P.G.: pronounced *pe pe hay*, an anti-impotence drug

puros: cigars

quedarse: to stay, meaning in Cuba 'to go to another country and stay there;' *se quedó en el exterior* means 'he stayed abroad'

resolver: to resolve (a problem), also meaning in Cuba to find goods and take possession of them, to settle an issue with the bureaucracy

ron: rum

ron añejo: rum aged more than seven years

rumbera: female rumba dancer; also, a folklorically dressed Cuban woman, in long, flounced skirt, white cotton or lace puffy-sleeved off-the-shoulder blouse, and head kerchief, sometimes seen smoking a cigar

El Señor: the Mister, the Sir, or the Lord, another name for Fidel Castro

serrucho: a fish

tostones: green bananas that are fried, then flattened

el triunfo: short for 'the triumph of the revolution'

vieja, viejo: old

yucas rellenas: mashed yuccas stuffed with meat, rolled in bread crumbs, and deep-fried

La Yuma: the United States

yuca: an edible tuber

A SELECTED LIST OF TRAVEL WRITING
AVAILABLE FROM TRANSWORLD

THE PRICES SHOWN BELOW WERE CORRECT AT THE TIME OF GOING TO PRESS. HOWEVER TRANSWORLD PUBLISHERS RESERVE THE RIGHT TO SHOW NEW RETAIL PRICES ON COVERS WHICH MAY DIFFER FROM THOSE PREVIOUSLY ADVERTISED IN THE TEXT OR ELSEWHERE.

81341 2	LIFE IN A POSTCARD	Rosemary Bailey	£7.99
99600 9	NOTES FROM A SMALL ISLAND	Bill Bryson	£7.99
99786 2	NOTES FROM A BIG COUNTRY	Bill Bryson	£7.99
99702 1	A WALK IN THE WOODS	Bill Bryson	£7.99
99808 7	THE LOST CONTINENT	Bill Bryson	£7.99
99805 2	MADE IN AMERICA	Bill Bryson	£7.99
99806 0	NEITHER HERE NOR THERE	Bill Bryson	£7.99
99703 X	DOWN UNDER	Bill Bryson	£7.99
99858 3	PERFUME FROM PROVENCE	Lady Fortescue	£7.99
81424 9	KITE STRINGS OF THE SOUTHERN CROSS	Laurie Gough	£6.99
81479 6	FRENCH SPIRITS	Jeffrey Greene	£6.99
14681 1	CASTAWAY	Lucy Irvine	£6.99
14680 3	FARAWAY	Lucy Irvine	£7.99
14595 5	BETWEEN EXTREMES	Brian Keenan and John McCarthy	£7.99
99841 9	NOTES FROM AN ITALIAN GARDEN	Joan Marble	£7.99
50667 6	UNDER THE TUSCAN SUN	Frances Mayes	£6.99
81250 5	BELLA TUSCANY	Frances Mayes	£6.99
81335 8	THE FULL MONTEZUMA	Peter Moore	£7.99
81238 6	THE WRONG WAY HOME	Peter Moore	£7.99
81451 6	NO SHITTING IN THE TOILET	Peter Moore	£6.99
81448 6	TAKE ME WITH YOU	Brad Newsham	£6.99
99852 4	THE ELUSIVE TRUFFLE:		
	Travels in Search of the Legendary Food of France	Mirabel Osler	£6.99
99928 8	INSTRUCTIONS FOR VISITORS	Helen Stevenson	£6.99

All Transworld titles are available by post from:
Bookpost, PO Box 29, Douglas, Isle of Man, IM99 1BQ
Credit cards accepted. Please telephone 01624 836000,
fax 01624 837033, Internet http://www.bookpost.co.uk
or e-mail: bookshop@enterprise.net for details.
Free postage and packing in the UK. Overseas customers: allow
£1 per book (paperbacks) and £3 per book (hardbacks).